DEATH

OF A

REVOLUTIONARY

DEATH

of a

REVOLUTIONARY

Che Guevara's Last Mission

RICHARD L. HARRIS

W. W. NORTON & COMPANY • NEW YORK • LONDON

For information about permission to reproduce selections from this book,
write to Permissions, W. W. Norton & Company, Inc.,
500 Fifth Avenue, New York, NY 10110

For information about special discounts for bulk purchases, please contact
W. W. Norton Special Sales at specialsales@wwnorton.com or 800-233-4830.

Manufacturing by RR Donnelley, Bloomsburg
Book design by Chris Welch
Production manager: Devon Zahn

Library of Congress Cataloging-in-Publication Data

Harris, Richard L. (Richard Legé), 1939–
Death of a revolutionary : Che Guevara's last mission / Richard L. Harris.—
Rev. and updated.
p. cm.
Includes bibliographical references and index.
ISBN 978-0-393-33094-6 (pbk.)
1. Guevara, Ernesto, 1928–1967—Death and burial. 2. Bolivia—History—
1938–1982. 3. Guerrillas—Bolivia—History—20th century. I. Title.
F2849.22.G85H3 2007
984.05'2092—dc22

2007024564

W. W. Norton & Company, Inc.
500 Fifth Avenue, New York, N.Y. 10110
www.wwnorton.com

W. W. Norton & Company Ltd.
Castle House, 75/76 Wells Street, W1T 3QT

3 4 5 6 7 8 9 0

This new edition of Death of a Revolutionary
is dedicated to
my son, Ricardo,
and
el hombre nuevo (*the new human being*)
of the twenty-first century

CONTENTS

photos follow chapter 10

BOLIVIA

Miles
0   100   200   300

Kilometers
0   100   200   300

BRAZIL

PERU

BRAZIL

Caracas

Lima   BOLIVIA

Rio de Janei

Santiago   Buenos Aires

uno   *Titicaca*

LA PAZ

Cochabamba   Santa Cruz

Oruro   Vallegrande

A L T I P L A N O   ZONE OF
GUERRILLA
OPERATIONS

Arica   Sucre

Puerto Suárez

Potosí   Ñancahuazú

Camiri

Tarija

GRAN CHACO   PARAGUAY

CHILE

ARGENTINA

A. M. JAUSS

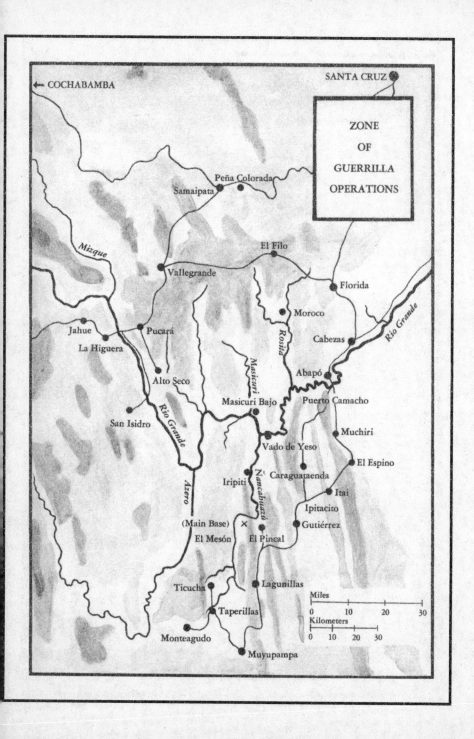

← COCHABAMBA

SANTA CRUZ

ZONE

OF

GUERRILLA

OPERATIONS

Peña Colorada

Samaipata

Mizque

El Filo

Vallegrande

Florida

Río Grande

Moroco

Rosita

Jahue

Pucará

Cabezas

La Higuera

Masicuri

Abapó

Alto Seco

Puerto Camacho

Masicuri Bajo

San Isidro

Río Grande

Muchiri

Vado de Yeso

El Espino

Iripiti

Caraguataenda

Ñancahuazú

Itai

Ipitacito

Azero

Gutiérrez

(Main Base)   ×

El Mesón   El Pincal

Lagunillas

Ticucha

Taperillas

Miles

0   10   20   30

Kilometers

Monteagudo

0   10   20   30

Muyupampa

PREFACE TO THE
NEW EDITION

Above all, always remain capable of feeling deeply whatever injustice is committed against anyone in any part of
the world. This is the finest quality of a revolutionary.
—Che Guevara, letter to his children (1965)

In October 1967, I was teaching at the University of Chile in Santiago when I learned that Che Guevara had been killed by the Bolivian army in an isolated part of southeastern Bolivia. Shortly afterward, I went to Bolivia to discover for myself why one of the most famous revolutionaries of the twentieth century had met his death in a remote area of this relatively isolated country and at the hands of one of the worst armies in Latin America. I wanted to know why Che Guevara and his comrades had given their lives in what appeared to be a hopeless mission. Upon my arrival in Bolivia, I told the Bolivian authorities and the officials in the U.S. embassy in La Paz that I wanted to conduct an "academic research project" on the failure of the revolutionary guerrilla force that Che had established in southeastern Bolivia in late

1966 and 1967. I hoped this explanation would open some official doors for me and allay suspicions about my presence there.

However, my real motivation was much more personal and political. I wanted to understand the revolutionary purpose and convictions of Che and his comrades, and the revolutionary spirit that was spreading throughout Latin America and the world at that time, in 1968. My journey to Bolivia was in fact an intellectual and spiritual quest that I hoped would help me better understand the revolutionary ferment in the world around me and define my own role in relation to it. I was already a socially concerned scholar and an embryonic political activist. I felt that a quest of this nature would help me decide what role I should play in the revolutionary events of the times. Little did I suspect then that I would still be thinking and writing about Che Guevara four decades later.

The field research upon which this book is based was carried out in Bolivia six months after Che's capture and death at the hands of the Bolivian military. At that time, the political ramifications of Che's tragic odyssey in Bolivia, in particular the uproar caused by the publication of his Bolivian diary (clandestinely sent to Cuba by one of the top members of the Bolivian government), were causing a great deal of trouble for the Bolivian government and military. Consequently, it was not an easy task to conduct research on Che's mission and death in Bolivia. I soon discovered that nearly all official doors were closed to the snooping gringo professor from California. Nevertheless, I found ample sources of information. In particular, members of the Bolivian press, progressive elements within the Catholic clergy, members of the Bolivian intellectual community, and the members of certain left-wing political parties proved to be extremely valuable informants. In addition, a number of questionable informants appeared at my doorstep, some of whom claimed to be members of the Bolivian military and intelligence services with firsthand knowledge of the circumstances surrounding Che's activities and death in Bolivia.

Because the politically relevant stratum of Bolivian society was at the time (and still is) relatively small, approximately equivalent to the political elite of a medium-sized American city, access to a few key insiders meant access to most of the political secrets of the country. And in a small political system like Bolivia's, it is almost impossible to hide the truth about a subject as popular and fascinating as the death of Che Guevara. In fact, the real problem in this case was one of coping with a superabundance of information, often conflicting, on many aspects of this subject. In the end, the success of my research efforts led to my being warned by a not too friendly official in the U.S. embassy that I knew too much and that "I should leave the country for my own safety." Since I felt that I had all the information I needed by that time, I heeded his warning. Over the years since I left Bolivia, the revelations that have been made public about Che's Bolivian mission and his death have confirmed nearly all of the findings of my research in 1968.

After my return to the United States in September 1968, I began writing the first edition of this book (which was released in January 1970). During the late 1960s and early 1970s, Che was one of the heroes of the student and antiwar movements in the United States, Canada, Western Europe, and Latin America—as well as the role model and the author of an important source of military strategy and tactics for revolutionary struggles around the world, particularly in Latin America. Because of my book on Che, I was invited to speak about him at universities, colleges, high schools, political gatherings, protest demonstrations, and academic conferences in various countries. As time went by, I discovered that my own identity was connected to Che Guevara, and I found myself often thinking about what he would have done or said in the situations that were taking place around me and in the world at large.

As one of the more recent biographies of Che states, "Many of us today owe the few attractive and redeeming features of our daily existence to the sixties, and Che Guevara personifies the era, if not the traits, better than anyone" (Castañeda 1997, 410). Since my first encounter with the death and revolutionary legacy of Che Guevara forty years ago, I have lived a life influenced to a considerable degree by his life and death. Consequently, I have often reflected on the personal as well as historical effects of his legacy. The republishing of this book has offered me another chance to reflect upon the life and death of this remarkable and controversial man, whose revolutionary legacy continues to inspire or incense those who knew or know of him.

The reader will find frequent quotations throughout this book taken from Che's Bolivian campaign diary as well as his earlier writings. In every case, these have been translated from Che's Spanish by myself, with the assistance of my Latin American friends. In general, they conform to the translations of Che's writings that have been published for commercial distribution. However, in certain cases, a different word or choice of phrasing has been used in order to convey the original meaning in the best possible manner. The version of Che's diary referred to throughout this book was published in 1968 by the Chilean leftist periodical *Punto Final*, which was involved in getting the copies of Che's diary out of Bolivia to Cuba.

It is impossible to acknowledge all the help I received in researching, writing, and revising this book, but I should like to mention in particular Allen Stevenson, Jorge Nef, the Gill family,

Genia Lane, David Kunzle, Peter McLaren, who convinced me that I should republish this book, my editor at W. W. Norton, Amy Cherry, and my wife, Melinda (Jun Ling) Seid. Finally, I want to express my deep appreciation and gratitude to the many Bolivians who provided me with most of the information presented in the pages of this book. Without their invaluable assistance, this genuine labor of love would not have been possible. In the original edition of this book, I did not name them, because in many cases their careers and lives could have been endangered by the exposure, and because most of them asked to remain anonymous. Since over forty years have passed since then, it seems senseless to name them now, although their faces and voices remain engraved in my memory. Many of them are no longer with us. It is still my fervent hope, as it was then, that their dreams and aspirations for the future of their country will one day be fulfilled. Indeed, recent developments in Bolivia give me much hope in this regard.

Much has happened in Latin American and the world since I wrote the first edition of this book in the fall of 1968 and the spring of 1969. Hundreds of books and articles, as well as films, paintings, sculptures, murals, songs, and poems, have been produced about Che Guevara, and many of his own writings have been published in numerous languages. However, the social injustices and social inequalities against which this Argentine-born revolutionary fought—first in the Cuban revolution, then in Africa, and finally in South America—are very much a part of the contemporary scene in many parts of the world today. Although armed revolution no longer appears to be the order of the day, as it did in the late 1960s and 1970s, the life, death, and revolutionary legacy of Che Guevara continue to be of great interest to people all over the world.

To commemorate the fortieth anniversary of his death in 2007 and the eightieth anniversary of his birth in 2008, I contacted W. W. Norton about the possibility of publishing a new edition of *Death of a Revolutionary*. Norton agreed that the book should be published in a revised and updated edition. Thus, together we have produced this new version of the original. I hope the reader finds it to be, as I originally intended, a concise, easy-to-read account of Che Guevara's life, the circumstances surrounding his last mission in Bolivia, and the historical legacy that his life and death as a revolutionary have left us.

That this new edition of my book is being published four decades after his death and thirty-seven years after it was first published is evidence of the continuing significance of Che Guevara's legacy. Today, his legacy is even more significant than it was in the past. His familiar face appears on banners, walls, billboards, flags, books, periodicals, and murals in cities, towns, and villages around the globe. His name is known to tens of millions of people everywhere. In Latin America, Che's image is known to everyone and always visible in the daily protests, rallies, mass marches, public celebrations, and popular assemblies that take place across the region. It is even displayed prominently in the offices of the elected leaders of Bolivia, Brazil, Ecuador, Nicaragua, Uruguay, and Venezuela. As a result, the expression *Che vive!* (Che lives!), which is frequently heard and seen throughout the region, is not an exaggeration.

Richard Legè Harris
Sacramento, California
March 22, 2007

DEATH

OF A

REVOLUTIONARY

Chapter 1

INTRODUCTION

◼

In the arduous profession of the revolutionary, death is a
frequent occurrence.

—Ernesto "Che" Guevara

On October 9, 1967, the half-nude body of Ernesto "Che"
Guevara was displayed on a stretcher to members of the
international press in the small town of Vallegrande,
Bolivia. Shot to death only a few hours earlier, he looked remark-
ably alive. His eyes were open and his lips were half parted in
an expression that could be interpreted as either a faint smile or
a mocking sneer. As the photographs of his almost Christ-like
face and the news of the death of this famous revolutionary were
spread around the world, people everywhere felt a sense of shock
and disbelief. The circumstances surrounding his death were per-
plexing. It did not seem possible that a person of his importance
and abilities could have been captured and killed by the army of
one of Latin America's weakest and poorest nations.

Since his death, Che Guevara has emerged as one of the greatest legendary figures of our times. His name, his ideas, and his romantic image have become part of the spirit and symbolism of those who believe that the social injustices of this world can be erased only by revolutionary means. Rarely in history has a single figure been so passionately and universally accepted as the personification of revolutionary idealism and practice. Moreover, even those who feel no sympathy for the ideals he upheld continue to be affected by the charisma of his almost mystical image and the enduring legacy of his revolutionary life.

Because he has become a revolutionary icon, those who admire the revolutionary example he set as well as those who abhor what he represents often possess a distorted conception of the man who was Che Guevara. The growing number of articles, pamphlets, books, and films on Che attest to the enduring importance of this man and his historical legacy. However, in much of the literature and many of the media presentations, his virtues are magnified out of all proportion or his faults and mistakes are exaggerated to the extreme, and in either case his true personality is distorted beyond recognition. The real Che Guevara lies buried beneath a mountain of propagandistic literature, sensationalism, antagonistic portrayals, and hopelessly biased analyses of his exploits, ideas, and words.

By sifting and interpreting the available evidence, one can rescue Che's life, death, and the circumstances surrounding his last mission from the distortions created by the propagandists, ideologues of the left and right, journalists, scriptwriters, and filmmakers. As an analysis of the historical facts nearly always reveals, behind every historical legend generally lies a reality far more fascinating and significant than the fabricated reality of the mythmakers and those who attempt to rewrite history for their own ends. The interpretation of facts, of course, provides the basis for drawing conclusions, and here human bias always colors the picture.

In researching Che's death and writing this book, I have sought to let the chips fall as they may. My intent is to provide an accurate account of Che's last mission and the circumstances that led up to his death. I have let the evidence answer various controversial questions: Did Che die a victim of his own tragic errors, the failure of Bolivia's pro-Soviet Communist Party to come to his aid, the assistance given to the Bolivian army by the U.S. military and CIA, or some other factors? Was his last mission to Bolivia doomed from the outset, or was there a possibility it could succeed? Was Che misled into thinking that his chances of victory were good, or did he know that his mission had very little chance of succeeding? Did he have the support and well wishes of his friend and Cuba's top leader, Fidel Castro? Did the Cubans do everything they could have done to aid him? Does his death in Bolivia and the failure of his Bolivian mission mean that his career as a revolutionary was a failure? What motivated Che? Was he a great revolutionary who died fighting for his revolutionary ideals, a psychopathic adventurer, or a ruthless renegade?

Thanks to the diary that Che kept during the period between his arrival in Bolivia and his capture some eleven months later, we have a primary source of exact and detailed information concerning this final episode in Che's life. This unique source has made it possible to see Che's Bolivian mission, in a sense, through his own eyes. Che's diary has provided not only a precise description of the daily incidents in the life of his guerrilla force but also a valuable insight into the critical reflections, miscalculations, mistakes, and personal recriminations that are inevitable in such an undertaking.

I carefully compared all the information that I obtained from my personal interviews and field research in Bolivia with Che's diary, and the high degree of congruence between these two sources of information convinced me that his diary is an authentic and honest account of what occurred during the last eleven months of Che's life. However, it does not give us much insight into what took place outside Che's guerrilla force during this period. For this information, I had to rely upon my own sources in Bolivia. In certain cases, however, Che's diary sheds light even on this subject, since he frequently commented upon news reports that he heard on the radio during the period he kept his diary.

I encourage you the reader to approach the subject of this book with an open mind. This is necessary because in all likelihood you have had the good fortune to be raised in a relatively comfortable and peaceful social environment—untouched personally by political oppression, economic exploitation, and social injustice. For this reason, you may not be in touch with many of the conditions, aspirations, and frustrations that lead people to believe in the necessity of revolutionary change, and at times to risk or even give their lives to bring about this kind of change. Today, armed revolution is not the order of the day around the globe, as it was during Che's lifetime, but it is still on the agenda in many parts of the world and will most likely continue to be there in the future. Thus, it is of great importance to understand why human beings like Che Guevara choose to live and die as revolutionaries.

Chapter 2

PROFILE OF A REVOLUTIONARY

I believe in the armed struggle as the only solution for those peoples who fight to free themselves, and I am consistent with my beliefs. Many will call me an adventurer, and that I am; only one of a different kind—one of those who risks his skin to prove his beliefs.

—Che Guevara, farewell letter to his parents (1965)

Che's life provides an excellent case study of how individuals become revolutionaries—how the conditions and circumstances in which they live can lead them to follow this path. Che the revolutionary was molded by specific historical circumstances, societal conditions, and social-psychological factors. The term "revolutionary" conjures up in the minds of many people a stereotype of a wild-eyed, bearded extremist who is driven by some fanatical urge to destroy the existing order of things, no matter what the cost in human life and property. Che Guevara does not fit this stereotype. In order to understand why Che Guevara became a revolutionary and why he died as one, one must put aside any preconceptions one has about revolutionaries and examine carefully his life and circumstances. Only by knowing something about the life of this remarkable man can one gain insight into why he became a famous revolutionary and why he died a tragic death as a guerrilla fighter in Bolivia at the age of thirty-nine.

Ernesto Guevara de la Serna was born on June 14, 1928, in the Argentine city of Rosario. (The biographical information on Che in this section comes from a biography written by Hugo Gambini, which I purchased in Argentina shortly before going to Bolivia in the spring of 1968.) His parents were of upper-class origin. His father was a contractor who had studied architecture but never received his degree. His mother was an intelligent, unconventional, and warm person who remained devoted to Ernesto, her firstborn, until her death just a few years before his own.

Soon after Ernesto was born, the Guevaras moved to San Isidro, Argentina. It was in this city along the banks of the La Plata River, his parents believed, that he contracted the asthma from which he suffered the rest of his life. His mother was an avid swimmer and used to take him with her to the yacht club in San Isidro when she went swimming. On one particularly chilly day, she did so again, and by the time she was ready to leave the club she discovered he was very ill. She and her husband rushed him to a doctor nearby, who informed them that their son had a severe asthmatic condition. For the next two years, Che's parents tried every possible cure, but in the end they were advised that they would have to move to a much drier climate if they wanted their son's health to improve. As a result, they relocated to the little town of Alta Gracia, in the central Argentine province of Córdoba.

Ernesto grew up in Alta Gracia and in Córdoba, along with his two brothers and two sisters, who were born there. The dry climate of the region greatly benefited his health, although he continued to suffer periodic asthma attacks. As he grew older, Ernesto spent as much time outdoors as possible. His childhood friends recall that he was always organizing hikes to the hills and playing games requiring physical skill and endurance. His friends also remember him as a decisive and bold youth who was very sure of himself. Above all else, though, they remember him for his enthusiasm and adventurousness. Evidently, he was willing to do almost anything, perhaps to prove to himself and others that in spite of his chronic illness he was just as good as they. This personality trait stayed with him in later years. Indeed, it appears to have been one of the most prominent aspects of his adult personality.

Ernesto's family life was relatively happy, although his parents ultimately separated. His father gave him considerable freedom, and his mother, who was never able to rid herself of the feeling that somehow she was at least partly responsible for his asthmatic condition, gave him a great deal of love and attention. Ernesto always confided in her, even years later when he became an important leader in the Cuban revolution. Because of his asthma, he was often unable to attend school for days at a time during the first years of his primary education. Consequently, his mother helped him with his studies at home. Later on, when he entered secondary school, she taught him to speak French, although by this time the frequency of his asthmatic attacks had decreased considerably, and his attendance at school was quite regular.

Ernesto's parents wanted their children to be freethinkers. At home, the parents never spoke of religion, and the children were given considerable freedom to think and talk about all kinds of subjects. Ernesto's father felt strongly that the children should not be overprotected and that they should begin to learn life's secrets and dangers at an early age. When Ernesto was sixteen years old, his father let him take his brother Roberto on a hitchhiking trip to the surrounding provinces. They were gone almost the entire two months of their summer vacation, and Ernesto so thoroughly enjoyed himself on this trip that he became a determined hiker.

Despite his asthma, Ernesto played both soccer (or "football," as it is called in Latin America and most of the world) and rugby. In the former, he usually played the position of goalkeeper, always with an inhaler in his pocket. However, it was at rugby that he really excelled. Hugo Gambini, in his biography of Che, claims that the position Ernesto played in this game helped to define his personality (Gambini 1968, 18). It seems his position was that of forward, which is generally the key position in rugby since the majority of advances depend upon the team members in this position. Ernesto played this position as though both his personality and his physical attributes had been made to order for it. Perhaps, as Gambini suggests, this game was instrumental in shaping Ernesto's personality as a daring leader.

All those who knew Ernesto as a youth were impressed by his intelligence and the ease with which he learned new things. However, he was not an exceptional student, because his interests lay outside of school. He was preoccupied with hiking, football, rugby, and chess. The last he learned at the age of eleven, and within a few years he was an excellent player. Later on, chess became his main hobby.

Ernesto grew up in a highly politicized environment. Both his mother and his father identified with the Republican cause during the Spanish civil war, and after the war they became close friends with two Spanish families who had been forced to flee to Argentina when the Spanish dictator Francisco Franco assumed power. Ernesto's family was also avidly anti-Nazi. His father belonged to an anti-Nazi and pro-Allies organization called Acción Argentina, and Ernesto joined the youth wing of this organization when he was eleven (Anderson 1997, 23). His mother formed a committee to send clothes and food to Charles de Gaulle's Free French forces during World War II. She was a leftist and far more progressive minded in her political views than his father, who was a libertarian conservative. However, both of Che's parents opposed Juan Perón's candidacy for the presidency of Argentina in 1946, and after Perón came to power, his mother in particular was an outspoken critic of Peronism.

In 1946, Ernesto enrolled in the Faculty of Engineering at the University of Buenos Aires. He also secured a part-time job to pay for his expenses. What little spare time he had he devoted to rugby, chess, and travel. He was eighteen when Perón became president, and, like most other students his age, he was not a supporter of Perón. However, he did not devote much time to political activities during this period, and his views regarding Perón have been characterized as "a-Peronism" (Castañeda 1997, 30–35). After the death of his grandmother, with whom he was very close, he decided to change his career to medicine and entered the Faculty of Medicine.

At the beginning of 1950, Ernesto toured all of northern and central Argentina by motorbike—a trip of four thousand miles (Gambini 1968, 22). On his return, he took the motorbike back to the store where he had bought it in order to have it reconditioned. When the store owner discovered the details of the trip, he was astounded and asked Ernesto to give him a letter attesting to his having made such a fantastic trip by motorbike. This letter, along with a picture of Ernesto sitting on his motorbike, was published in a local sports magazine as an advertisement for the type of motorbike which he had used.

Ernesto's trip in 1950 served to whet his appetite for more travel and adventure. Almost two years later, in December 1951, when he was only one year short of receiving his medical degree, he and his friend Alberto Granados, a biochemist, set out to explore all of Latin America by motorcycle. His now published "motorcycle diaries" provide a valuable personal narrative of this journey (Guevara 1995). They shed light on a little-known period in his young adulthood and provide important insights into his personality and the development of his views about the world. Written while he was traveling around South America in his early twenties, they allow the reader to gain an intimate contact with him at an important and formative period in his life.

The reader of these lucid and brief accounts can almost hear Che's thoughts, view the world through his eyes, and sense his spirit. They allow the reader to travel back in time to meet the man before he became a revolutionary and before he made his grand entrance on the stage of world history as one of the most charismatic young leaders of the Cuban revolution.

From Buenos Aires, Ernesto and Alberto went to the south of Argentina and crossed into Chile. As they neared Santiago, the motorcycle gave out and they were forced to continue on foot. They panhandled and worked at various odd jobs in order to obtain their room and board. In this way, they managed to hitch-hike their way from northern Chile to the Peruvian frontier.

In Peru, they came into close contact with South America's suffering Indian masses. They saw how the Indians of the Peruvian altiplano (high plateau), whose ancestors were the great Incas, were (and still are) exploited and oppressed. Because of their interest in leprosy, they visited a leprosarium on the banks of one of the tributaries of the Amazon River at San Pablo, Peru. There they worked in the leprosarium's laboratory and endeared themselves to the inmates. They played soccer with them, took them on hikes, and even led them on hunting expeditions. When it came time for Ernesto and Alberto to leave, the inmates gave them a very emotional farewell party.

From San Pablo, Ernesto and Alberto crossed the river to Leticia, Colombia, on a raft built for them by the inmates of the leprosarium. In Leticia, they managed to obtain free passage on a flight to Bogotá by playing for the town's football team. At the time, Colombia was under the dictatorship of Laureano Gómez, and all foreigners entering the capital were regarded by the authorities as potential subversive agents. When Ernesto and Alberto arrived in Bogotá looking like two expeditionaries, they were arrested and interrogated by the police. Indignant, they reacted angrily toward their captors, which only made their situation worse. A local student group heard of their plight and convinced the authorities that they should be released and allowed to leave the country. From these students, Ernesto and Alberto learned that one of the agents they had berated had a reputation for having killed a number of people in Bogotá with less provocation than they themselves had given him. With this information and the financial assistance of the Colombian students, the two harassed travelers left Bogotá on a bus to Venezuela.

In Caracas, Venezuela, they met a doctor who was a specialist in leprology. Impressed by Alberto's interest in leprosy, he offered him a position in his laboratory at a hospital for lepers. At about the same time, Ernesto ran into an uncle who had an airplane, which he used to transport race horses between Buenos Aires and Miami. He told Ernesto that he could return with him to Buenos Aires if he wanted to resume his studies at medical school. Ernesto and Alberto made a pact: Alberto would accept the job offered him and stay in Venezuela, while Ernesto would go back to Buenos Aires to graduate from medical school and then return to Venezuela to work with Alberto. At the end of July 1952, they said good-bye in Caracas.

From Caracas, Ernesto's plane went to Miami before returning to Buenos Aires. The plane had to lie over in Miami because of mechanical problems, so Che took advantage of the opportunity to get to know the city (Guevara 1995, 153–54). As it turned out, he had to wait a whole month for the plane to be repaired. He had no money, but he was able to stay with one of the cousins of his former girlfriend in Argentina. This young Argentine was a student at the University of Miami. During his month in Miami, Che visited the beaches and hung around with this student, who helped him find a place to stay and a job as a dishwasher in one of Miami's restaurants. When the plane was repaired, he flew back to Buenos Aires in September 1952.

After he returned to Argentina, Ernesto undertook a crash program to complete the requirements for his graduation from medical school. He met all the remaining requirements in less than a year and obtained his medical degree in March 1953. Since he did not have the money to go directly to Venezuela and join Alberto, he decided to travel to Venezuela in the same romantic manner that he and Alberto had traveled there a year earlier. He used what little money he had to buy a train ticket from Buenos Aires to La Paz, Bolivia. He figured he would travel from Bolivia to Venezuela as best he could.

In July 1953, Ernesto and his friend Carlos "Calica" Ferrer made the three-thousand-mile train trip from Buenos Aires to La Paz (Anderson 1997, 100–11). They arrived in the Bolivian capital a year after the country had undergone a dramatic popular revolution in which the major foreign-owned mines had been nationalized and the peasants had taken possession of the feudal estates on which they had formerly labored as serfs and tenant farmers. Thus, they found in La Paz an atmosphere filled with revolutionary fervor and excitement.

Soon after their arrival, Ernesto and Calica met a group of Argentine exiles who had been forced to leave Argentina because of their opposition to the Perón regime. One of these exiles was a young lawyer named Ricardo Rojo. In a short time, Rojo and Ernesto became friends and traveling companions. After Che Guevara's death, Rojo wrote about his friendship with Che and their joint experiences in Bolivia and elsewhere in Latin America (Rojo 1968). Rojo recalls that when he met Ernesto in La Paz, he was living in a miserable rented room in one of the oldest parts of the city. Ernesto spent most of his time visiting ancient Inca ruins or passing the day in the noisy cafés along the capital's main boulevard, Avenida 16 de Julio. From these cafés, Ernesto, Ricardo, and Calica were able to look out on the broad and sunny boulevard and watch the continuous parade of the Bolivian people as they stopped to look at the large signs propagandizing the revolutionary goals of the new regime.

Rojo remembers that Ernesto expressed little interest in politics at the time and that he was pessimistic about the fate of the Bolivian revolution. Ernesto regarded the new regime as merely reformist and not truly revolutionary. On one occasion, Ernesto and Rojo visited the Ministry of Peasant Affairs, where they saw long lines of peasants being methodically sprayed with DDT to rid them of lice. Ernesto reportedly was incensed by the humiliating way these peasants were being treated by a regime that claimed to be the instrument of their interests. According to Ernesto, the new regime was not solving the causes of Bolivia's problems but merely trying to ameliorate their effects (Rojo 1968, 33). In the case of the peasants, the government was spraying them to rid them of lice, rather than improving the social and economic conditions that were the cause of their lice.

During this period, Ernesto was neither a Marxist nor a revolutionary. He was definitely a political nonconformist with a keen sense of social justice, but these traits had not yet led him to espouse any particular political cause or ideology. Rojo recalls that when they first met, Ernesto was uncertain about what he wanted to do with his life, but very sure about what he did not want to do with it.

In September 1953, Ernesto, Calica, and Rojo left Bolivia for Peru. According to Rojo, Ernesto demanded that his traveling companions be willing to walk interminably, be devoid of any concern about the condition of their clothing, and accept without anguish the state of being absolutely without money. Soon after they entered Peru, they separated. Ernesto and Calica went to visit Machu Picchu, the lost city of the Incas, and Rojo went on to Lima. A few weeks later, they met again in Lima, and from there they traveled together to Guayaquil, Ecuador. After several weeks in Guayaquil, Ernesto decided to follow Rojo to Guatemala, instead of going with Calica to Venezuela to join Alberto Granados. His decision appears to have been based on two considerations. First, he seems to have been influenced by Rojo's enthusiasm to observe at first hand the popular reformist regime then in power in Guatemala. Probably even more important was the reality that he had no money to travel any farther, and he had managed through friends in Guayaquil to obtain free passage on a ship owned by the infamous United Fruit Company that was bound for Panama.

Ernesto did not reach Guatemala until January 1954, having spent a number of weeks on the way in Costa Rica and Panama, where he met Juan Bosch, the famous nationalist leader of the

Dominican Republic. When he finally arrived in Guatemala City, he located himself in a pension where a number of young Peruvian exiles were staying. These Peruvians were militant members of Peru's left-wing APRA party (American Popular Revolutionary Alliance, known as the Partido Aprista Peruano), then under attack in Peru because of its opposition to the dictatorial regime of Manuel Odría. Offered asylum by the Guatemalan authorities, these Peruvians had found employment in the various agencies of the Guatemalan government that were engaged in economic planning and agrarian reform, subjects on which they were regarded as experts. Through his association with the Peruvians staying at the pension, Ernesto was introduced to a number of interesting people, including some Cuban political exiles. Among these people was a young Peruvian exile named Hilda Gadea, whom he later married.

Since Ernesto needed money to pay his bills at the pension and wanted to stay in Guatemala, he went to the Ministry of Public Health to seek employment as a doctor in one of the government's public assistance programs. He was interested in working with one program in particular, which was being carried out among the Mayan Indians in the region of the ancient temple of Tikal. Apparently, he never succeeded in getting an interview with the elusive minister of health, and finally Hilda arranged a job interview for him with the head of the youth wing of the Partido Guatemalteco de los Trabajadores (the former name of the Guatemalan Communist Party). She recalls that everything went fine until she told him that the party leader wanted Ernesto to join the party (Anderson 1997, 138). According to Hilda, Ernesto told her that the day he decided to affiliate himself with a particular political party it would be out of conviction and not out of necessity.

Having failed to secure employment as a doctor, Ernesto

started selling encyclopedias. Before long, however, Hilda was able to obtain a position for him in one of the agrarian reform programs. Through Hilda, he became friends with a number of Guatemalan leftists, and at their suggestion he began to read the works of Marx and Lenin. From this point forward, he seems to have begun to take a serious interest in politics.

At the end of February 1954, Ricardo Rojo received some money from his parents in Argentina, and he decided to travel to the United States. Ernesto chose to remain in Guatemala City because of his interest in Hilda and the revolutionary programs of the Guatemalan regime. But events soon brought his stay to an abrupt conclusion.

Before 1944, Guatemala had been just another "banana republic," ruled by a series of dictators who served the interests of the local oligarchy and the American-owned United Fruit Company (Schlesinger and Kinzer 1982). But in 1944, the ruling strongman, Jorge Ubico, was overthrown by a popular revolt led by junior army officers and students. On the surface, the revolt appeared to be aimed primarily at replacing Ubico's oppressive regime with a more democratic government. In reality, though, the groups that participated in the revolt demanded the complete reform of Guatemala's exploitative economic and social order. Following the overthrow of the Ubico regime, elections were held, and Juan José Arévalo became Guatemala's first popularly elected president. Under Arévalo's rule a major effort was made to bring Guatemala's large Indian population into the twentieth century, and a large number of farm and city workers were unionized. The revolutionary policies of Arévalo's regime were continued and in fact accelerated by Arévalo's successor, Jacobo Arbenz, who was elected president in 1951. By the time Ernesto arrived in Guatemala, in early 1954, the Arbenz regime had distributed to some

100,000 Guatemalan peasants uncultivated land that the government had expropriated from the country's large feudal estates, including eleven thousand hectares of uncultivated land belonging to the United Fruit Company. The response from the United States was almost immediate.

At the March 1954 foreign ministers' meeting of the Organization of American States (OAS), U.S. Secretary of State John Foster Dulles accused the Arbenz regime of being "Communist-infiltrated" (Schlesinger and Kinzer 1982). He also succeeded in having passed the famous Resolution 93, which indirectly condemned the Arbenz regime and expressed the right of the OAS members "to take the necessary measures to protect themselves against Communist intervention." The necessary measures in the case of Guatemala involved the preparation of a mercenary invasion force in neighboring Honduras and El Salvador. On June 17, this force, under the command of Carlos Castillo Armas, crossed the frontiers of Guatemala and began marching toward the capital. The invasion was supported by the CIA, which supplied the invaders with arms and planes and also arranged for the betrayal of the higher echelons of the Guatemalan army. In a matter of days, the Arbenz regime collapsed and Castillo Armas assumed control of the country. One of his first acts was the issuance of a decree returning expropriated lands to their former owners.

When the invasion began, Ernesto and his Peruvian friends watched in exasperation as Arbenz naïvely relied upon the army to repulse the attacks and refused to give arms to the various left-wing parties and organizations that were demanding them so that they could help defend "their revolution" (Castañeda 1997, 67–76). As Castillo Armas's small force of mercenaries neared the capital with hardly any resistance from the army, Ernesto could no longer contain his frustration with what he saw happening around him. In a desperate effort to save the revolution that he had only recently adopted, he went to the leaders of the various left-wing youth organizations and exhorted them to assume immediate control of the capital and defend it against the mercenaries who were advancing against it. However, his frantic efforts to mobilize popular support for the Arbenz regime succeeded only in drawing the attention of the CIA and Castillo Armas's agents in the capital.

Ernesto would almost certainly have been imprisoned, and probably executed, if it had not been for the Argentine ambassador. Having been advised that there was an Argentine on the list of those who would be executed by the new regime, the ambassador went to Ernesto and offered him asylum in the Argentine embassy. At first Ernesto refused, but the ambassador convinced him that he couldn't do alone what the Guatemalans themselves were not disposed to do.

Ernesto remained approximately a month in the Argentine embassy in Guatemala City along with a number of other Latin Americans who were given asylum there. For the purposes of quartering these individuals, the embassy classified them either as "Communists" or "moderates." Because of his activities during the invasion, Ernesto was classified as a Communist and located in a special part of the embassy. Later, the ambassador offered him space on an Argentine military plane if he wanted to return to Argentina, but Ernesto declined the offer and asked the ambassador whether he could secure a guarantee of safe conduct for him so that he could travel to Mexico. This was arranged, and he departed by train for Mexico City.

When Ernesto arrived in Mexico City, he discovered that it was a haven for exiles from all over Latin America. In addition to the latest influx of Guatemalan exiles, there were political refugees from the Dominican Republic, Peru, Cuba, Colombia, Venezuela, Haiti, and his own Argentina. Most of these exiles lived in the same pensions and frequented the same bars and cafés. Hilda was expelled from Guatemala and followed Ernesto to Mexico City, where they subsequently rented a flat in the section of the city where most of the exiles were living. Shortly afterward they were married, and in February 1955 they had a child, a girl whom they named Hilda and called Hildita.

Ernesto managed to make ends meet as a photographer and by working in hospital laboratories. He became a regular member of the exile community and was friendly in particular with the Cubans. As time went by, he became increasingly bitter about his Guatemalan experience and developed a deep hatred for the United States, which he blamed for the overthrow of the Guatemalan regime and for most of Latin America's economic and political ills.

In one of the many gatherings of his fellow exiles, Ernesto met Raúl Castro, Fidel Castro's brother (Anderson 1997, 173–74). Shortly after arriving in Mexico in early September 1954, Guevara renewed his friendship with Ñico López and the other Cuban exiles he had known in Guatemala. In June 1955, López introduced him to Raúl Castro. Some weeks later, Fidel Castro arrived in Mexico City, following his release from a Cuban prison, where he had been incarcerated for the abortive attack he had led against the Moncada barracks in 1953. On the evening of July 8, 1955, Raúl introduced Guevara to Fidel. Ernesto was impressed by Fidel's intelligence and his determination to return to Cuba and fight for the liberation of his people from the dictatorship of Fulgencio Batista.

They immediately took a liking to each other and became close friends. In the journal he was keeping at the time, Che wrote, "I

met Fidel Castro, the Cuban revolutionary. He is a young, intelligent guy, very sure of himself and extraordinarily audacious; I
think we hit it off well" (Guevara 2002, 32). Fidel and Raúl told
Ernesto of their plans to invade Cuba with a contingent of well-
armed men and appeal to the peasants to join them in revolting
against the dictatorial Batista regime. Ernesto asked whether they
could use a doctor in the contingent, and when they said yes, he
volunteered to join them. From this point on, Hilda said, Ernesto
spoke of nothing but the Cuban revolution, and in the end she
lost her husband to this cause.

Fidel left Mexico for a time to seek support from the Cubans
living in the United States who were opposed to Batista (Castañeda 1997, 76–98). From these fellow exiles, he collected funds
and recruits for his planned invasion, and when he returned to
Mexico he obtained the services of a Colonel Alberto Bayo to
train his recruits in the tactics of guerrilla warfare. Colonel Bayo,
a former officer in the Spanish Republican Army, had gained a
great deal of experience in guerrilla warfare in Morocco against
the Arabs and in the Spanish civil war against Franco's fascist
forces. With his assistance, Fidel established a secret training
camp for his group at a large ranch in the mountainous Chalco
district of Mexico. Fidel brought eighty men to the training camp,
including Ernesto. At the end of the training period, Colonel Bayo
singled out Ernesto as his best student.

It was during this training period in Mexico that Ernesto's
Cuban comrades gave him the nickname Che. They called him
Che because like most Argentines he used the word "che" constantly, which is similar to both "Hey!" or "buddy" in English
and is used by most Argentines to catch attention and/or express
familiarity. He accepted this nickname with pride because it
marked him as Argentine.

In November 1956, Che and the others departed for Cuba on an old launch named *Granma* (Guevara 1968c, 40). Because of the poor condition of the boat, which was designed to carry twenty persons instead of over eighty, and the bad weather at sea, it took them a week to reach Cuban waters. When they finally reached the Cuban coastline near Cape Cruz, it was dark, and the launch got stuck in a marsh along the shoreline. As a result, the guerrillas were forced to abandon their heavy equipment and most of their supplies and make their way to dry land by wading through the muddy marsh. For several days, they marched toward the neighboring Sierra Maestra mountains without encountering any resistance, but on December 5, they were surprised by the army on a sugarcane plantation where they had stopped to rest. Only Che, Fidel, Raúl, and nine others managed to escape and make their way to the Sierra Maestra. In the fighting, Che was wounded in both the throat and the chest, but his wounds were not serious and he survived with only the most rudimentary medical treatment.

The twelve survivors of the *Granma* were joined by five discontented peasants in January 1957, and this minuscule group began operating as a guerrilla force from its hiding places in the Sierra Maestra. As the months went by, the guerrillas managed to carry out a number of daring attacks against small military outposts in the region, and the news of their actions attracted the support of student groups all over the country. In time, the ranks of the guerrilla force swelled with recruits from these groups and from the sympathetic peasantry.

Che was to have been the medical officer of the force, but his value as a guerrilla leader soon became evident. He so distinguished himself in the group's first encounters with the army that Fidel gave him increasingly greater military responsibilities.

In March 1957, Fidel appointed him, along with Ramiro Valdés, Ciro Redondo, and Camilo Cienfuegos, to the rank of captain. A short time later, Che was promoted to the rank of comandante (major), the highest rank in the guerrilla army, and in July 1957 Fidel placed Che at the head of a new column with instructions to operate apart from the main force.

By March 1958, the guerrillas had succeeded in defeating every effort by the regular army to dislodge them from the Sierra Maestra. Consequently, Fidel decided to extend the scope of the war and sent his brother Raúl to the northern end of Cuba's Oriente province to establish a second guerrilla front in the mountains there. At the beginning of April, he also called on the Cuban people to support a general strike against the Batista regime. But his call for a strike did not receive widespread popular support, and Batista decided the moment had arrived to launch an all-out attack against Castro. He threw the full weight of the Cuban army, air force, and navy against the guerrillas. This massive offensive forced the guerrillas to give up 90 percent of the territory over which they exercised some control. However, the offensive failed to destroy the rebel army, and by July 1958 it began to take the initiative away from Batista's troops. In fact, during the first eleven days of combat in July, the guerrillas captured over two hundred of Batista's soldiers, who were no match for Fidel's men in the rugged terrain of the Sierra Maestra.

Having turned Batista's offensive into a guerrilla victory, Fidel attracted major political support. On July 20, the leaders of the various Cuban political parties opposing the Batista regime, moderates and conservatives alike, signed a declaration in Caracas in which they threw their support behind the guerrillas. The only party that refused to sign the Caracas declaration was the Cuban Communist Party.

In August 1958, Fidel gave Che instructions to take his column down from the Sierra Maestra toward the province of Las Villas, in the central portion of the island. As his column moved across the lowlands toward Las Villas, it won one battle after another, and the almost suicidal character of its maneuvers began to seriously demoralize the regular army. In a desperate attempt to shore up his shaky regime, Batista tried to stage a rigged national election in November 1958. But the election was boycotted by a majority of the citizenry and by all the political parties that had signed the Caracas declaration.

The public's repudiation of the election so infuriated Batista that he launched a reign of police terror against the general populace. The guerrillas took this as the cue to begin their general offensive. Fidel ordered Camilo Cienfuegos to take a column down to the plains and support Che in his drive toward Las Villas. From there, the two columns proceeded to cut the country in half and liquidate Batista's main forces in the eastern half of the island.

The decisive battle of the war was fought by Che's column in the city of Santa Clara in December 1958. He arrived at the city at the head of a convoy of confiscated trucks and jeeps, which were filled with his guerrillas from the Sierra Maestra, as well as students and peasants who had joined his force in increasing numbers as he moved across the plains. The column headed first to the university, and from there Che sent contingents to capture various strategic sites in the city. It was at this point that an armored train arrived in the city with four hundred government reinforcements. Che gave his men instructions to concentrate their fire on the train when it stopped to unload its cargo of troops. As a result, the soldiers could not disembark. Moreover, when the train tried to reverse its direction, it was derailed; Che had ordered a patrol to separate the rails behind it after it arrived. Surrounded, and with no hope of escape, the soldiers had no choice but to surrender to the rebels.

As word went through the city of the capture of the reinforcements, the citizenry began barricading the streets with cars and buses in order to obstruct the movement of the army's tanks and armored cars. Then, from the balconies of their houses and apartments, the city's inhabitants and the guerrillas threw Molotov cocktails on the military vehicles as they attempted to pass through the barricaded streets. Batista ordered his air force to bomb the city, but, although many sections were reduced to rubble, the situation could not be reversed. Che's column had gained control of the city. On January 1, 1959, word reached Santa Clara that Batista and his immediate family had fled to the Dominican Republic. Informed of this, the troops still holding out in certain parts of the city surrendered to Che.

On January 3, 1959, Che and Camilo Cienfuegos arrived with their men in Havana. Meanwhile, Fidel marched with his troops to Santiago de Cuba to capture the Moncada, the same fortress where he had made an abortive attempt six years earlier to bring down the Batista regime. On January 5, five Latin American countries recognized Fidel's provisional government. Great Britain and a number of other nations followed. On January 7, the United States recognized the new regime and recalled Ambassador Earl Smith, who was unanimously condemned by Cuban public opinion for having supported Batista. Finally, on January 8, Fidel arrived in Havana, where Che and Camilo Cienfuegos awaited him.

As Fidel triumphantly rode into the city, his brother Raúl was on his right and Che on his left. In less than three years, the young Argentine had risen from the obscure existence of a roving young adventurer to become one of the most popular and important leaders in the Cuban revolution. Three years earlier, he had only begun to think seriously about his political convictions and commitments, but now, at the age of thirty-one, he found himself an accomplished military commander and one of the three most powerful leaders in the new government of Cuba.

While historical circumstances, destiny, or fate—call it what you will—must be given some of the credit for Che's meteoric rise to fame and power, the importance of the man's personality must not be underrated. By the time he arrived in Havana, Che seems to have acquired all the characteristics of a true revolutionary and charismatic leader. He demonstrated an amazing capacity for personal sacrifice, and he never compromised his ideals. From the time he became a guerrilla, he appears to have lived according to the motto *"todo o nada"* (all or nothing). In fact, he was so demanding of himself that he did not permit himself a single indulgence. This, of course, made it possible for him to demand a great deal from those around him.

Che had that quality of personal magnetism that attracts and inspires the loyalty and devotion of others. In the Sierra Maestra, his boldness and determination evoked the enthusiasm of his comrades, and it soon became clear to Fidel that Che was a natural leader. Once having elevated him to a position of leadership, Fidel found that Che was an extremely capable and resourceful military commander. He gave Che increasingly greater responsibilities and, in the end, entrusted him with the most important and crucial campaign of the Cuban revolutionary war.

Fidel had complete confidence in Che, since he knew that Che had no personal political ambitions. He recognized that Che, as an Argentine, felt it was not his place to question the basic political objectives chosen by his Cuban comrades. Fidel knew that he could count on Che's loyalty and unquestioning devotion to the goals of the revolution. Their relationship was close, largely because of the similarity of their thinking, and it was only much later that Che ever differed with Fidel on any major issues.

After Fidel's seizure of power, there followed a period in which the new regime suffered a series of strains and internal struggles. On May 17, 1959, Fidel put into effect a new agrarian reform law that eliminated Cuba's large estates and turned these lands over to the formerly landless peasantry through a form of collective ownership. This was immediately interpreted by the press and government officials in the United States as a threat to private property. In the ensuing months, the value of shares in Cuban sugar companies dropped to an all-time low on the New York Stock Exchange, and Cuba's relations with the U.S. government rapidly deteriorated.

During the first six months of the new government, Che became one of Fidel's closest confidants and advisers. In February 1959, Che was proclaimed by an official decree to be a Cuban by birth. He brought his estranged wife, Hilda, and their daughter, Hildita, to Cuba; but Che and Hilda were divorced shortly after her arrival. On June 2, he married Aleida March, who had joined his guerrilla column six months before the end of the war. Aleida was one of the leaders of the underground network of the 26th of July Movement, and she served as Che's assistant during the last months of the war. They had been living together since that time. Less than two weeks after their marriage, the first serious crisis of the new Cuban government occurred, and five cabinet ministers who disagreed with Fidel over the direction the new regime resigned. A few days later, Che left Cuba on a goodwill tour to Yugoslavia, the Middle East, and Asia. His departure was the result of pressure brought to bear on Fidel by those in the government who considered Che too radical.

Che returned to Cuba in September 1959, after an absence of three months. In the meantime, Fidel had purged his government of the more moderate elements and had decided to sell five million tons of sugar to the Soviet Union. Shortly after Che's return, Fidel presided over a meeting of the new National Institute of Agrarian Reform and announced that he was appointing Che head of the Department of Industries in that organization (later Che was made minister of industries and given control over both Cuba's agrarian reform and its industrialization programs). At the end of November, Fidel appointed Che to the important post of president of the National Bank of Cuba, which placed him in charge of all the country's financial affairs. Shortly after Che assumed this position, he made a public declaration in which he indicated that Cuba would not give any special guarantees to foreign capital and that the country would seek trade and financial ties with the Communist bloc.

Throughout the early sixties, Che remained one of Fidel's closest advisers and one of the most important members of his cabinet. He was second only to Raúl Castro in his proximity to Fidel. In addition to his political responsibilities, he wrote what has now become a classic work on guerrilla warfare, *La guerra de guerrillas* (Guevara 1961), plus books and articles on various subjects, perhaps one of the most famous being *Reminiscences of the Cuban Revolutionary War* (Guevara 1968c).

To most of those who knew and observed him during the years he served at Fidel's side, Che was the model revolutionary leader. He was dedicated to his duties, absolutely convinced of the rightness of his cause, and devoted to Fidel. In the opinion of many, he was the most intelligent and persuasive member of Fidel's cabinet. But he was dissatisfied with the routine and bureaucratic aspects of his ministerial responsibilities. On a number of occasions, he told his friends of his desire to return to the revolutionary struggle. As time went by, he spoke increasingly of the possibility of leaving his ministerial post and devoting his future efforts to the revolution against imperialism in Latin America and in other parts of the world.

Moreover, Che's own personal austerity and disregard for flattery and personal gain presented a sharp contrast to the self-indulgent lifestyles, womanizing, and personal excesses of many of the people around him (Anderson 1997, 571–72). In this regard, it is interesting to note that even though he was one of the most important and high-ranking members of the Cuban revolutionary government, he was famous for his careless appearance—he always wore his uniform shirt out of his pants and open at the throat, and the laces of his boots were never laced to the top. Moreover, when he visited Cuba's industries, he always entered the workshops first to talk with the workers, and only later would he go to the offices of the managers (Taibo 1996, 467).

His casual dress and unconventional behavior can be traced to his "vagabond" trips around South America as a young man, when he seems to have taken delight in traveling for days without bathing or changing his clothes, and was not distressed by having little or no money or having no idea where he would stay the night. All of these traits helped him later as a guerrilla fighter, when he often had to go without bathing, food, water, or a roof over his head.

In the prologue to Che's *Motorcycle Diaries* written by his father, the latter notes that it is from Che's letters about his travels through South America that we can "come to understand that he was following a truly missionary impulse which never left him" (Guevara 1995, 3). As his father claims in the following passage, we can see in Che's motorcycle diaries that Che "had faith in himself as well as the will to succeed, and a tremendous determination to achieve what he set out to do. Add to this an intelligence of which he gave ample evidence and you can understand how he achieved so much in such a short time" (Guevara 1995, 4). His motorcycle diaries also reveal his growing sense of indignation and his early leanings toward socialism as he became aware through his travels of the extreme conditions of social injustice in Latin America. What is most striking about the motorcycle diaries, however, is that while they reveal his strong desire to help others less fortunate than himself they reveal he did not possess the kind of self-righteousness or exaggerated piety that one often associates with zealous do-gooders and missionaries. Che had an ironic and sarcastic wit and a sharp tongue, but he could also laugh at himself. He practiced a curious blend of romanticism and pragmatism; and while he did demand a great deal of those around him, he demanded even more of himself (Anderson 1997, 572).

In his lifestyle and personal conduct, he exemplified the principles of individual sacrifice, honesty, loyalty, and dedication. Women flocked to him, and he was constantly approached by people who wanted to do him favors, but he spurned all attempts at flattery and pandering, hated brownnosers, and remained monogamous throughout his days in Cuba (Anderson 1997, 572).

In the fall of 1960, Che was asked by a reporter from *Look* magazine whether he was an orthodox Communist. His answer was no—he preferred to call himself a "pragmatic revolutionary." In fact, he was neither a pragmatic revolutionary nor an orthodox Communist. To be sure, his outlook, his prejudices, and the events in which he participated located him among the Communist ranks. But, as the *New York Times* correspondent Herbert Matthews said after interviewing him in 1960, Che would have had no emotional or intellectual problem in opposing the Communists if the circumstances had been otherwise (Matthews 1961). He made common cause with the Communists because they were opposed to the same things in contemporary Latin American society that he was opposed to. Che differed from the orthodox Communists in that he refused to accept their rigid ideological position on the lack of the proper conditions for a socialist revolution in Latin America and the rest of the Third World. He firmly believed that the Cuban experience demonstrated that socialist revolutions in the Third World could be successfully launched without the direction and control of an orthodox Communist party. Such "heretical" views earned him the disfavor of the pro-Soviet Communists.

Che's unorthodox political views and his distrust of the Soviet Union made him a prime target of the pro-Soviet Communists in Cuba. This group, led by Aníbal Escalante, was in constant conflict with Che, right up to the time of his resignation from the cabinet in 1965. According to them, Cuba's economic instability and its strained relations with the Soviet Union were a direct result of Che's impractical projects and his "pathological" revolutionary adventurism.

The assertion by members of this group that Che was a pathological adventurer must be discounted as an obvious attempt on their part to discredit a man who stood in the way of the policies advocated by these pro-Soviet Communists. Nevertheless, Che was a dreamer and an adventurer. He was prone to dreaming up grandiose plans and projects, especially when he was confined to bed by his as asthma. One of his dreams was to lead a revolution in his native Argentina. And only a dreamer could have believed, as he did, that the revolutionary liberation of Latin America was an objective capable of realization in the mid-1960s.

As for the assertion that Che was an adventurer, this he admitted himself in his farewell letter to his parents (Gerassi 1968, 412), which he wrote in the spring of 1965 (shortly before he departed from Cuba on a secret mission to help the rebel forces in the Congo).

Dear Parents:

Once again I feel below my heels the ribs of Rosinante [Don Quixote's scrawny horse]. I return to the road with my shield on my arm.

Almost ten years ago, I wrote you another farewell letter. As I remember, I lamented not being a better soldier and a better doctor. The second doesn't interest me any longer. As a soldier I am not so bad.

Nothing in essence has changed, except that I am much more conscious, and my Marxism has taken root and become pure. I believe in the armed struggle as the only solution for those peoples who fight to free themselves, and I am consistent with my beliefs. Many will call me an adventurer, and that I am; only one of a different kind—one of those who risks his skin to prove his beliefs.

It could be that this may be the end. Not that I look for it, but it is within the logical calculus of probabilities. If it is so, I send you a last embrace. I have loved you very much, only I have not known how to express my love. I am extremely rigid in my actions and I believe that at times you did not understand me. It was not easy to understand me. On the other hand, I ask only that you believe in me today.

Now, a will that I have polished with the delight of an artist will sustain my pair of flaccid legs and tired lungs. I will do it!

Remember from time to time this little condottiere [Italian term for the captain of a band of soldiers of fortune] of

the twentieth century. A kiss to Celia, to Roberto, Juan Mar-
tín and Pototín, to Beatriz, to everyone. A large embrace from
your recalcitrant prodigal son.

                                                    Ernesto

Che knew full well that his life might come to a tragic end. In
addition to his reference to this in his farewell letter to his parents,
he also acknowledged the possibility in a letter that he sent at
about the same time to his old friend and traveling partner Alberto
Granados. There he prophetically wrote, "My rolling house has
two legs once again and my dreams will have no frontier—at least
until the bullets speak."

Che was not a fanatic, and he did not have a pathological love
of bloodshed or human cruelty. He was not, however, a normal
and contented man. If he had been, he would never have become
a revolutionary. He was a dreamer, an adventurer, and an unre-
lenting rebel against the established order of things. He was a
man deeply incensed by the social injustices that he saw in the
world all around him, and he was motivated by a sincere desire
to rectify them.

He was the personification of the true revolutionary—a super-
idealist who insisted on bringing heaven immediately to earth.
Moreover, his willingness to die for his ideals is proof that he
possessed far more courage and conviction than the ordinary man
or woman. Indeed, the fact that he fought and died for what he
believed in makes him stand out in sharp contrast to the vast
majority of Latin America's political leaders, whose opportunism
and lack of conviction have left the poor majority of the region's
population with little hope that their condition will ever be
improved by the existing political order.

Chapter 3

CHE'S THEORIES ON
REVOLUTIONARY WARFARE

Above all it must be made clear that this type of struggle
is a method: a method for achieving a purpose. That
purpose, indispensable and unavoidable for every revolutionary, is the conquest of political power.
  —Che Guevara, "Guerrilla Warfare: A Method" (1963)

Any book written on the history of Latin American social
and political thought in the twentieth century must
include a discussion of Che Guevara's ideas about revolution and guerrilla warfare. His writings on this subject are required
reading for all those interested in understanding the nature of
guerrilla warfare and the conditions that recommend its use.
Che's book *La guerra de guerrillas* (entitled *Guerrilla Warfare* in
the English translation, 1985), which was first published in 1961,
is now considered one of the most important works on guerrilla
warfare ever written. This book, along with certain articles written by Che, in particular his "Guerra de guerrillas: Un metodo"
(translated in English as "Guerrilla Warfare: A Method," in Ger-

assi 1968, 266–79), put forward a complete theory of revolution-ary guerrilla warfare, largely based upon the Cuban experience. This theory has influenced revolutionary movements throughout Latin America and the rest of the world, and it inspired many radical groups to go off into the hills to start a revolutionary guer-rilla *foco* (a Spanish word used to refer to the focal point or center of guerrilla operations) like the one established by Fidel Castro, Che, and their comrades in the Sierra Maestra of Cuba.

While a guerrilla leader in the Sierra Maestra, Che made it a daily habit to write down his observations in a personal campaign diary. At the end of a long day's march or after an engagement with the enemy, he always sat down somewhere apart from the others to write about the events of the day. On the basis of these notes, he was later able to formulate his theories about guerrilla warfare and to write an excellent historical account of the Cuban revolutionary war, entitled *Pasajes de la guerra revolucionaria* (the English edition is entitled *Episodes of the Revolutionary War*, 1996).

Che believed that the Cuban revolution clearly demonstrated that the people of Latin America can liberate themselves from dictatorial rule if they resort to guerrilla warfare. In his book *La guerra de guerrillas*, Che wrote that the Cuban revolution had made three fundamental contributions to revolutionary thought in Latin America. First, the Cuban experience proved that popu-lar, irregular forces could win a war against a professional army. Second, it showed that it is not necessary to wait until all the con-ditions for revolution are present. According to Che, the insurrec-tional guerrilla *foco* can itself create the necessary conditions.

Finally, Che believed that Cuba demonstrated that in Latin America, which has a large rural population, a revolutionary struggle must initially concentrate on the rural areas and not the cities if it is to succeed. Che claimed that the first two of these contributions refuted the arguments of those who claimed to be revolutionaries but refused to take any revolutionary action, on the pretext that they could not defeat a professional army or that the necessary "objective conditions" for revolution did not exist in Latin America.

Che contended that a nucleus of from thirty to fifty determined men could establish and consolidate a revolutionary guerrilla *foco* in any country of Latin America, provided they had the cooperation of the people and a perfect knowledge of the terrain upon which they would be operating. He also stressed that the people must believe it is impossible for them to obtain social and economic reforms through peaceful means before they will be inclined to support an insurrectionary guerrilla *foco*. Moreover, where a government has risen to power by some form of popular consultation, including fraudulent elections, and maintains at least the appearance of constitutional legality, it is impossible to establish and consolidate a guerrilla *foco* because many of the people will still believe that there is some chance of improving their social and economic conditions through legal means.

Che was very critical of those who argued that the revolutionary struggle in Latin America depended primarily upon the political mobilization of the discontented urban masses in the cities. He felt that it was far more difficult to carry out a successful insurrection in the cities, where the armed forces and police can be effectively concentrated and utilized, than in the rural areas, where regular troops are at the mercy of a highly mobile guerrilla force supported by the rural population. The support of the rural population, according to Che, is the sine qua non of guerrilla warfare. In fact, he defined guerrilla war as a war of the people, led by a fighting vanguard (the nuclear guerrilla force) against the forces of the ruling oligarchies (elites) and their foreign backers (the U.S. government and the transnational corporations with investments in the Third World). Thus, in Che's view, the guerrilla force does not seize power by itself; rather, it serves as a catalyst that inspires the masses themselves to take up arms and overthrow the established regime.

In *La guerra de guerrillas*, Che wrote that without the support of the people, a guerrilla force is nothing more than a roving gang of bandits. Both have the same characteristics: homogeneous membership, respect for their leaders, courage, knowledge of the terrain, and appreciation of the correct tactics to employ against numerically superior forces. They differ, however, in a fundamental respect: one has the support of the people, and the other does not. Consequently, bandits are inevitably hunted down and eliminated, whereas guerrilla forces, which count upon the support of the people, can defeat a professional army and bring about the downfall of the most oppressive regime.

The guerrilla force, according to Che, wins the support of the masses in the rural areas largely by championing their grievances. This means that the guerrillas must present themselves as crusaders intent upon righting the injustices of the prevailing social order. Che believed that the major grievances shared by the rural masses throughout Latin America arise from the concentration of landownership in the hands of a small wealthy landed elite. The great majority of the peasantry do not own the land upon which they live and work. Consequently, land reform is the key issue to be used by guerrilla forces in their effort to win the support of the rural masses. In other words, the guerrilla fighter must be an agrarian revolutionary who uses the peasantry's hunger for land as the basis for mobilizing their support.

Che also believed that any revolutionary guerrilla force must be the conscience of the people, and that the moral behavior of each guerrilla must be such that the people regard him as a true priest of the social reforms that he advocates. The guerrilla must always exercise rigid self-control and never permit himself a single excess or weakness. This means that the guerrilla must be an ascetic whose moral behavior earns him the respect and admiration of the local population. In addition, it is the duty of guerrillas to give technical, economic, and social assistance to the peasantry. In this way, they develop a close relationship with the peasantry, which allows them to win their trust and confidence. Once this relationship has been achieved, it becomes the task of the guerrillas to indoctrinate the peasants about the fundamental importance of the armed struggle as the only way in which they can liberate themselves from their present state of exploitation and oppression. Che believed that the successful execution of this task brings about a true people's war and the inevitable destruction of the existing regime.

One of Che's most original contributions to the literature on guerrilla warfare is his discussion of the qualities of the guerrilla fighter. According to him, the ideal guerrilla soldier is an inhabitant of the zone in which the nuclear guerrilla *foco* is established. This is because the two most important prerequisites of successful guerrilla warfare are a thorough knowledge of the terrain and the cooperation of the local population. The guerrilla who is an inhabitant of the region in which he is operating knows the terrain and has friends in the area to whom he can turn for help. It follows that in Latin America the local campesino (peasant) makes the best guerrilla soldier, although Che emphasized that a guerrilla force should not be composed exclusively of campesinos.

Che seems to have been describing himself without knowing it when he listed the personal qualities that the ideal guerrilla soldier should have. He stressed audacity and a readiness to take an optimistic attitude at times when an analysis of existing conditions does not warrant it. He also indicated that the guerrilla fighter must be ready to risk his or her life on an almost daily basis and voluntarily to give it up if the circumstances require it. This, of course, demands a high degree of devotion to the cause for which the guerrillas are fighting, and, according to Che, such devotion can be sustained only if the guerrilla movement is based upon an ideal or ideals that are meaningful to each guerrilla fighter. He concluded that among nearly all campesinos such an ideal is the right to have a piece of land as their own, while the ideal of adequate wages and better social conditions plays a comparable role among guerrillas from the urban working classes, and more abstract ideals, such as political freedom and social equality, motivate students and intellectuals.

In addition to the moral and psychological qualities that make a good guerrilla fighter, he or she must also have certain important physical qualities and be able to adapt to the most difficult environmental conditions. As Che himself knew well from his own experience, the conditions of guerrilla life require the endurance of severe privations, including the lack of food, water, proper clothing, shelter, and medical attention. Moreover, the guerrilla must be able to adapt to a life of almost constant movement in which he or she is required to march long distances and traverse areas where no ordinary man or woman would ever venture.

Che wrote that, in terms of the general pattern of the guerrilla's day-to-day life, combat is the most interesting event that befalls them. Combat, therefore, is both the climax and the greatest joy of the guerrilla's life, and only through combat do they fulfill the purpose for which they exist. Che emphasized that the guerrillas must perform their role as combatants without any reluctance or weakness, since they must give the enemy no quarter and expect none in return. On the other hand, Che also made the point that wounded and captured enemy soldiers must be treated benevolently by the guerrilla soldier, unless they have committed criminal acts requiring that they be tried and perhaps executed.

The final objective of a revolutionary guerrilla war, according to Che, is the defeat of the enemy's army and the seizure of political power in the name of the people. However, he made it quite clear that guerrilla warfare cannot in itself bring about victory. He emphasized that it is important to remember that guerrilla warfare is only the first phase of a war of national liberation and that, unless it develops into a conventional war, the enemy cannot be completely defeated.

Che wrote that in the earliest stages the primary strategy of a revolutionary guerrilla force is to assure its own survival. This means that it must flee from and avoid the enemy forces sent to destroy it. During this phase, it must restrict its offensive activities to lightning attacks on unsuspecting enemy posts or units, and in each case retreat to a secure hiding place before the enemy has a chance to react with its superior forces and weapons. If the guerrilla force succeeds in eluding the forces sent to destroy it, Che assumed it will increasingly attract recruits from the rural population and gradually enlarge the scale of its operations, striking more frequently at the enemy troops in the zone surrounding the guerrilla *foco*. In this way, the guerrillas begin to weaken and demoralize the enemy's forces. By systematically harassing the enemy through surprise attacks, they also disrupt his communications and force him onto the defensive.

The next phase involves extending the territory of guerrilla activity by sending small groups deep into enemy territory to sabotage and terrorize the enemy's key centers of supply and communications. Meanwhile, the original base of guerrilla operations must be continually strengthened and measures taken to indoctrinate the inhabitants of the guerrilla zone. Later, when more recruits and arms have been obtained and the circumstances appear to warrant an expansion of the conflict, new guerrilla columns are formed and sent to operate in areas behind the enemy's lines.

The final phase of the struggle begins, according to Che, when the guerrilla columns unite and engage the enemy's forces in a conventional war of fixed fronts. It is at this moment that the "people's army" comes into existence and the drive toward the cities begins. The death knell of the old order arrives when the urban masses turn upon the defending troops, and the last strongholds of enemy resistance surrender to the people's army. This outcome clears the way for the revolutionary leaders to seize power and begin the building of a new society.

Che warned that a people's army does not emerge spontaneously and that victory is obtained only after a long and difficult struggle, in which the people's forces and their leaders are exposed to repeated attacks by superior forces intent upon annihilating them. He also pointed out that the guerrillas must expect to suffer greatly at the hands of the enemy. Che made this point most effectively in the following passage from his article "Guerrilla Warfare: A Method," which prophetically describes the situation his guerrilla force encountered in Bolivia:

> The enemy army will punish them severely. At times they will be split up into groups, and those who fall prisoner will be tortured. They will be hounded relentlessly like hunted animals in the areas they have chosen for their operation. They will suffer the constant uneasiness of having enemies at their

heels, and they will constantly have to suspect all they encounter, since the frightened peasants will in some instances hand them over to the repressive troops in order to rid themselves of the latter by removing the reason for their presence. Their only alternative will be death or victory, at times when death is a thousand times present and victory is a myth about which only a revolutionary can dream. (Gerassi 1968, 276)

However, Che argued that even if only a fragment of the original guerrilla nucleus survives, it can continue to spark the revolutionary spirit of the masses and can organize anew to carry on the struggle.

Che believed that war is governed by a series of scientific laws, and that those who disregard these laws are destined to be defeated. Since guerrilla warfare is merely one type of war, he claimed, it is governed by the same laws. Because of its special aspects, however, guerrilla warfare is also governed by a series of accessory laws or principles that any guerrilla force that hopes to succeed must recognize.

Since one of the precepts of guerrilla warfare is the enemy's vast superiority in troops as well as in equipment, the guerrillas must utilize special tactics that will allow them to offset the enemy's superiority in troops and equipment. These tactics are based, as already mentioned, upon two essential preconditions: (1) the guerrillas must be highly mobile, and (2) they must possess a much greater knowledge of the terrain over which they will be operating than the enemy. Unless these two preconditions are met, the guerrillas will lack the minimal capabilities required for effectively utilizing the special tactics of guerrilla warfare.

Extreme mobility and a detailed knowledge of the terrain of operations make it possible, in Che's opinion, for the guerrillas to outmaneuver and surprise the numerically superior and better-equipped forces sent against them. With these capabilities, they can strike the enemy when it is off-guard, and then quickly disappear before it can retaliate, thus inflicting heavy casualties with very few or no losses of their own. "Strike and run, wait, watch carefully, and then again strike and run." This, in Che's words, is the primary tactic of guerrilla warfare, to be repeated over and over again until the enemy is demoralized and forced to take a static and essentially defensive posture. The basic characteristics of this tactic are the element of surprise and the rapidity of the guerrillas' attacking and withdrawal maneuvers. The speed and surprise inherent in this tactic give the guerrillas a great advantage over the enemy's larger and better-equipped forces. Moreover, it is particularly effective when used at night, and for this reason one of the basic features of guerrilla warfare is night fighting.

Somewhat more static than the hit-and-run technique, but just as effective, is the ambush. This tactic is, of course, as old as war itself and has always been used by the weak against the strong. It requires that the enemy be on the move—ideally, marching in file through a ravine, canyon, or pass, where it can be caught in a devastating crossfire. However, Che made an original contribution to this age-old tactic. In his writings, he mentions the psychological damage that can be inflicted upon the enemy if the guerrillas follow the practice of always concentrating their fire upon the advance elements of the army units they catch in their ambushes. This makes the enemy's soldiers realize that they can expect almost certain death if they are in the advance positions of a column. This tactic, Che claimed, creates panic among the soldiers and may even lead them to mutiny if they are ordered to take the lead positions in a column marching through a suspected guerrilla area.

In addition to the ambush and the rapid hit-and-run attack,

Che wrote about what is called the "minuet tactic." The kind of movement used with this tactic somewhat resembles the dance of the same name and involves surrounding an enemy column with several small groups. These groups alternately engage the enemy from different points. As soon as one group retreats, another one initiates an attack from a different direction. As a result, the enemy column is constantly kept off balance and demoralized. In fact, if the guerrillas have enough men and ammunition, and if the surrounded enemy column cannot receive outside aid, the guerrillas can annihilate the entire column by means of this tactic.

A guerrilla force must never allow itself to be encircled, for experience had shown, Che said, that the only really effective way of stamping out a guerrilla force is to encircle the guerrillas in a given area, concentrate as many troops in the circle as possible, and progressively close in around the guerrillas until they are completely liquidated. For this reason, guerrilla warfare is a war without any fixed front or battle lines. According to Che, the guerrillas must appear and disappear at the enemy's rear, at its flanks, and in its midst. In the initial stages, they rarely attempt to hold a given position, since their concern is to avoid encirclement or a frontal encounter with the enemy's superior forces. Instead, they aim to inflict as many casualties on the enemy's forces as possible without jeopardizing themselves. Confronted with this type of irregular warfare, the enemy's regular army is rendered powerless. Since it is equipped and trained to fight a conventional war or control the street demonstrations of students and workers, it becomes frightened and completely demoralized when forced to combat the tactics of the guerrillas.

Since one of the most important aspects of guerrilla warfare is the relationship that exists between the guerrillas and the local population, Che believed, the guerrillas should conduct themselves at all times in the most respectful manner toward the civilian population. For this reason, they should always pay for any goods taken, or at least give a certificate of debt to be paid at some future date. The zone of guerrilla operations must never be impoverished by the direct action of the guerrillas, and the local inhabitants must be permitted to sell their products outside the guerrilla zone, except under extreme circumstances. As their effort progresses and the whole area of a country comes under their control, then, the guerrillas must assume responsibility for governing the civilian population and regulating economic activity in the areas under their control.

Although Che considered sabotage one of the most effective tactics available to a revolutionary guerrilla movement, he was opposed to terrorism per se. He believed that terrorism is a negative weapon that can turn the people against a revolutionary movement. Moreover, the results of terrorist attacks are not worth the cost in lives that they entail. On the other hand, he distinguished sabotage (the destruction of essential industries and public works) from terrorism (the systematic use of violence to coerce the population) and advocated the destruction of nearly everything necessary for normal, modern life—telephone lines, electrical power stations, water mains, sewers, gas pipelines, railroads, radio and television stations, and so on. Yet even in the case of sabotage, a guerrilla force must consider the social consequences of each act of destruction so as not to cause unnecessary suffering among the urban and rural masses.

For Che, one of the most important characteristics of guerrilla warfare is the difference between the information possessed by the guerrillas and that possessed by the enemy. He saw the situation as one in which the enemy's regular forces must constantly operate in areas where they encounter the sullen silence of the local inhabitants, while the guerrillas can count upon a friend in every house who will pass information about the enemy's movements along to the guerrilla headquarters or the guerrilla force operating in the area. Che deemed this one of the greatest advantages enjoyed by the guerrillas, which they should utilize to the fullest extent.

However, a guerrilla force should never confide too much in the local peasantry, since peasants have a natural tendency to talk to their friends and relatives about everything they see and hear. Moreover, given the brutal way in which the regular troops treat the local population in an area where guerrillas are known to be operating, it is to be expected that certain members of the population will give the enemy information about the guerrillas in order to escape torture or mistreatment.

Since Che conceived of guerrilla warfare as a revolutionary war of the people in which the guerrillas serve as the revolutionary vanguard, he emphasized throughout his writings that the support of the masses is crucial to the success of any guerrilla insurgency. He therefore treated in detail how a guerrilla force secures and develops popular support. For this reason, his writings on revolutionary guerrilla war come closer to being a manual on how to organize and successfully execute a popular revolution than a theoretical work on military strategy and tactics per se.

Perceptive and eloquent as Che's writings on guerrilla warfare are, they do not provide a valid blueprint for replicating the Cuban revolution elsewhere. To make generalizations based upon one case is always inadvisable, and to do so with a view toward providing others with a formula for fomenting revolution elsewhere is especially dangerous.

Most revolutionary movements in Latin America following the Cuban revolution were based on Che's contention that a small band of from thirty to fifty guerrillas can create the conditions required for a revolutionary victory in any country of Latin America. Most of these movements, including the one directed by Che himself, failed to demonstrate that an insurrectionary guerrilla *foco* located in the rural areas can, by itself, produce a successful popular revolution.

The Cuban revolution was not purely a peasant revolution, mounted by a small guerrilla force that came down out of the mountains to liberate the cities. Che knew this. There is much more to the story of the Cuban revolution than this. To be sure, the guerrillas were the symbol of the revolution, and they played a crucial role in its development. However, Cuba's urban working and middle classes who threw their weight behind the guerrillas because of their hatred of the corrupt Batista regime, and the weakness of the Cuban army, which was unhappy about defending an unpopular regime, were also decisive factors. Moreover, if Castro had put forward a more radical program of social and economic reforms prior to his seizure of power, the revolutionary movement against Batista would not have been able to acquire the magnitude of popular support that made its victory possible. Castro cleverly presented himself as a moderate leader, who promised elections and a constitutional government once Batista's dictatorial regime was toppled.

In fact, the Cuban experience may well have made another Cuban type of revolution in Latin America very difficult to achieve. It is hard to imagine a revolutionary guerrilla movement today that would either (1) deceive the upper and middle classes into believing that it has moderate political aims or (2) win the support of U.S. and international public opinion as romantic freedom fighters combating a tyrannical regime. The political elites in Latin America have learned a lot from the Cuban revolution and subsequent attempts to replicate it. They now know that a revolutionary guerrilla force must be eliminated as soon as it appears, that the army must be effectively trained in counterinsurgency warfare, and that serious efforts must be made to win the support of the peasantry or at least to forestall their giving support to a revolutionary movement.

The apparent flaw in Che's theory of revolutionary guerrilla warfare was his overemphasis upon the rural population as the popular base for a successful revolutionary movement in Latin America. The armies of a number of Latin American countries, using modern counterinsurgency tactics that their officers have learned from U.S. advisers and training programs, have shown that they can defeat or at least contain a Cuban type of guerrilla movement that relies principally on a rural base of support.

Even more important is the obvious fact, recognized by most Latin Americans interested in revolution, that the main breeding grounds for any kind of radical popular movement in Latin America are the cities and towns. The cities are being inundated with migrants from the rural areas. Hoping to break away from the poverty and misery of rural Latin America, they generally find waiting for them in the cities unemployment and worse living conditions than they had in the rural areas. The frustration and discontent that derive from this situation provide a fertile soil for radical political groups. Thus, today and in the future, the exploding urban centers offer an important base of potential popular support for radical political movements in Latin America and in other parts of the world with similar social and economic conditions.

That said, it is important to note that in a modified form, Che's ideas on guerrilla warfare and the Cuban model of the catalytic guerrilla *foco* were adopted with some success by armed revolutionary movements in Central America in the 1970s and 1980s. The success of the Sandinista Front for National Liberation (Frente Sandinista de Liberación Nacional, or FSLN) in overthrowing the Somoza dictatorship in Nicaragua at the end of the 1970s is perhaps the best example of a successful revolutionary movement in Latin America that began with a rural-based guerrilla force similar to that recommended by Che. However, the FSLN, which was backed by Che and the Cubans, succeeded in overthrowing the Somoza regime in the 1970s because it combined guerrilla warfare in the countryside with a successful campaign of urban guerrilla warfare and the development of a multiclass, multi-party political alliance—not that different from what occurred in Cuba. This broad-based political alliance helped them mobilize a nationwide popular insurrection that toppled the Somoza regime (Harris and Vilas 1995).

Moreover, for those who assumed that a rural-based armed insurrection had been eclipsed by the end of the Cold War, the surprise appearance on the contemporary scene of the Zapatista movement in southern Mexico in the mid-1990s is evidence that guerrilla movements similar to the type advocated by Che Gue-vara will most likely continue to occur in Latin America and other parts of the world where extreme social injustices persist. And the striking resemblance of the Zapatista's charismatic spokesperson, Subcomandante Marcos, to Che is certainly no accident of history. The Zapatista movement has more modest political goals and has used less aggressive military tactics than Che and his comrades, but this insurrectionary movement among the indig-enous peasant population of Chiapas clearly reflects the legacy of Che's example and his ideas about revolutionary guerrilla warfare (Anderson 1997, 753).

Chapter 4

WHY CHE LEFT CUBA

Other lands of the world now claim the assistance of
my modest efforts. I can do what you now are prevented
from doing because of your responsibility at the helm
of Cuba, and so the time has come to separate. Let it
be known that I do this both in pleasure and sorrow:
hereI leave the purest of my hopes as a builder and the
most cherished of my loved ones and I leave a people
who admitted me as one of their sons. . . .
—Che Guevara, letter to Fidel Castro (1965)

Any analysis of why Che Guevara died in Bolivia must take
into account the reasons he left Cuba in 1965, for it was
the motives behind his departure from Cuba that eventually led him to Bolivia. There was a great deal of speculation over
why Che resigned his cabinet post in Fidel Castro's government
and disappeared from public view in 1965 (Deutschmann 1994,
27–31). At the time of Che's disappearance, some believed that
Che and Castro had come to a serious disagreement and that Che
had been either imprisoned or secretly executed. There were also
reports that Che had been killed in the Dominican Republic dur-

ing its civil war in the spring of 1965. Later on, it was speculated that Castro or elements within the Cuban regime had eliminated Che because of his opposition to certain policies advocated by the pro-Soviet wing of the Cuban Communist Party.

By the beginning of 1964, it was evident even to Che that his four-year plan initiated in 1961 to industrialize Cuba was having great difficulties. He realized that he had underestimated the difficulties involved in transforming Cuba from a largely agrarian economy dominated by the production and exportation of sugar to an industrialized economy characterized by diversification and the extensive application of modern technology (Taibo 1996, 482–500). Despite his own herculean efforts, the sixteen- to eighteen-hour workdays that he imposed on himself and those around him, his genius at finding innovative solutions to the country's shortage of the technology and technical skills needed for industrial development—his exemplary leadership could not overcome the many organizational deficiencies, widespread lack of equipment and replacement parts (caused largely by the U.S. economic blockade of Cuba), and lack of properly trained cadres that vexed the development of both Cuba's agricultural production and its manufacturing sector in the early 1960s.

On the basis of what Che told friends, we can ascertain what his thinking was during this period. In the first place, it is clear that Che was forced to admit that Cuba would have to return to its historical mode of livelihood—that is, the production of sugar for export. Yet he was not willing to accept the recommendations of the Soviet advisers that Cuba abandon the goal of becoming an industrialized country. He felt strongly that Cuba's economic relations with the socialist bloc of nations should not be the same as those between capitalist countries. If Cuba could not industrialize by itself as a result of its underdeveloped economy, then the more developed socialist countries had an obligation to help Cuba. Che thought that the Soviet Union should finance Cuba's long-term efforts to industrialize, instead of expecting Cuba to remain the socialist bloc's sugar mill.

Che's ideas found little sympathy among the Soviets. They regarded his plans to industrialize Cuba as impractical. Even if Cuba were to succeed in transforming its economy with Soviet assistance, they argued, there would be an insufficient market for Cuba's manufactured goods and the island lacked most of the raw materials needed for heavy industries (Anderson 1997, 488–89). They pointed out that Cuba's internal market was not large enough to make the production of its own manufactured items economically justifiable and that, given its political isolation, Cuba could not expect to export its products to any of its neighbors. When Che countered that Cuba would have an export market in Latin America as soon as the revolution was carried to other countries of Central and South America, the Russians made it quite clear that they were not willing to risk basing their support on this eventuality.

Che was also critical of the Soviet Union's economic system and its reliance upon what he regarded as basically capitalist methods of organization, management, and investment. In particular, Che felt that the Soviet system's reliance on material incentives and its system of decentralized financial management of state industries were contradictory to the development of a socialist economy and adoption of a socialist consciousness on the part of the workers (Gerassi 1968, 292–316). Moreover, he knew that Moscow and Washington had entered into a tacit agreement to respect each other's spheres of influence and that, as part of this agreement, Moscow had promised to restrain Havana from promoting revolution in Latin America.

Che felt strongly that Cuba should firmly align itself with the neutral nations of Africa, the Middle East, and Asia and assist national liberation struggles and socialist revolutions throughout the Third World. This idea motivated him to travel extensively throughout Africa and Asia during early 1965. He went on an extended state visit to Africa, China, and then Africa again during the first three months of 1965. In Africa, Che visited Algeria, Mali, Congo-Brazzaville, Guinea, Ghana, Dahomey, Tanzania, and Egypt, where he met with important African and Arab leaders such as Ahmed Ben Bella of Algeria, Kwame Nkrumah of Ghana, Julius Nyerere of Tanzania, and Abdel Nasser of Egypt (Anderson 1997, 620–21).

After going to Africa, Che made a trip to the People's Republic of China, with the official purpose of explaining Cuba's position with regard to the growing division between the Soviet Union and China. The Chinese were upset over what they considered to be Cuba's increasing support for the Soviet Union. Because of the tension between Cuba and China, Che had only a brief formal meeting with Chairman Mao Zedong, but he was able to meet at length with other top Chinese leaders and discuss with them his ideas about a united anti-imperialist front to liberate the Third World from Western imperial domination.

Actually, Che's views were closer to those held at the time by the Chinese leadership, and he had become increasingly critical of the split between the Soviet Union and China. He considered the course adopted by the Soviet Union under Premier Nikita Khrushchev to be a "rightist" deviation from socialism. He also considered the emphasis that the Soviet advisers in Cuba placed on continuing the country's specialization in sugar production and on using material incentives to increase labor productivity and giving financial self-management to the state enterprises to be contrary to the revolutionary regime's commitment to rapid industrialization of the economy and the replacement of capitalist material incentives with Communist moral incentives. He predicted (correctly as it turns out) that the Soviet Union and the Soviet bloc of East European countries would return to capitalism if they continued to rely upon market mechanisms, material incentives, and enterprise self-management (Anderson 1997, 697).

After his visit to China, he returned to Africa via Paris, where he learned definitively of the death of his friend Jorge Masetti in Argentina, following the latter's abortive effort to start a guerrilla *foco* there. From Paris, he flew to Dar es Salaam, Tanzania, where he met with President Nyerere and with the representatives in Dar es Salaam of the armed guerrilla movements fighting for national independence at that time in Angola, Mozambique, Rhodesia (Zimbabwe), and the Congo (Taibo 1996, 514–15). Among the representatives were Gaston Soumaliot and Laurent Kabila, two of the leaders of the Congolese rebel movement that was then in control of the eastern portion of the Congo. Although he did not form a good impression of Soumaliot and most of the representatives he met, he was favorably impressed by Kabila's leftist views, which he found similar to his own. Acting on the authority that he had previously received from Fidel Castro, Che offered to send Kabila's forces Cuban arms and military advisers.

From Tanzania, he went to Egypt, where he told President Nasser of his desire to go to the Congo at the head of the contingent of Cuban advisers he had promised Kabila. In February 1965, Che appeared as a "Cuban observer" at the second conference of the Organization of Afro-Asian Solidarity in Algeria, where he initiated a personal crusade to create an anti-imperialist front among the neutral nations of the Third World. In the speech he delivered at this conference, he criticized the socialist countries for being the "accomplices of imperialist exploitation" and called upon them to support popular revolutions in the neocolonial and colonial countries of the Third World, instead of pursuing a selfish foreign policy (Gerassi 1968, 378–86). The Soviet observers who were in attendance were outraged. Following the conference, both President Ben Bella, of Algeria, and President Nasser, of Egypt, tried to talk Che out of the idea of heading a Cuban contingent to the Congo. Nasser warned him that if he went to the Congo, he would be considered a white man and that his involvement there could only turn out badly (Taibo 1996, 517). Ben Bella was more supportive and allowed Che to establish a base in the hills overlooking Algiers that he and the representatives of other Latin American revolutionary groups supported by Cuba were able to use for training purposes and maintain as a sanctuary until the military coup that overthrew Ben Bella took place in June 1965.

When Che returned to Cuba in March 1965, he was ready to resign his position in the Cuban government in order to devote all his efforts to furthering the armed struggle against imperialism. Since he had played such an important role in the Cuban revolution without being Cuban, he assumed he would be able to do the same elsewhere, not only in Latin America but this time also in Africa.

Shortly after Che returned to Havana, he met with Fidel Castro to discuss the results of his travels and his views regarding the position Cuba should take in international affairs. At this meeting, it appears that Fidel reproached Che for criticizing the Soviet Union and the other socialist countries in his speech at the Organization of Afro-Asian Solidarity (Taibo 1996, 522). Fidel also made it clear that he was under both external and internal pressures to move Cuba closer to the Soviet Union in the growing Sino-Soviet split. In fact, the Soviets and the old-guard Communists within the Cuban regime were pressing Fidel to come out openly in favor of the Soviet Union and against the People's Republic of China.

Che realized that Cuba had no alternative but to side with the Soviets. Che also knew that his continued presence in the government was a liability, in light of his disagreements with the Soviets over their foreign policy, Cuba's growing dependence on Soviet aid and trade, and his desire to participate directly in the revolutionary struggle against imperialism. He realized that it would be impossible for him to participate directly in such a struggle in Latin America or Africa if he continued to hold a high position in Cuba. Under the circumstances, Che decided to resign from his positions in the Cuban government and leave Cuba. Fidel Castro evidently encouraged Che to go to the Congo, since he knew that he had become increasingly restless in his responsibilities in Cuba and anxious to carry out what he considered to be his historic mission (Anderson 1997, 628).

Fidel Castro supported Che's idea of assisting the rebels in the Congo. It appears Fidel did this in part to keep Che from going to Latin America to start a guerrilla *foco* without sufficient previous preparation, especially in view of the recent rather disastrous failure of the guerrilla *foco* in northern Argentina led by Che's friend and operative Jorge Masetti (Taibo 1996, 522–23). According to Che's second-in-command in the Congo, Víctor Dreke, "Che did it [he went to Africa] contrary to his original idea of going to fight in Argentina" (Taibo 1996, 523). And according to Pablo Rivalta, the Cuban ambassador to Tanzania who assisted Che's Congo mission, Che regarded the Congo as a training base for liberation movements that would revolutionize all the African countries, particularly South Africa, which was then dominated by an infamous white supremacist regime.

Che's disagreement with Castro regarding Cuba's relationship with Moscow did not end the long-standing friendship between them. Nor did it lead Castro to abandon his desire to see Cuba play an important role in the international struggle against U.S. and European imperialism. Castro was therefore quite willing to send a contingent of Cubans, headed by Che, to assist the left-wing rebels in the Congo, who were fighting against the pro-Western regime of Prime Minister Moise Tshombe.

The Congo appealed to Che largely because of his fascination with the idea of linking the nations of Africa, Asia, and Latin America together into a powerful struggle against Western imperialism. And despite the lack of enthusiasm for this idea among many of the Africans he met, Che contemplated a Cuban-led training center based in the eastern Congo, where revolutionaries from all over the African continent would come to train and gain valuable fighting experience, which they would then take back to their own countries (Anderson 1997, 623).

Che removed himself from public view at the end of March 1965. But by the end of April, his disappearance had begun to cause a great deal of speculation both inside and outside Cuba. On April 30, Castro was interviewed by a number of reporters, and in response to their questions about Che, he answered that he could say only that Che would always be where he could be of most use to the revolution. This statement, however, only served to intensify the speculation and rumors regarding Che's disappearance. As a result, Che wrote a personal letter of resignation, which he hoped would squash the speculations about his disappearance. This letter (Gerassi 1968, 410–11), which Castro did not make public until October 1965, also appears to have been designed to absolve the Cuban government of all responsibility for Che's actions in the Congo.

Fidel:

I remember at this hour many things, when we met at Maria Antonia's house in Mexico, when you suggested that I come to Cuba, and the tension of the last minute preparations. One day they came around asking who to advise in case of death, and its real possibility struck us all. Afterward, we knew that it was certain, that in a revolution you die or triumph (if the revolution is a true one). Many of our comrades were left behind on the long road to victory. Today everything has a less dramatic tone because we are all more mature, but the same thing is repeating itself. I feel I have completed that part of my duty that has tied me to the Cuban revolution and so I say good-bye to you, our comrades, and to your people, who are now mine too.

I formally renounce my post in the directorate of the party, my post as minister, my rank of comandante, and my status as a Cuban. There is nothing legal that ties me to Cuba, only ties of another type that cannot be broken as in the case of offices. Making a summary of my past life, I think that I have worked with sufficient honesty and dedication to consolidate the success of the revolution. My only fault of any gravity is that I did not confide in you at the beginning in the Sierra Maestra and have not understood with sufficient clarity your qualities as a leader and revolutionary.

I have lived magnificent days at your side and I have felt the pride of belonging to our people in the dark and bright days of the Caribbean crisis [Bay of Pigs invasion by U.S.-backed Cuban exiles]. Rarely has a statesman shone as brightly as you in those days. I feel proud of having followed you without hesitation, identifying myself with your way of thinking, seeing and appreciating both the dangers and principles. Other lands of the world now claim the assistance of my modest efforts. I can do what you now are prevented from doing because of your responsibility at the helm of Cuba, and so the time has come to separate. Let it be known that I do this both in pleasure and sorrow: here I leave the purest of my hopes as a builder and the most cherished of my loved ones and I leave a people who admitted me as one of their sons; this lacerates part of my spirit. To new fields of battle I will take the faith that you have given me, the revolutionary spirit of my people, and the feeling of carrying out the most sacred of duties: to fight against imperialism wherever it exists; this comforts and cures my pain abundantly.

Once again I say that I free Cuba of all responsibility, except that which comes from her example. If my last hour should come under other skies, my last thought will be for the Cuban people and especially for you. I am grateful for your teaching and example, and I will be faithful to you until my last act. I have always identified myself with the foreign policies of our revolution and will continue to do so. Wherever I go I will feel the responsibility of being a Cuban revolutionary, and I will act as one. I leave nothing material to my wife and children; and this doesn't bother me for I am happy that it is this way. I ask nothing for them, since the state will provide them enough to live and will educate them. There are many things I could tell you and our people, but I feel that this is not necessary. Words cannot express what I want to say, and it is not worth while to fill sheets of paper. Victory always! Country or death! My embrace with all revolutionary fervor.

Che

Che left for the Congo on April 1, 1965, leading a handpicked group of approximately one hundred black Cubans who had fought with him and Castro in the Sierra Maestra. Their departure was carefully planned by Cuban intelligence, which even managed to plant a false report in the Dominican Republic indicating that Che had arrived in Santo Domingo in April and had been killed shortly thereafter in one of the street battles that took place there in the local civil war (Anderson 1997, 638). Thus, while the CIA was looking for evidence of Che's presence in the Dominican Republic, he and his companions were able to leave Cuba and enter the Congo under the cover of complete secrecy.

In sum, Che's reasons for leaving Cuba to go fight in the Congo and then afterward for going to Bolivia appear to have been two-fold. On the one hand, he wanted the freedom of action that would come from no longer being a government minister who had to be careful to speak in the name of the government he served and to act in accordance with established government policy and protocol (Taibo 1996, 530). And he had to free himself from the constraints and conventional obligations imposed upon him by his official obligations as an important leader in the Cuban government, if he wanted to return to the life of a revolutionary guerrilla fighter and carry out the global struggle against capitalism and Western imperialism, which he had come to consider his main mission in life. His commitment to this conviction was his primary reason for leaving Cuba in 1965.

Che wrote a 153-page manuscript on his Congo mission, which has been edited and published by his wife Aleida March and Richard Gott (Guevara, March, and Gott 2001). The *Library Journal* has accurately described it as "an honest, detailed account of the life and work of a great 20th-century revolutionary." He prepared this manuscript during his stay in the Cuban embassy in Dar es Salaam, Tanzania, after the failure of his Congo mission and the forced withdrawal of his contingent of Cuban volunteers from the eastern Congo.

This manuscript reveals, among other things, that Che had decided that he would lead the contingent of armed Cubans that went to the rebellious eastern region of the Congo, without first informing and obtaining the consent of the Congolese rebel leaders. Thus, Che states in his Congo diary,

> I hadn't told any of the Congolese about my decision to fight there. In my first conversation with Kabila I had not been able to do so because nothing had yet been decided, and after the plan was approved [by Fidel] it would have been dangerous for my project to be known before I arrived at my destination; there was a lot of hostile territory to cross. I decided, therefore, to present a fait accompli and act according to however they reacted to my presence. I was not unaware of the fact that a negative would place me in a difficult position, because now I couldn't go back [to Cuba], but I calculated that it would be difficult for them to refuse me.

Although the Congolese rebel leaders did not object to Che's presence as the commander of the Cuban contingent, he soon understood that there was little prospect for the rebels to overthrow the corrupt, neocolonial regime that had been established in the Congo with the backing of the Belgian, British, and U.S. governments.

He realized almost immediately that the rebels could not win, because of their corrupt and weak leaders, failure to organize the local population, distrust of one another, and lack of discipline. In this regard, Che's Congo diary includes the following observation:

> The leaders of the movement pass most of their time outside of the territory. . . . Organizational work is almost null,

due to the fact that the mid-level leaders do not work, in fact they do not know how to work, and every one distrusts every one else. . . . Lack of discipline and lack of self-sacrifice are the dominant characteristics of the guerrilla troops. Naturally, with these troops one cannot win a war.

Che also recognized his own responsibility for the failure of his mission. He wrote, "I have left with more faith than ever in the guerrilla struggle, but we have failed. My responsibility is large; I will not forget the defeat nor its precious lessons." And he made the following scathing critique of his own actions:

> I was the leader of a group of Cubans, a company no more, and my function was to be their true leader, their guide to a victory that would give impulse to the development of an authentic popular army; but at the same time my peculiar situation converted me into a soldier, the representative of a foreign power, an instructor of Cubans and Congolese, a strategist, a high flying politician in an unknown setting. And I was a Canton-censor, repetitive and tiresome in my relations with the leaders of the revolution. With so many threads to deal with, a Gordian knot formed which I didn't take the decision to cut. If I had been a more authentic soldier I would have been able to exercise more influence over the rest of my complex relations. I have narrated how I arrived at the extreme of saving my own skin (my precious person) in the moments of particular disaster in which I saw myself enveloped and how I didn't overcome subjective considerations in the final instance.

This passage in his diary makes it clear that Che was deeply critical of his own behavior and the many limitations he confronted in the Congo. He engaged in this self-critique with a view to avoiding the repetition in the future of the errors that he felt he had committed in the Congo. However, Che's subsequent mission to Bolivia appears to have failed for some of the same reasons as the Congo mission. Che repeated the tactic of inserting himself secretly into another country at the head of foreign military group, and into a situation that was devoid of both the objective and the subjective conditions necessary for a successful revolutionary movement.

Although Che's Congo mission was a bitter defeat for him and his Cuban companions, his brief presence in the Congo changed dramatically the life of the Congolese teenager who served as his translator during the months Che and his companions operated in the Fizi Baraka mountain range near the border between the Congo and Tanzania. Freddy Ilanga, who spoke both Swahili and French, had been a newspaper vendor and was just sixteen years old when he was assigned by the rebel leadership to serve as Che's translator during the time the Cubans carried out their then secret support of the Congolese leftist rebels in their attempt to overthrow the Western-backed Tshombe regime.

This brief encounter with the legendary revolutionary and his companions placed Freddy Ilanga on the path of an incredible journey that took him from being a teenage rebel in the eastern Congo to Cuba, where he ended up studying medicine, married a Cuban woman, and became a brain surgeon. As a young African who saw the whites in his country as an oppressive force, he knew nothing about the Cuban revolution, and he at first considered Guevara to be "that sarcastic white" (Doyle 2005). But he soon came to admire Che, growing particularly impressed with how he treated the Africans around him with the same respect as the whites in his company. In those days in the Congo, that was something Freddy had never seen. Shortly before Che and his companions pulled out of the Congo, they arranged for Freddy to be sent to Cuba, where he finished his schooling, trained as a doctor, and specialized in pediatric neurosurgery. Although Freddy never returned to the Congo before he died, today there are hundreds of Cuban and Cuban-trained African doctors in Africa.

In November 1965, Che left the Congo as secretly as he had entered. It was a bitter blow for him to return furtively to Cuba after spending seven months in the Congo without having anything to show for his efforts. The experience, however, seems to have made Che even more determined than ever to undertake a successful revolutionary mission outside of Cuba, but this time in his native Latin America.

Che's return to Cuba was never made public (Deutschmann 1994, 119). He remained in hiding during the entire period that he stayed there. Almost immediately after his return, he began to prepare a new mission that would not have the limitations of his abortive undertaking in the Congo. He chose Bolivia as the site for a revolutionary guerrilla *foco*, which he would organize and lead himself. In October 1966, he once again left Cuba, as secretly as he had entered, to begin this undertaking.

Chapter 5

WHY CHE CHOSE BOLIVIA

We have maintained for quite some time now that, owing to the similarity of their characteristics, the struggles in our America will achieve in due course continental proportions.

—Che Guevara, "Message to the Trincontinental: Create Two, Three, Many Vietnams" (1967)

The land where Che met his tragic death is a hauntingly beautiful and almost primeval country of towering mountains, dry windswept plateaus, and deep tropical valleys. It has such an otherworldly atmosphere and such unusual colors and geography that visitors feel as if they were in Tibet or perhaps on another planet rather than in the heart of the South American continent.

Bolivia is divided into two distinctive parts by the massive wall of the Andes Mountains, which traverses the country from north to south. Bolivia west of the Andes can best be described as a Latin American Tibet. This part of the country is situated on the altiplano, the great high plateau of South America. Here the descendants of the Incas, with their herds of llamas, live a bleak existence some two and a half miles above sea level. The vastness and barrenness of this windy plateau give it a beauty all its own, and anyone who has been to this part of the world takes away unforgettable memories of magnificent panoramas, azure blue skies filled with clouds that look close enough to touch, and snow-covered peaks bathed in the soft, multicolored light of an indescribably beautiful sunset.

Located on the altiplano are Bolivia's major mining centers and the focal point of national politics, the capital city of La Paz. Situated at 11,900 feet in a basin on the altiplano, La Paz is the highest capital city in the world. The only approach by land to the city is from the altiplano. Consequently, one's first view of La Paz is from some 2,000 feet directly above it. The view is breathtaking. Far below sprawls the glittering city and, in the distance beyond, the snowy peaks of Mount Illimani, which tower to a height of over 21,000 feet.

La Paz is a fascinating blend of the old and the new. Together with modern buildings and late-model cars, one sees churches built by the Spaniards over four centuries ago and, in every street, Indian women with their characteristic bowler hats, colorful shawls, and babies carried on their backs. It is a bustling, sunny city, filled with color and an atmosphere of excitement.

Over the mountains from La Paz lies the city of Cochabamba, an important agricultural center in the heart of an 8,400-foot-high valley where the climate is mildly temperate and the soil quite fertile. Farther east, the mountains drop toward the tropical savannas and plains of eastern Bolivia. The most important city in this area is Santa Cruz, located at the foot of the eastern slopes of the Andes. Santa Cruz is known for its colonial Spanish architecture and its beautiful women of Spanish descent, but today it has all the characteristics of a boom city. The Bolivian government, with U.S. assistance, has invested heavily in the region and has encouraged people from the altiplano to come to the various colonization projects located in the surrounding province. The growing local economy is based on sugar, cotton, rice, oil, and cocaine. Approximately two hundred miles south of Santa Cruz lies the town of Camiri, the only other sizable urban community in the eastern part of the country. Camiri is Bolivia's oil and gas center, and although not comparable to Santa Cruz in either importance or size, it too has experienced an economic boom.

Even though the eastern portion of Bolivia accounts for approximately 70 percent of the total land area of the country, only about one-fourth of Bolivia's small population lives east of the Andes. This means that the heartland of Bolivia is located on the altiplano. It is there that the vast majority of the country's people live and that the main loci of economic and political power are to be found. Most of the important events in Bolivian political history have taken place on the altiplano.

In 1825, Bolivia formally declared independence from Spain after some sixteen years of almost uninterrupted warfare (Klein 1984). During this time, most of the major battles were fought on the altiplano, the focal point being Lake Titicaca, the sacred sea of the Incas and one of the highest lakes in the world. Since independence, the stormy political history of Bolivia has been scarred by hundreds of uprisings, revolts, and coups d'état. Nearly all of these have been centered in the altiplano cities of Sucre (the country's first capital), Oruro (Bolivia's main mining center), Cochabamba, and La Paz. The two most important exceptions to this geographic pattern were the war of the Pacific in 1879, in which Bolivia lost its seacoast to Chile, and the Chaco War of 1930–32, a bloody dispute with Paraguay that led to the loss of more than fifty thousand Bolivian troops and a sizable chunk of the Gran Chaco area in the southeast.

Bolivia's humiliating defeat and territorial loss to Paraguay in the Chaco War provoked much internal political turmoil and the demand for major reforms (Malloy 1989). Returning veterans of the Chaco War organized and provided the fuel for radical political movements among the miners and urban workers that ultimately brought about the revolution of 1952. This event broke the historical pattern of Bolivian politics and destroyed the traditional social order. The Movimiento Nacionalista Revolucionario (MNR, or National Revolutionary Movement), led by Víctor Paz Estenssoro, eliminated the professional army with the help of armed workers and miners. Shortly thereafter, the new government nationalized the major foreign-owned mining operations in the country and set about diversifying the economy. Of even greater significance, however, was that the government decreed universal suffrage and enacted a national land reform program. As a result, Bolivia's Indian masses gained at least the formal dignity of citizenship and were freed from their centuries-old serfdom.

In November 1964, Paz Estenssoro's MNR government fell victim to the new army that it had established after the 1952 revolution. In classic Latin American style, the military staged a coup d'état and forced Paz Estenssoro to leave the country. His successor was General René Barrientos, who had been Bolivia's vice president and former air force chief of staff. Following the coup, Barrientos appointed a large number of military officers to key posts in the government and doubled the country's defense budget. Under the pretext of correcting the revolutionary excesses of the former regime, he also took a variety of measures designed to stifle all effective political opposition to his regime, particularly the miners and the MNR. Barrientos, who was referred to as a Latin American "Captain Marvel" because of his flamboyant behavior, built a popular base of support around the peasant unions created out of the 1952 revolution. Consequently, in 1966 he felt confident enough to allow a government-controlled election, in which he was formally elected to the presidency of the country. However, his main source of support was the military. Behind Barrientos loomed the very visible figure of General Alfredo Ovando, the commander in chief of the Bolivian armed forces at the time and subsequently the head of the military regime that was established after Barrientos's demise.

Meanwhile, upon his return to Cuba from the Congo, Che found solace in the fact that one of his grandest dreams, an intercontinental organization representing the underdeveloped countries of the world, with its headquarters in Cuba, had been founded only a few months before his return by Fidel Castro. From January 3 to 15, 1966, the first conference of the Organization of Solidarity of Asian, African, and Latin American Peoples—referred to thereafter as the Tricontinental—was held in Havana, with some four hundred delegates from the underdeveloped world attending. As it turned out, Che's revolutionary ideas were the central topic of discussion among the delegates, and this undoubtedly reinforced his determination to carry out the realization of one of his oldest dreams: the liberation of Latin America's oppressed and exploited masses. This dream was bolstered by his belief that Cuba would become truly independent of the Soviet Union only when additional revolutionary governments were established in Latin America that could provide support to Cuba.

As Fidel Castro has stated on a number of occasions (Deutschmann 1994, 120), Che assigned himself to the mission in Bolivia. However, he would never have gone to Bolivia without Fidel's approval and his support. Why, then, did Fidel support Che's mission to Bolivia? By the spring of 1966, Fidel and the Cuban leadership had become quite alarmed at Cuba's faltering international prestige and isolated position in the Western Hemisphere. They were determined to make good on Cuba's promise to carry the armed revolutionary struggle to the rest of Latin America. It seems Fidel decided to support Che's desire to establish a revolutionary guerrilla movement based in Bolivia, because he shared Che's desire to see the revolution extended to Latin America and because, if successful, it would strengthen Cuba's revolutionary position in the Americas and throughout the world. Evidently, he was also willing to risk incurring the Soviet Union's displeasure and any sanctions that the Soviets might bring to bear against Cuba for supporting such an operation (Anderson 1997, 677).

Che considered several other countries—Argentina (his homeland) and Peru, in particular—before choosing Bolivia as the site of his guerrilla operation. There was nothing he would have liked better than to bring the revolution to his native Argentina. He had planned that for many years. But the situation in Argentina was clearly not favorable for such an undertaking in 1966. As was mentioned above, in 1964 a Cuban-backed and Che-inspired guerrilla force attempted to establish itself in northern Argentina, but the effort ended in total failure a few months later without having realized a single military engagement (Castañeda 1997, 247–50). The leader of this group, an Argentine named Jorge Masetti, had been a close friend of Che's in Cuba, and together they planned the Argentine undertaking in early 1963. Their objective at the time was to establish a chain of guerrilla *focos* from northern Argentina to Peru. However, Masetti's small force was defeated by the harsh environment of northern Argentina, by its poor organization, and by its inability to attract any popular support. In the end, those members of his guerrilla band who did not die of starvation and exposure were either taken prisoner or killed by the Argentine police and armed forces. The death of Masetti, and of the three Cubans from Che's own bodyguard who had gone with him to help establish the guerrilla movement in Argentina, was a bitter reminder to Che that Argentina was not the most suitable place for him to establish an armed revolutionary movement.

As for Peru, the situation there was no more favorable than in Argentina. In 1966, that country had an elected civilian regime with a moderately progressive program (Taibo 1996, 612–16). Moreover, the government and the army had effectively suppressed several guerrilla uprisings in isolated parts of the country during the preceding two years. Che also considered Colombia, Venezuela, and Brazil, but never very seriously (Anderson 1997, 678). In the end, Bolivia was chosen because it was considered to have the best revolutionary potential and because it afforded the ideal strategic location.

Since Che had been in Bolivia for a short time after he finished medical school in 1953, his impression of the country at that time undoubtedly influenced his choice of Bolivia in 1966. As was previously mentioned, he was there during a period when the country was infected with revolutionary enthusiasm. Less than a year before, thousands of miners, campesinos, and deserters from the Bolivian army had revolted and brought down the then existing military regime. When Che arrived in La Paz in 1953, the old army had been destroyed, the largest foreign-owned mines in the country had been nationalized, and the campesinos had taken possession of the land under the sanction of the new government's agrarian reform law. The streets were filled with singing and loud demonstrations, and everywhere he saw the armed campesinos and workers of the revolutionary militia. He surely must have thought of these armed campesinos and workers in 1966 when he chose Bolivia as the place to initiate his revolutionary movement, firmly believing that the revolution of those days had been subsequently betrayed by opportunistic politicians and generals corrupted by Yanqui dollars, military advisers, and the CIA.

Most of Che's information on Bolivia appears to have come from several Bolivian Communists, who had helped previously with the Masetti operation, and Che's aide, José María Martínez Tamayo (Papi),who was sent to Bolivia in March 1966 to make the preliminary preparations for Che's new operation (Castañeda 1997, 334). Some of these Bolivian Communists had received military training in Cuba. They assured Papi that the country was ripe for a Cuban type of revolution and that all that was needed was Cuban support. They told him of widespread discontent in Bolivia with the military-backed regime of President Barrientos, and said that his government could fall at any moment. They also spoke of the country's strong revolutionary tradition, of the visible and often resented U.S. presence in the country's economic and political affairs, and of how the mining centers were virtual caldrons of rebellion. Finally, they confirmed what Che and the Cuban intelligence service already knew—that the Bolivian security and military forces were perhaps the most ineffective and badly organized in Latin America.

As a result, Che decided that Bolivia was the appropriate location for his operation. He minimized the fact that Bolivia's Communists were badly split along pro-Soviet and pro-Chinese lines and that the leader of Bolivia's pro-Soviet Communist Party, Mario Monje, had told Fidel during the Tricontinental conference in 1966 that he was interested in establishing a guerrilla *foco* himself in Bolivia.

One of the other reasons Che chose Bolivia was its strategic importance, for it lies in the *corazón* ("heart") of South America and borders most of the major countries on the continent (that is, Argentina, Brazil, Chile, and Peru). From Bolivia, Che hoped that his revolutionary effort could extend in every direction and involve all of South America. It would provide a training base and jumping-off point for what he hoped would ultimately become a continental revolutionary struggle (Siles del Valle 1996, 29–38).

Having decided on Bolivia, Che selected the southeast of the country for his initial guerrilla *foco* or base of operations. He chose the southeast because it offered access to neighboring Argentina, Brazil, and Paraguay. In addition, he assumed that in this area, because of its isolation and sparse population, his guerrilla force would be able to develop without being discovered before it was ready to begin operations.

The specific location chosen as the central base of operations was the Ñancahuazú River valley. In this tropical, heavily forested valley, Che planned to train the nucleus of his guerrilla movement, build fortifications, and establish caches of supplies and arms. Once his force was ready for combat, it would move north and threaten three of Bolivia's major cities: Cochabamba, Santa Cruz, and Sucre. This would enable the guerrillas to control the railway line that runs from northern Argentina to Santa Cruz, as well as to cut the U.S.-owned Gulf Oil Company pipeline that ran from Santa Cruz to Camiri. Che planned later to locate a second guerrilla base farther east, on the slopes of the Andes.

His schedule forecast the beginning of military operations in the spring of 1967, following six months of preparation. In the opening phase, he planned to divide his force into several small bands and have them strike simultaneously at a number of widely dispersed points north of the Ñancahuazú. In this way, he hoped to force the Bolivian army to disperse its forces over a large area, while his guerrillas made a slow withdrawal toward the Ñanca-huazú, where they could rely upon previously established caches of supplies and fortifications. If the inexperienced Bolivian army attempted to follow the guerrillas into the Ñancahuazú River valley, it would be at the mercy of Che's guerrilla bands. As his guerrillas demonstrated their capacity to win victories against the Bolivian army, Che reasoned, the campesinos and miners would come to the support of the movement.

Che assumed that once his guerrilla movement was well established and drawing widespread support and public attention, conditions would become more favorable for guerrilla operations in Peru and Argentina (Taibo 1996, 615). He planned to have a guerrilla group operating in the Ayacucho region of Peru by the end of 1967 and another force in northern Argentina sometime after that. The Bolivian movement was to be a training ground for the nucleus of both the Peruvian and the Argentinean forces.

Che revealed his overall strategy in the message he sent to the second conference of the Tricontinental in 1967. It was entitled "Create Two, Three, Many Vietnams." In this message, he clearly believed that a successful guerrilla insurgency in Latin America would force the United States to commit itself directly to the contest, creating a second Vietnam in the heart of South America. That Che planned to create another Vietnam in Bolivia is evident from his message to the conference. His conception of the course of events that would follow the appearance of his guerrilla movement in Bolivia is revealed in the following passage:

> New outbreaks of war will appear in these and other Latin American countries, as has already occurred in Bolivia. And they will continue to grow, with all the vicissitudes involved in

this dangerous occupation of the modern revolutionist. Many will die, victims of their own errors; others will fall in difficult combat to come; new fighters and new leaders will arise in the heat of the revolutionary struggle. . . . The Yankee agents of repression will increase in number. Today there are advisers in all countries where armed struggle is going on. . . . Little by little the obsolete weapons that are sufficient for the suppression of small armed bands will be converted by the Americans into modern arms, and American advisers will be converted into combatants, until, in a given moment, they will see themselves obligated to send increasing quantities of regular troops to assure the relative stability of a power whose puppet national army disintegrates before the attacks of the guerrillas. This is the road of Vietnam. It is the road that other people will follow, and it is the road that Latin America will follow. . . . We must definitely keep in mind that imperialism is a world system, the final stage of capitalism, and that it must be beaten in a great worldwide confrontation. (Deutschmann 1997, 322–23)

From this message, it is clear that Che was counting on American involvement in Bolivia and that he saw this as a means of gaining the support of both Bolivian and international public opinion.

As for the ultimate goal of the continental revolutionary movement that Che was hoping to start in Bolivia, it too was revealed in his message to the Tricontinental conference. He said,

We can summarize our hopes for victory as follows: the destruction of imperialism through the elimination of its strongest bulwark: the imperial dominion of the United States of North America. This will be accomplished through the gradual liberation of its subject peoples, either one by one or by groups, drawing the enemy into a difficult struggle outside of its territory; and cutting it off from its bases of support, i.e., its dependent territories.

Thus, for Che, Bolivia was to be the first step in a grandiose plan to liberate all of Latin America from U.S. influence and convert it into a bastion of socialism. Everything therefore depended upon successfully establishing in Bolivia a guerrilla force that would develop into a successful revolutionary movement of continental dimensions. Prophetically, the final sentences in his message to the Tricontinental conference suggested what was to come:

> Wherever death may surprise us, let it be welcome if our battle cry has reached even one receptive ear; if another hand reaches out to take up our arms, and other men come forward to join in our funeral dirge with the rattling of machine guns and with new cries of battle and victory.

Chapter 6

PREPARATION OF THE GUERRILLA *FOCO*

> At the beginning, the relative weakness of the guerrilla
> force is such that it must work to establish itself in the
> area in order to become acquainted with the environ-
> ment, establishing connections with the populace and
> reinforcing the places that may possibly be converted
> into their support bases.
> —Che Guevara, "Guerrilla Warfare: A Method" (1963)

C he could not seek the support of the pro-Chinese Communists in Bolivia, because the leaders of the pro-Soviet
Communists in Bolivia had told Fidel Castro that their
party would set up a guerrilla *foco* in the country. It appears they
deliberately misled Fidel into believing this in order to outflank
the more militant, pro-Chinese Communists, who they feared
were interested in doing this with Cuban help (Anderson 1997,
682–87). On the other hand, Che distrusted Monje and the other
leaders of Bolivia's pro-Soviet Communist Party. Consequently,
he relied primarily upon a small number of Castroites within

Monje's pro-Soviet Communist Party to make the preliminary preparations for his guerrilla operation. These were individuals who had previously spent some time training in Cuba, and Che knew many of them personally. He felt they could be trusted to lay the groundwork for his operation without telling even the leadership of their party what they were doing.

The most important of Che's Bolivian contacts were two brothers—Roberto "Coco" and Guido "Inti" Peredo. The brothers helped to convince Che that Bolivia was the ideal base for a guerrilla operation. Because of this and perhaps because Che saw the two as the future Raúl and Fidel Castro of Bolivia, he entrusted them with the most important aspects of the preliminary preparations for his guerrilla *foco*.

Coco and Inti had participated in the efforts made in 1960 to establish guerrilla *focos* in Salta, Argentina, and Puerto Maldonado, Peru. They had joined the Communist Party's youth wing at an early age, and their participation in these attempts to establish Cuban-style guerrilla *focos* made them ideal candidates for the guerrilla force that Che organized in Bolivia. They also owned and operated a taxi in La Paz; this gave them a perfect cover for their clandestine activities. Sometime during the summer of 1966, they both traveled to the southeast and located themselves in Camiri, Bolivia's petroleum center. There they made friends with some of the local inhabitants and let it be known that they were interested in buying land in the area north of Camiri for the purpose of establishing a ranch and cereal farm.

In September, they succeeded in buying an abandoned ranch in a largely uninhabited region near the Ñancahuazú River, some fifty miles north of Camiri. In addition, they rented some adjacent property from their only neighbor, Ciro Argañaraz, a local landowner and cattle rancher. While Inti returned to La Paz to take care of their personal affairs, Coco began readying the ranch for the arrival of Che and his Cuban comrades. He contracted two local men to work the ranch and planted several different varieties of cereals. He also bought some cattle, hogs, and poultry. During this period, Coco traveled the winding dirt road from the ranch to Camiri in his new Toyota jeep almost daily. On this road, about twelve miles from the ranch, is the small village of Lagunillas. Coco stopped there on several occasions to buy vegetables and fruits. The large amounts of supplies that he transported to the ranch in his jeep aroused the suspicion of local villagers. Many of them, as well as the landowner Argañaraz, assumed that the Peredo brothers were either cocaine merchants or cattle thieves.

Meanwhile, in La Paz, Che's other Bolivian collaborators made arrangements for receiving Che's group and their equipment. They obtained a house and a warehouse in the center of the city, where they stored arms and ammunition, which they received hidden in bags of cement mix. These were shipped from Cuba to the port of Arica, in northern Chile, and from there sent by rail to La Paz.

One of Che's prime contacts in La Paz during this period, and later the only female member of his guerrilla force, was a woman known by the code name of Tania. Her real name was Haydée Tamara Bunke. She was a German-Argentine whom Che met in Communist East Germany and who had come to Cuba on his invitation. While there, she became a member of the small circle of Argentines who met frequently at Che's house. Tania left Cuba and entered Bolivia in 1964 with a false Argentine passport. In early 1965, she obtained a job working for Gonzalo López, director of information in the presidential palace. In addition to working for López, Tania successfully passed herself off as a professor of languages. This gave her an opportunity to travel throughout the country, ostensibly for the purpose of studying the languages and folk songs of the indigenous (Indian) population. In her spare time, she worked her way into some of the capital's artistic, cultural, and diplomatic circles. Her contacts provided Che with valuable information and assistance. Her direct access to documents and forms in the Information Office of the Presidency later enabled her to provide Che and some of his Cuban companions with very impressive credentials that allowed them to travel quite freely within the country.

Che arrived in Bolivia around the first of November 1966, on a plane from São Paolo, Brazil. He entered Bolivia as a clean-shaven, bald man wearing glasses. He had two false Uruguayan passports, and it is not clear which of the two he actually used to enter Bolivia. The passports were issued under the names of Ramón Benitez and Adolfo Mena. The fingerprints on the passports are exactly the same as those that have been identified by various governments as belonging to Che. The photographs on the passports are also the same. On close examination, they reveal a clean-shaven, bald Che Guevara wearing glasses. The two passports have the same dates of entry and departure from the Madrid airport.

Che was accompanied by one of his longtime Cuban comrades, Alberto Fernández (whose code name was Pacho). Upon arrival, they contacted Tania, and she gave Che a truly extraordinary document: it accredited Che (Adolfo Mena, in this case) as a special envoy of the Organization of American States. According to this document, he was in Bolivia for the purpose of conducting research on the social and economic relations prevailing in the rural areas of Bolivia.

November 3, 1966

The Director of Information of the Presidency of the Republic has the pleasure of presenting:

ADOLFO MENA GONZÁLEZ

Special Envoy of the Organization of American States, who is undertaking a study and collecting information on the social and economic relations that prevail in the Bolivian countryside.

The undersigned, who has presented this credential, asks all national authorities and private persons and institutions to lend Señor Adolfo Mena all the cooperation that they can in order to facilitate his research effort.

signed:

Gonzalo López,

Director of Information

Presidency of the Republic

La Paz, November 3, 1966

With Che carrying this document, Che and Pacho traveled to the Ñancahuazú ranch in two separate jeeps, arriving there the night of November 6. Che brought to Bolivia a contingent of twelve Cubans. Most of the members of this handpicked group were veterans of Che's guerrilla column in the Sierra Maestra. Some held the rank of *comandante* in the Cuban army. Many of them had served in important posts in the Cuban government and armed forces, and several were members of the Central Committee of the Cuban Communist Party. All were tied to Che by unquestioning personal loyalty. Some had been with him in the Congo. They were willing to follow him to hell if he asked them to do so, and in the end only three of them returned home to Cuba alive.

Che's Cuban comrades traveled to Bolivia in separate groups. Like him, they all had excellent documents supporting their false identities. The first group arrived in Bolivia sometime in October and the remaining groups in November and December. Some entered Bolivia via the rail line from Arica, in nearby Chile. Others came by plane from São Paolo, Brazil. One group flew from Cuba to Prague, from there to Frankfurt, and from Frankfurt to La Paz via New York and Miami.

The Bolivian members of the guerrilla force were largely recruited by Coco and two other Bolivian agents, known by the code names of Rodolfo and Sánchez. The latter two men also served as liaisons between Che's group and the support network in the urban areas during the period before the guerrilla force was discovered. The entry in Che's diary at the end of November 1966 indicates that he hoped to increase the number of Bolivians in his force to at least twenty before beginning military operations. In December, he met with Mario Monje, the leader of the pro-Moscow Bolivian Communist Party, to discuss the possibility of receiving men and assistance from his party. Monje refused, however, to support the guerrilla operation and to send more men unless he was in charge of it.

By the end of March 1967, Che had succeeded in recruiting approximately twenty Bolivians. Some of these recruits were Bolivians who had been trained in Cuba specifically for the purpose of fighting in the guerrilla operation. The remainder were dissident members of the youth wing of Monje's party and unemployed miners from the tin-mining areas on Bolivia's high plateau.

The unemployed miners were recruited by Moisés Guevara (no relation to Che), an important union leader among the tin miners in Oruro. Moisés had broken away from the pro-Chinese Communist Party in Bolivia and traveled several times to Cuba, where he had met Che. Although Monje was opposed to involving Moisés in the guerrilla force, Che's Bolivian contacts invited him to join with some of his miners. Moisés agreed and brought eight men with him to the Ñancahuazú camp in February 1967.

In addition to the Cubans and Bolivians, Che's guerrilla force included among its members three Peruvians known by the code names of El Chino, Negro, and Eustaquio. El Chino (Juan Pablo Chang, a Peruvian of Chinese descent) was supposed to establish Che's planned guerrilla *foco* in Peru. He brought Eustaquio, a radio operator, and Negro, a physician, to Che's camp during the latter part of February. They were to be joined later by additional Peruvians who were supposed to train with Che's force.

The total number of combatants in the guerrilla force stood at forty-four when the first encounter between the army and Che's group took place, in March 1967. The composition of the guerrilla force at that time was as follows:

17	Cubans
22	Bolivians
3	Peruvians
2	Argentines (Che and Tania)
44	Total

Most of the leadership positions were held by Cubans. Che appointed his old comrade-in-arms from the Sierra Maestra, Comandante Juan Vitalio Acuña (code name Joaquín) as his second-in-command of the guerrilla force and as leader of the rear guard. He also appointed Cubans to the posts of leader of the vanguard, chief of operations, chief of services, and chief of supplies. Inti and Coco were the only two Bolivians entrusted with any leadership responsibilities. Inti was placed in charge of finances and appointed political commissar to the Bolivians. Coco, initially given charge of urban contacts and recruitment, was later incorporated into the guerrilla force and assigned various responsibilities.

No additions to the guerrilla force took place after the outbreak of hostilities in March. Instead, the size of Che's force was steadily reduced as each encounter with the army took its toll. Che had hoped to recruit peasants from the local area once his force began operations, but he failed to recruit even a single peasant after the fighting began.

In November and December of 1966, the Cubans arrived at the ranch, and the first Bolivian recruits were brought by Coco and Rodolfo. During this time, the Bolivian called Bigotes acted as the operator of the ranch, while Che and his comrades established their camp in a densely wooded area some distance from the ranch house. Then, in twos and threes, Che and his men began exploring the Ñancahuazú River valley and the general area north of the ranch.

They soon discovered that the area they had chosen for their guerrilla *foco* was unlike anything they had expected. They found themselves in a hostile region characterized by innumerable deep and densely wooded ravines. The Ñancahuazú River twists its way through a very steep canyon. Along the river is a very narrow beach that occasionally disappears, forcing anyone walking along the river's edge to climb one of the steep walls on either side. This is extremely difficult because of the thickets that grow from the river's edge to the top of the ravine walls. These thickets are by far the worst enemy of humans in the region. They are inhabited by clouds of voracious mosquitoes and consist of thin reeds, twisting vines, and various types of cacti. The vines are so numerous in some places that it is impossible to see more than a few feet ahead. One of the more prevalent cactus plants in these thickets has large leaves with serrated edges. Anyone attempting to move through the thickets in which these plants abound can count on leaving some flesh and clothing behind. Injuries and accidents were common in this hostile terrain, and Che lost several of his men in fatal accidents before the fighting ever began.

In mid-December, Che and his group moved farther away from the ranch house and deeper into the densely wooded area surrounding the Ñancahuazú River. There they established a second camp and spent the remainder of the month digging trenches and supply caves, building observation posts, cutting trails through the undergrowth surrounding the campsite, and practicing the defense of the area. Che also gave his men classes in guerrilla warfare and the political objectives of their operation. On January 6, for example, he wrote in his diary that he had given the group that day a lecture on the qualities of the guerrilla soldier and explained to them that their mission was to form a nucleus of steel that would serve as an example for others to follow. The group also studied Quechua. This is an important Indian language in the highland areas of Bolivia and Peru, but it is of little use in the area where Che was planning to initiate his guerrilla operation.

In January 1967, a number of serious problems emerged that were to vex Che and his group during the months ahead. First of all, they found themselves so short of food that they had to send out regular hunting parties as well as buy supplies in Lagunillas and Camiri. In addition, their neighbor Argañaraz told Bigotes that he "knew many things" and was willing to collaborate in "whatever they were doing." Thus, it was obvious that Argañaraz suspected that something illegal was going on at the ranch and that he might inform the authorities. Che gave Bigotes instructions to accept Argañaraz's offer of collaboration, while at the same time threatening to kill him if he went to the authorities. Nevertheless, a few days later the ranch was visited by a Lieutenant Fernández and four policemen, who claimed they were looking for "the cocaine factory." The lieutenant made it clear to Bigotes that he expected to be bribed in return for permitting him to continue operating the cocaine factory. He took Bigotes's pistol and suggested that he come to Camiri in a few days, under the pretext of reclaiming his pistol, to discuss the whole matter. Following this visit, Bigotes and some of the others discovered that one of Argañaraz's men was spying on the ranch. They chased him away and established an observation post from which they could keep a close watch on Argañaraz. As if the problem of Argañaraz and the police had not been enough, a number of Che's men fell sick with malaria, and the radio equipment was ruined by water seepage into the cave where it had been stored for safekeeping.

In view of the increasing possibility that the guerrilla force might be discovered by the authorities if it continued to remain at the ranch, Che decided to take his group on a training and reconnaissance march to the north. He had previously intended to undertake this exercise in mid-February, but the exigencies of the moment forced him to advance the date of departure to the first of February. Somewhat earlier, Che had instructed Tania to go to Argentina to interview his contacts there and bring them to the Ñancahuazú camp to discuss establishing a guerrilla *foco* in the north of Argentina. Che had expected Tania to return with the Argentines before February, but when she did not arrive by February 1, he decided to start the march north without waiting for her. He left Bigotes and four men behind to watch the ranch. They were instructed to wait for Tania, the Peruvians, and Moisés Guevara, who was due to bring his first group of recruits around the middle of February.

The morning of February 1, Che and his men left the ranch, heavily laden under their knapsacks and weapons. Their progress the first few days was painfully slow because of the constant rain and the fact that a number of the men, suffering from malaria, held the entire group back. They soon discovered that their maps of the area were incomplete and, in places, useless. On the sixth day, they reached the Rio Grande and had difficulty crossing it. Once having crossed the river, they encountered some peasants and attempted to win their sympathy by giving medical treatment to their children. But the peasants were suspicious of them and uncooperative.

During the next few weeks, the guerrillas roamed across the broken terrain north of the Rio Grande, occasionally losing their way or encountering steep cliffs that forced them to double back over ground already covered. The difficult terrain, the heat, and their dwindling food supply began to affect their physical and psychological condition. By the end of the third week, Che himself was so exhausted that he was on the verge of collapse. On February 23, he wrote in his diary that he had made it on guts alone that day. He wrote the sun was so hot at noon that it cracked stones, and he had nearly fainted climbing a hill. Che also noted that he had overheard Marcos (Comandante Antonio Sánchez Díaz), who was in charge of the vanguard, telling his comrades to go to hell.

A few days later, Marcos threatened Pacho with a machete. The incident was so serious that Che was forced to reprimand both of them before the entire group. He took the occasion to explain that the kind of physical discomfort they were experiencing was an introduction to what they could expect in the future, and that lack of discipline under such circumstances produced shameful incidents such as those that had occurred between the two Cubans. At the same time, he asked the Bolivians to be truthful and to tell him if they felt like quitting. He assured them they would be permitted to leave freely if their convictions weakened. Later the same day, one of the Bolivians, a young student named Benjamin, was forced to drop back because of exhaustion. As the remainder of the group was climbing a cliff alongside the Rio Grande, Benjamin strayed off the trail and fell into the river. He didn't know how to swim, and the current dragged him under almost immediately.

Although Che had planned to return to the Ñancahuazú camp by the first of March, the second week of March found his group still a long way from the camp and at the end of its food supplies. The scarcity of food seriously affected the morale of the men, and they soon became so weak they could make very little progress each day. Their preoccupation with their lack of food emerges from Che's diary notations for this period. They are very short and deal almost exclusively with whether or not any game was killed each day and how many rations they had remaining.

On March 14, they finally reached the Ñancahuazú River, which was very turbulent because of the heavy rainfall in the area the preceding weeks. Rolando, one of the best swimmers in the group, swam across the river and went on ahead to notify those at the camp that Che and the others would be arriving in a few days. However, it took Che three days to move the entire group and the equipment across the swollen river. A raft was built for this purpose, and on the last crossing another fatal accident occurred. The raft was overturned by a whirlpool, and Carlos, one of the best of the Bolivian recruits, was lost in the swirling water, along with most of their ammunition.

The next day, the weary group resumed the march to the camp still some two days distant. In the afternoon, Che and the others noticed a light airplane circling the area ahead of them. This alarmed Che considerably, particularly since he had not received any news from the camp in many weeks. He decided to get to the camp as quickly as possible and told his exhausted men they would have to keep marching beyond nightfall. At about five-thirty that evening, they met the Peruvian named Negro, who had been sent by El Chino to find Che and tell him what had happened in his absence. The news was upsetting. Two of the recruits recently brought to the camp by Moisés Guevara had deserted, and the police had visited the ranch again.

At some point during the last two weeks of the march, Marcos and the vanguard had separated from the main force and gone ahead to the ranch. They evidently reached the ranch several days in advance of Che. As Che and his men approached the ranch, they encountered Pacho, who had been sent by Marcos with a message indicating that the situation was becoming increasingly critical. In addition to the two desertions and the police visit to the ranch, a large number of soldiers had moved into the area and had captured one of Moisés Guevara's recruits. There was even some fear at this point that Bigotes had been taken prisoner as well.

During Che's long absence, a number of people had gathered at the ranch. In mid-February, Coco had returned with Moisés Guevara and his first group of recruits from the mines. They were followed by El Chino and his two comrades, Negro and Eustaquio. In addition, Tania came with several visitors. Only two of these visitors remained at the ranch to wait for Che's return. They were Régis Debray, the young French leftist writer, and Ciro Bustos, one of Che's Argentine contacts. This group had moved to a small campsite apart from the main base to wait for the return of Che and his men.

When Che arrived at the visitors' campsite, he found everyone there in a state of great confusion. The news that soldiers were in the area, that two of Moisés Guevara's men had deserted, and that a third had been captured had set everyone's nerves on edge. Moreover, Che discovered that Marcos and the vanguard were not at the visitors' campsite or the main camp. In fact, as Che and his men reached the visitors' camp, one of the members of the vanguard arrived with instructions from Marcos that everyone in the camp should prepare for a complete withdrawal from the area. Che noted in his diary that there was an atmosphere of defeat and complete chaos among those present, and that no one appeared to know what to do.

Che immediately sent Marcos an angry message reminding him that "wars are won with bullets" and ordering him and the men with him to go at once to the main camp and defend it. In view of this situation, one wonders what would have happened if Che had not arrived at this moment. Marcos and the others would have withdrawn from the area and quite possibly fallen into an army ambush. Alternatively, Che and his group might have arrived at the camp to find it deserted. Unaware of the army's presence in the area, Che and his group might have then unsuspectingly run headlong into them. Indeed, it is difficult to understand how Che could have made the error of remaining away from the main camp for over a month and a half. In his absence, something was sure to go wrong at the ranch, particularly given the arrival of a number of undisciplined new recruits.

Having ordered Marcos and the vanguard to the main camp, Che spent the entire day of March 21 talking with El Chino, Debray, Bustos, and Tania. With El Chino, he discussed the details of the Peruvian guerrilla *foco*. He agreed to give El Chino five thousand dollars monthly, provided he and his men took to the mountains in the Ayacucho region of Peru within six months. He next spoke to Debray, who indicated that he had come to join the guerrilla force. However, Che convinced him that he could do more for the guerrilla operation if he returned to France and organized international support for the Bolivian operation. Bustos made it clear he was willing to place himself at Che's disposal. Che therefore proposed that Bustos serve as a kind of coordinator of the Argentine contacts and make arrangements for the first five men from Argentina to be sent for training with the Bolivian group.

Tania told Che that she had contacted the right people in Argentina and brought them to the ranch. However, they had insisted she travel with them in their own jeep from Camiri to the ranch. She was thus forced to leave her jeep parked on a side street in Camiri. But the Argentines, with the exception of Bustos, had left the camp and returned to Argentina when they discovered that Che was not there. Tania decided to wait at the ranch for Che's return, since she was afraid her long absence from La Paz had created too much suspicion. As it was, the jeep she had left parked in Camiri for several weeks did attract the attention of the local police, and upon investigation they discovered some documents in the jeep that later enabled them to link her to the guerrillas.

On March 22, Che moved everyone in the second campsite to the main camp, where Marcos and the vanguard were waiting. Upon arriving, he ordered Coco and five others to go down to the river and set up an ambush that would stop the soldiers if they attempted to approach the main camp from the river. He also sent several of his men on reconnaissance patrols in order to try and locate the exact position of the soldiers. Soon after Che's arrival at the main camp, Inti informed him that Marcos had treated him disrespectfully. Che became furious at Marcos and told him that if what Inti had reported was true, he could be expelled from the guerrilla force. Marcos, on the point of tears, answered that he would rather be shot than expelled from the group. However, the problem presented by Marcos's behavior was soon eclipsed by the news that a column of soldiers was marching in the direction of the guerrillas' camp.

Chapter 7

THE DISCOVERY OF
THE GUERRILLAS

Evidently, we will have to start the march sooner than
I thought and get a move on, leaving a group in reserve,
and with the handicap of four possible informers. The
situation is not good, but another stage of testing now
begins for the guerrilla. . . .

—Che Guevara, *Bolivian Diary* (1967)

On the morning of March 23, an army patrol led by
Major Hernán Plata approached the guerrillas' main
camp through the canyon of the Ñancahuazú River.
The patrol, which was under orders to investigate the reported
presence of Cuban-style guerrillas in the area, advanced along
the river in three sections. The first section was led by Captain
Emilio Silva, the second by Major Plata, and the third by Lieutenant Loayza. A fourth officer and a civilian guide, Epifano Vargas,
accompanied the section led by Captain Silva. In all, there were
approximately thirty soldiers. At about seven in the morning,

Captain Silva discovered near the river footprints that led in the direction of the guerrilla camp. He halted the column and consulted with Major Plata. The major gave his consent to follow the footprints, and Captain Silva led the column up a path along one side of the river canyon. A few minutes later, the first section of the patrol approached the area where Coco and his men had set up their ambush. The guerrillas were positioned on both sides of the canyon so that they could catch anyone moving up the river in a crossfire.

As Captain Silva's section came within fifty feet of the guerrillas, the soldiers were startled by Coco's cry of "Viva la liberación nacional." Before the soldiers had time to react, they were caught in a rain of bullets. In a few minutes, the civilian guide Vargas, the officer accompanying him, and five soldiers lay dead along the path. The remainder of the first section, as well as the second section led by Major Plata, was hopelessly pinned down under the guerrillas' crossfire. Coco called on the soldiers to surrender. Seeing the futility of any resistance, Captain Silva ordered his men to cease firing and raise their hands. The men in Major Plata's section followed, while the third section, under Lieutenant Loayza, quickly retreated along the river.

As the smoke cleared, Coco and the other guerrillas in the ambush began collecting the soldiers' weapons and evaluating the results of the action. They counted seven dead, four wounded, and fourteen prisoners. Major Plata was found in a clump of bushes, suffering from a heart attack brought on by the shooting. He and the wounded soldiers were given medical attention by one of the Bolivian guerrillas who had formerly been a doctor. Coco ran back to the main camp to inform Che of the ambush and to ask for more men to guard the prisoners. He brought with him papers found on Major Plata that indicated the army's plan of operations. On the basis of this information, Che was able to ascertain that the army was advancing on the main camp from the two extremes of the Ñancahuazú River, and he was forewarned of the possibility of another patrol's arriving at the rear of his camp from upriver.

Major Plata and Captain Silva were afraid they were going to be killed; Che's diary indicates that when Inti interrogated them, they "talked like parrots." According to Che, Major Plata said he was going to retire from the army, and Captain Silva claimed that he had reentered the army a year earlier at the request of "the Party," implying that he was a Communist. He also said he had a brother studying in Cuba, and that he knew two officers who would be willing to collaborate with the guerrillas. Actually, Captain Silva was not a Communist, and he did not have a brother studying in Cuba. He thought that if he could convince the guerrillas he was sympathetic to their cause, he might save his life. Both he and Major Plata, therefore, were quite surprised when they learned the next day that the guerrillas were going to set them free and allow them to return unharmed to Lagunillas. They were also surprised by the cordial treatment they received. Of course, that was all part of Che's strategy. He hoped that such chivalrous treatment would earn the guerrillas the admiration of the soldiers and perhaps induce some of them to join the guerrilla force.

On March 24, some twenty-four hours after they had been captured, the soldiers were set free. Inti asked them first whether they would like to join the guerrilla movement, and when they all refused, he ordered all but the officers to strip to their underwear. In exchange for their camouflage uniforms, they were given the olive-green fatigue pants and jackets of the guerrillas, and permitted to leave by the same trail they had been on when they were ambushed. That afternoon, they reached the remainder of their unit and reported to the Fourth Army Division headquarters in Camiri what had transpired. Naturally, they exaggerated greatly the number of guerrillas who had captured them. Word was flashed to La Paz that perhaps as many as five hundred Castroite guerrillas were operating in the Ñancahuazú region, and that an army patrol led by Major Plata had made contact with them near their main camp. In this manner, the news of the guerrillas' first and most successful military action was transmitted to the outside world, although at the time there was no official recognition that Che Guevara was the leader of the guerrilla operation.

Che's original plan was to begin military operations north of the Rio Grande and then slowly withdraw southward across a terrain carefully prepared with caches of arms and ammunition, food supplies, and fortified bases. He needed perhaps another month before this plan would have been ready to be put into operation. But he had to discard it when the army discovered his main base in the Ñancahuazú area. The army was able to do this because during the first few weeks of March it had received a number of credible reports about the presence of guerrillas in that area.

On the morning of March 11, two of Moisés Guevara's new recruits left the main camp, ostensibly to go hunting. They took the path leading down to the river, but instead of going to the east, where the best hunting area was, they disappeared in the direction of Camiri. A few days later, they were arrested and brought to the headquarters of the Fourth Army Division in Camiri. There they gave their captors a detailed report concerning all they knew about the guerrilla operation.

They identified themselves as Vicente Rocabado and Pastor Barrera, both unemployed miners from the Oruro area. They said they had been recruited by the Communist union leader Moisés

Guevara to join a group in the southeast that was planning to launch a Cuban type of revolution in Bolivia. Because they were unemployed and Moisés Guevara had promised them payment for their services, they said, they agreed to join the guerrilla force. But after a month at the guerrillas' camp, where they claimed they had been made to work as peons, they decided they were fed up with guerrilla life and would desert at the first opportunity.

Rocabado and Barrera gave the army detailed information about the location of the guerrillas' camp, the number of people there, and the fact that most of the guerrilla force was away at the time on a training and reconnaissance march to the north. They said they had been told that Che Guevara was the leader of the operation and that he was with the others in the north. They also told their captors about the large number of Cubans in the guerrilla group and about the presence at the camp of Régis Debray, Ciro Bustos, and Tania.

The senior officers at the divisional headquarters in Camiri received this information with considerable skepticism, if not disbelief. "Guerrillas in Ñancahuazú, with Che Guevara as their leader? Impossible!" was the response of the divisional commander, Colonel Humberto Rocha, who thought it more likely that they were dealing with a gang of cocaine merchants or perhaps even a band of cattle thieves. But his skepticism was soon dispelled by the arrival at the divisional headquarters of Epifano Vargas, an oil worker from Vallegrande. Vargas told Colonel Rocha that he had encountered a number of men, clad in olive-green clothing and armed with automatic weapons, near the Ñancahuazú River around the first of March (this was undoubtedly Marcos and the vanguard). He said they had presented themselves to him as foreign geologists who were interested in buying food. Vargas had sold them some of his food and, because he suspected they were not geologists, had followed them at a safe distance until they reached the ranch. He then went directly to the army headquarters in Camiri to report what he had seen. This report, together with the information given by the two deserters, prompted Colonel Rocha to dispatch troops to the Ñancahuazú ranch. He also ordered an immediate aerial surveillance of the entire zone. Vargas was asked to go along with the troops and serve as a guide. There is some evidence that he refused to go voluntarily and had to be taken along as a prisoner.

On March 16, units from the Fourth Division reached the ranch and seized the house and the portion of the ranch closest to the road. The next day, they captured Salustio Choque, one of Moisés Guevara's recently arrived recruits. If the army had any doubts about the presence of guerrillas in the Ñancahuazú area, the capture of Choque erased them. He confirmed everything that Rocabado and Barrera had told the military authorities in Camiri. He also volunteered to guide the soldiers to the guerrilla camp. Major Plata's column apparently preferred to rely on Vargas instead of Choque as a guide, but Choque subsequently led another column, under Major Sánchez, to the guerrilla camp at the beginning of April. At that time, he showed them where the guerrillas had hidden their supplies, film, documents, and various other items of importance.

The information that Choque, the two deserters Rocabado and Barrera, and the oil worker Vargas gave the Bolivian authorities led to the discovery and subsequent annihilation of Che's guerrilla force. This information enabled the army to locate Che's main base before his men were ready to begin military operations. It also gave the army the initiative from the beginning of the conflict until its tragic termination some six months later. Timing was a crucial factor in Che's strategy, and the premature initiation of hostilities threw his whole operation off balance. His small force of men was never really able to recover from the shock of having its central base discovered before it was ready to begin fighting. All of Che's subsequent efforts were little more than valiant, but futile, attempts to put up a good fight in the face of overwhelming odds. He and his men seem to have deluded themselves during the first few months of fighting that their operation still could succeed, but in reality their fate was sealed from the beginning.

Che had written of the extreme danger that a guerrilla force faces during its preparatory stage in his article "Guerrilla Warfare: A Method." He pointed out that the future of a revolutionary movement depends upon the way in which the nuclear guerrilla force handles itself when the enemy moves against it. Unless the guerrillas are able to develop their capacity to attack the enemy during the early stage of the struggle, they have little prospect of surviving.

Régis Debray, in his work *Revolution in the Revolution?* (Debray 1967), also noted that the crucial moment for a guerrilla force is the moment of its entry into action and that here the question of timing is critical. Debray stated that the destruction of the guerrilla *foco* in its embryonic stage, before it has linked itself closely to the local population or gained sufficient experience, is the ideal accomplishment of any counterinsurgency operation. He went on to emphasize that once the guerrilla force has been discovered, it must not allow itself to be contained within a specific zone, for this deprives the guerrillas of their main weapon, mobility, and allows the regular army to utilize its forces most effectively. This was the precise situation in which Che's force found itself after March 23. As a result of the army's discovery of their main base, Che and his men were forced to withdraw into a relatively confined area. Whereas he had originally planned to have his force withdraw across a zone carefully prepared with caches of supplies and fortified bases, the army's discovery of their main base forced Che and his men to move into an area about which they knew very little and where they had difficulty finding food and places to hide.

Only Che's will to succeed and his refusal to accept defeat can explain his optimism about the future of his guerrilla operation after the discovery of his force in the Ñancahuazú area at the end of March. Anyone else undoubtedly would have concluded that the circumstances left no choice but to abandon the entire venture and escape while it was still possible to do so. But not Che; until the end, he continued to believe that his effort would succeed. Perhaps he kept thinking of how high the odds had been against the success of Castro's operation after the *Granma* disaster, when only twelve members of the original eighty-man invasion force survived the landing on Cuban soil and made their way to the Sierra Maestra.

Chapter 8

THE CAPTURE OF RÉGIS DEBRAY AND CIRO BUSTOS

Dantón (Debray) and Carlos (Bustos) fell victims of their own haste, almost desperation, to get out, and my lack of energy in trying to prevent them, so we have lost our communications with Cuba (Dantón) and we have lost our plan of action in Argentina (Carlos).

—Che Guevara, *Bolivian Diary* (1967)

Following their first clash with the army, the guerrillas were forced to withdraw from their main base in Ñancahuazú. As they moved north toward the little town of Gutiérrez, they discovered that a large number of troops were stationed in the area immediately ahead of them. Che was forced to hastily modify his plans. Instead of heading north toward the Vallegrande region, he decided to make a diversionary move toward the south. By staging a surprise attack against the town of Muyupampa, some thirty miles to the southwest, Che reasoned he and his men would have no trouble marching north along the series of ridges leading from the Muyupampa area toward the Rio Grande.

In addition to the shortage of food, the lack of preparation of his force, and the precariousness of their position, Che faced the problem of slipping Régis Debray and Ciro Bustos out of the combat zone without their being captured by the Bolivian authorities. As previously mentioned, Che had convinced Debray that he would be of more value to the movement if he returned to France. As for Bustos, Che was depending on him to return to Argentina and lay the groundwork for the future Argentine phase of his operation.

Faced with the difficulty of transporting them safely out of the area after the ambush of the army patrol on March 23, Che had initially offered Debray and Bustos three alternatives: (1) they could stay with the guerrilla force until a later date, when it might be easier for them to depart safely, (2) they could try to get out of the combat zone right away, or (3) they could stay with the guerrilla force until it reached the town of Gutiérrez and from there take their chances at escaping. They chose the third alternative. But when they discovered that a large number of troops were defending Gutiérrez, they decided to accompany Che and the others to Muyupampa.

Not far from Muyupampa, Che's men captured an Anglo-Chilean reporter named George Roth, who had paid some youths in Lagunillas to lead him to the guerrilla force. Needless to say, Che was not happy to learn that the general location of his force was a matter of public knowledge in Lagunillas. On the other hand, Roth's arrival gave Debray an idea how he and Bustos could leave the guerrilla force and get past the Bolivian authorities without arousing their suspicion. Both of them, pretending to be reporters, could leave in the company of Roth and, if they were stopped, could explain that all three of them had entered the area to interview the guerrillas.

Debray had entered the country legally, with credentials from the leftist Mexican magazine *Sucesos* and the Paris publishing house of Maspero. He therefore thought he would have no difficulty convincing the authorities that his presence in the area was legitimate. Bustos presented a problem, however, since he had entered the country with false documents and had no credentials that would support his contention that he was a journalist. Nevertheless, Debray persuaded Bustos that they would be able to convince the Bolivian authorities that he was a fellow journalist if they were questioned. After consulting Bustos, Debray went to Che with his plan. Aware that there were as many troops around Muyupampa as in the Gutiérrez area, Che told Debray it would be better if they waited. But when Debray insisted on going and Bustos indicated he was willing to give the plan a try, Che reluctantly gave his consent.

Meanwhile, Roth was being held under guard a short distance from the main body of the guerrilla force, so that he would not discover that Che was the guerrillas' leader and that a large number of Cubans were in the force. When Inti presented Debray's plan to Roth, he readily agreed to it. Roth not only thought the undertaking would provide him with an excellent story but was afraid of what might happen to him if he refused to help Debray and Bustos. Up until the point Inti presented Debray's plan to him, Roth had been afraid the guerrillas were not going to let him go. He knew that they were suspicious of him because his passport indicated he had spent some time in Puerto Rico, regarded by the guerrillas as the training ground for all U.S. agents in Latin America. Actually, Roth had been employed in Puerto Rico by the U.S. Peace Corps to teach Spanish to Peace Corps volunteers training there for assignments in Latin America.

On April 19, Debray and Bustos, together with Roth, left the guerrilla force just outside the town of Muyupampa. Debray had some last-minute doubts about leaving when he learned that Muyupampa was under heavy guard, but Bustos had made up his mind and Debray had no choice but to leave with him. Before they left, Che gave Debray a message that he was to deliver personally to Fidel. He also gave Bustos some money and final instructions regarding his mission to Argentina. A few hours later, the three were stopped and arrested by an army patrol on the outskirts of Muyupampa.

Since the Bolivian authorities had already been informed that a Frenchman and an Argentine were among the guerrillas, Debray and Bustos were immediately identified. At first, the Bolivians thought Roth was a guerrilla, but he was later released and allowed to return to Chile. On Bustos, who was quite an artist, were found a series of sketches that he had drawn of the most important members of the guerrilla force, including Che. These proved very helpful to the Bolivian authorities in identifying many of the guerrillas.

The capture of Debray and Bustos gave the Bolivian authorities a propaganda field day. Above all, it provided them with visible proof of the "foreign" character of the guerrilla operation, and they did not fail to get as much mileage as possible out of this fact. They realized that in the eyes of most Bolivians they could effectively discredit the guerrillas by depicting them as foreign invaders intent upon intervening in the internal affairs of their country. Debray, in particular, was a perfect instrument for agitating and mobilizing the nationalistic sensibilities of the Bolivian people against the guerrillas. Not only was he a foreigner; he was also a well-known European Marxist, a friend of Cuba, and the author of several works on revolution in Latin America, the latest being *Revolution in the Revolution?*, widely publicized at the beginning of 1967 as a primer for Marxist insurrection in Latin America.

Soon after the capture of Debray and Bustos, the Bolivian authorities announced that both would be publicly tried by a military tribunal for their crimes against the Bolivian people. During the months preceding this trial, the government waged an intensive propaganda campaign against the prisoners, in particular Debray. When the trial was finally held, during October 1967, Debray was accused of a long list of crimes. According to the prosecutor, he had come to Bolivia as a spy on two previous occasions (he had visited the country several years earlier as a journalist). The prosecutor also accused him of bringing maps as well as money to the guerrillas, of being a member of the general staff of the guerrilla force, and of giving them training in guerrilla warfare. Finally, he claimed that Debray had personally participated in the guerrillas' ambush of the army column on March 23 and that he was the intellectual architect of the entire guerrilla operation.

Acting as his own attorney at the end of the trial, Debray made a brilliant, though perhaps too intellectual, defense of his actions. He argued that the government was pretending to condemn him for having performed a major role in the guerrilla operation, while in fact it was condemning him because he was a Marxist, an admirer of Fidel Castro and Che Guevara, and an advocate of revolution in Latin America. Debray said that if this was what he was to be punished for, he admitted to being guilty. But although he admitted his political and moral complicity, he reminded the members of the tribunal that if they were going to continue with the pretext of trying him for violations of criminal law, then they could not condemn him for his beliefs or even his intentions, but only for whatever criminal acts they could prove he had committed. In this regard, he asserted that the government had failed to produce any evidence proving that he had participated either directly or indirectly in the military activities of the guerrilla force. Furthermore, he claimed that Che's diary (introduced during the last part of the trial) supported his innocence in this respect.

Debray was correct about Che's diary. This journal makes it quite clear that both he and Bustos were considered visitors and that they did nothing more bellicose than occasionally take a turn at guard duty. To be sure, the diary also reveals that Debray asked Che for permission to join the guerrilla force as a combatant and indicates that Che convinced him that he would be much more useful to the movement outside Bolivia. At the trial, Debray said that Che had also wanted him to leave because he was suffering from malnutrition and Che didn't have much confidence in his physical resistance. He claimed that Che alluded to his lack of experience and poor physical condition by telling him that one campesino was worth more to him than ten intellectuals from the city.

Che's diary also leaves little doubt that Debray was neither the intellectual architect of the guerrilla operation nor one of its planners. Che mentioned Debray's book *Revolution in the Revolution?* only twice throughout the twelve-month period covered in his diary. These references show, too, that Che had not read Debray's book until Debray himself gave him a copy in the guerrilla camp. At any rate, the book is based upon the revolutionary theories and practices of the leaders of the Cuban revolution, in particular those formulated by Che. Therefore, it is hard to believe that Debray was the intellectual architect or that his book served as the primer for an operation organized and led by Che Guevara, one of *the* most prominent authorities on the theory and practice of revolutionary guerrilla warfare.

Apart from being caught trying to leave the guerrilla force, Debray never did anything more than serve as a messenger for the guerrillas. Che's diary reveals that he brought information with him from Cuba when he arrived at the guerrilla camp in March. However, this information had already been received by Che through other sources. Debray was subsequently instructed by Che to deliver a message to Fidel and, upon his return to France, to contact Jean-Paul Sartre and Bertrand Russell about organizing an international fund to help the Bolivian guerrilla movement. Actually, it was not Debray but Bustos to whom Che had given the responsibility of carrying out an important and truly subversive mission—that of laying the groundwork for an Argentine guerrilla *foco*.

It has been suggested that after he was captured, Debray gave the Bolivian intelligence service and the CIA information that they were able to use against Che and his guerrilla force. Indeed, it seems Che himself suspected that Debray and Bustos might have done this. In his diary entry on June 30, Che referred to having heard over the radio a declaration made by the head of the Bolivian armed forces, General Ovando, in which Ovando stated that Che was the leader of the guerrillas. Che noted that General Ovando had said his declaration was based on certain statements made by Debray. Che commented that it appeared Debray had said more than was necessary. Later, on July 10, Che wrote that the public statements made by both Debray and Bustos were not good, and he was especially upset that they had confessed the continental purpose of the guerrilla movement.

At a press conference permitted by the army on July 9, Bustos did in fact tell reporters that Che was in Bolivia for the purpose of launching a revolutionary movement that would eventually encompass the entire continent. He also told them that Che had no more than forty or fifty guerrillas with him and that a number of them were foreigners. He specifically mentioned Coco and Inti Peredo as the two leading Bolivian members of the guerrilla force. The fact that Bustos's wife was allowed to visit him a few days after this interview, and that he later received better treatment than Debray, suggests that he may have made a deal with the Bolivian authorities.

As for Debray, it is quite possible that he unwillingly gave the CIA and the Bolivian intelligence authorities information about the guerrilla force. He obviously was very frightened after he was taken prisoner in Muyupampa. In the defense declaration he made at his trial, he mentioned that he had been beaten by Bolivian intelligence agents after he was captured. Under the circumstances, he may have broken down and told the authorities everything. Moreover, at his trial he spoke of having been interrogated by a CIA agent who called himself Dr. Eduardo Gonzales (a Cuban exile whose real name is Gustavo Villoldo). According to Debray, Gonzales knew from the outset that he was not a guerrilla. Instead, he assumed that Debray had a confidential political mission to perform for the guerrillas outside of Bolivia. He questioned Debray about his mission, about his relations with the Cuban government, about the guerrilla movement's sources of support outside Bolivia, and, of course, about Che.

During the course of his testimony, Debray stated that he told Gonzales he had visited the guerrilla camp solely to interview Che but that upon arriving he had discovered that a Bolivian named Inti was the guerrilla leader. But several weeks later, according to Debray, Gonzales returned to interrogate him again, and this time he had precise testimonies and detailed documents that proved beyond any doubt that Che was the leader of the guerrillas and that Debray had "interviewed" him. At this point, Debray stated that he was forced to admit that he had interviewed Che, and he gave Gonzales a summary of this interview. What Debray really told Gonzales we can only guess. If he did give Gonzales any valuable information about Che and the guerrilla movement, he would, of course, have been too ashamed to admit it.

Debray's motivation for going to Bolivia remains unclear. Did he go to the guerrilla camp so that he could write a sensational eyewitness account of Che's guerrilla operation in Bolivia, or did he go there in order to perfect his theories on revolutionary guerrilla warfare by directly participating in the operation? Perhaps his book *Revolution in the Revolution?* offers a partial answer. In it Debray wrote that "the Latin American revolutionary war possesses highly special and profoundly distinct conditions of development, which can only be discovered through a particular experience." He argued that to understand this kind of war in the Latin American context, it does no good to consult previous theoretical works on this subject. Instead, he used the analogy of learning a foreign language to support his point that this kind of war must be observed firsthand. He stated, "A foreign language is learned faster in a country where it must be spoken than at home studying a language manual." It would seem that Debray tried to follow his own advice by going to Bolivia to learn at first hand the "language" of revolutionary guerrilla warfare.

Why, then, was Debray so anxious to leave the guerrilla force so soon after he arrived? Did he perceive that Che's guerrilla operation was doomed to failure, did he become frightened for his own safety, or was he merely trying to relieve Che of the added problem of worrying about him and Bustos at a time when Che had more than enough to worry about? According to Debray, he felt that he and Bustos were greatly interfering with the mobility of the guerrilla force, particularly in view of his own bad health.

He claims he insisted on leaving the guerrilla force as soon as the first opportunity arose, so as to reduce the burdens on Che. But if this was Debray's motivation for wanting to leave Che and the others, there is no evidence in Che's diary to substantiate it.

Che made no reference in his diary to Debray's having been ill. On the other hand, his diary suggests that Che suspected that Debray was anxious to leave the guerrilla force because he was frightened. On March 28, for example, Che wrote in the diary that Debray was "too vehement about how useful he could be to the movement outside of Bolivia." Moreover, after Debray and Bustos had been captured and imprisoned, Che wrote that they were victims of "their own near desperation to leave the guerrilla force, and of my lack of energy to prevent them from doing so." He also noted that as a result of Bustos's and Debray's capture, his communication link with Cuba was cut off, and his plan for establishing a guerrilla force in Argentina was lost.

After Che's death, both Debray and Bustos made a number of interesting statements about the failure of Che's guerrilla operation. Both were confined to a rather comfortable existence in a former officer's club in Camiri, which was converted into a special prison for them. According to reporters who were allowed to visit them, they both admitted that Che's guerrilla operation failed because of its lack of popular support and the betrayal of the pro-Soviet Bolivian Communists.

In addition, Debray confessed to reporters that he thought the Bolivian government acted very intelligently in response to the guerrilla threat. Referring to the way in which the government used the people's sense of national pride against Che and the guerrillas, he told Georgie Anne Geyer of the *Chicago Daily News*, "They made me the stranger. They put me in an untenable position. This thing of nationalism is very important. You cannot go beyond feelings of nationalism." He also claims that he had changed some of his ideas about revolution in Latin America. For example, in the same interview, he said that he now felt that the armies of Latin America, including the Bolivian army, presented a major obstacle to revolution. In several other interviews, Debray declared that the guerrilla operation led by Che was condemned to failure from the start. He also claimed that the CIA knew about the guerrilla operation in February 1967 and that from that time forward the guerrillas were in an extremely precarious position.

Of the two, Bustos made the more critical statements about Che and his guerrilla operation. He told Geyer that "Che did everything wrong" and that "the biggest problem was Che's vision of the revolution as continental." Because of this idea, Bustos said, Che failed to see Bolivia in its proper perspective, and "he underestimated . . . the army, the people's will, and [Bolivian] nationalism." Bustos also criticized the number of Cubans Che brought with him to Bolivia, indicating that their presence tainted the entire undertaking as a form of foreign intervention.

Although they were sentenced to thirty years in prison, both Debray and Bustos were released after three years by General Juan José Torres, who headed a short-lived reformist regime in Bolivia that took power in 1970 (Anderson, 1997, 746–47). Debray wrote a book, largely based on his experience in Bolivia, entitled *La guerrilla de Che* (Debray 1975). It provides his perspective on the conditions that were responsible for the failure of Che's effort in Bolivia as well as the overthrow of the socialist government of Salvador Allende in Chile in 1973. He became a celebrity in European leftist circles and served as an adviser on Latin American affairs in the French socialist government of President François Mitterrand in the 1980s. In more recent years, he has been highly critical of Fidel Castro and Cuba.

Chapter 9

THE HIGH POINT OF GUERRILLA ACTIVITIES

The plan, in the face of the enemy's general superiority, is to find a tactical means of achieving relative superiority in one chosen place. . . .

—Che Guevara, "Guerrilla Warfare: A Method" (1963)

Throughout April, May, June, and July, the guerrillas foiled the army's efforts to trap and annihilate them. In fact, because of the ineptitude and inexperience of the Bolivian army, the guerrillas badly mauled some of the units sent out to encircle them and lost very few of their own men. Thus, they humiliated the army and embarrassed the government during the first months of their short-lived campaign.

Following their initial encounter with the army near their main camp, on March 23, over two weeks passed before the guerrillas clashed with the army again. The second encounter took place on April 10 some twelve miles north of the guerrillas' main camp, at a place along the Ñancahuazú River named Iripiti. On the morning of the tenth, the guerrillas were making their way toward the town of Gutiérrez by proceeding up the Ñancahuazú when they discovered that a patrol of fifteen soldiers was coming downriver. Che quickly ordered his men to set up an ambush on both sides of the river. A short time later, the soldiers arrived, and in the ensuing exchange of gunfire the lieutenant in charge of the patrol and two of his men were killed. Two soldiers were wounded, six were taken prisoner, and four managed to escape. On the guerrilla side, there was only one casualty, the Cuban called El Rubio (Jesús Suárez Gayol). He was found near the wounded soldiers with a bullet in his head and his jammed rifle and a grenade at his side.

The guerrillas learned from the prisoners that they were part of a company of soldiers currently in possession of the guerrillas' former main camp. Che calculated that the remainder of this company would most likely come in search of his group just as soon as the soldiers who had escaped the ambush reported back to their company commander. Therefore, he had his men establish another ambush, and at around five that evening a column of about forty-five soldiers under the command of Major Rubén Sánchez was caught in it. The first volley of gunfire killed a lieutenant, a sergeant, and several soldiers who were at the head of the column. The guerrillas called upon the remainder to surrender, but the major ordered his men to keep shooting. Since they could not see the guerrillas hidden in the thickets around them, it soon became obvious, however, that the situation was hopeless, and Major Sánchez and most of his men surrendered. The rear guard of the column, accompanied by two reporters from La Paz, managed to escape the ambush and return to the army field headquarters in El Pineal, a few miles south of the guerrillas' former main base. The final results of this second ambush were seven soldiers killed, five wounded, and twenty-two taken prisoner (including the major and several junior officers). Che's force suffered no casualties.

The wounded soldiers were cared for by the two doctors in Che's force, and Inti Peredo took charge of interrogating the prisoners. After interrogation, the captured soldiers had their rations and boots taken from them, and they were set free. The major and his men, carrying their dead and wounded, walked some six miles on their bare feet before they finally reached their comrades. The news that the guerrillas had successfully ambushed the army twice on the same day, killing ten men and capturing more than thirty, was a source of considerable humiliation to the Bolivian military high command.

Meanwhile, Che decided to divide his force into two groups. He appointed Joaquín (Comandante Juan Vitalio Acuña) as the leader of the second group. He was a member of the Central Committee of the Cuban Communist Party and one of the first campesinos to join Castro's guerrilla movement in the Sierra Maestra. Joaquín's group consisted of fourteen persons, including those who were too ill to march at anything but a very slow pace, and the Bolivian recruits whom Che regarded as misfits. Among the sick were Tania and the Cuban called Alejandro (Gustavo Machín de Hoed), both of whom were running high fevers, plus Moisés Guevara, who had recently been disabled by a gall bladder attack.

Che wanted Joaquín to stay in the area immediately to the west of the Ñancahuazú River and make a demonstration there, while he and the second group, including Debray and Bustos, went to Muyupampa. It was from the soldiers taken prisoner in the Iripiti ambushes that Che had learned that the town of Gutiérrez was being used as a staging area by the army. This information led

Che to forget Gutiérrez and march in the opposite direction to attack Muyupampa. After the raid on Muyupampa, he hoped to rejoin Joaquín's group and then head north toward the Rio Grande. As Che and his group approached Muyupampa, however, they discovered that the town was under heavy guard and in a state of alert. Consequently, Che was again forced to change his plans, and, after dropping off Debray and Bustos, he and his group marched north toward the village of Ticucha.

On April 22, Che's group set up an ambush on the road running from the little village of Taperillas to Ticucha, some six miles farther north. During the course of the day, the guerrillas stopped a small truck belonging to the government-owned petroleum company, also a considerable number of peasants, and another truck loaded with a large quantity of bananas. They confiscated the petroleum company truck and let the peasants go. At dusk a plane began to circle above their position, indicating that their presence had been detected. Nevertheless, they casually went about making the preparations for their departure and were still not ready to leave when they were surprised by shooting and the voices of troops calling upon them to surrender.

According to the entry in Che's diary, at this point there was general confusion and a near-panic among his men. However, they had already loaded their supplies and equipment into the small truck, and with the aid of this truck and six horses they managed to withdraw from the scene before they were encircled by the opposing troops. They could not find Loro, one of the Bolivian members of the guerrilla force, and left without him. They also left behind some merchandise that they had bought from the local inhabitants and a packet of U.S. dollar bills that fell from the bag of one of the Cuban guerrillas.

Having narrowly escaped encirclement by the army, the members of Che's group moved north of Ticucha to a place called El Mesón, where they established camp and waited for Joaquín's group. But on April 25, a column of sixty soldiers arrived in the area. The guerrillas, having very little warning of their approach, were forced to set up a hastily improvised ambush along the path leading to their camp. Much to the surprise of Che and his men, the advance element of the army column was led by a soldier with three trained German shepherds. As the dogs excitedly advanced into the ambush area, Che shot at the first dog and missed; he was about to shoot at the soldier guiding the dogs when his carbine jammed. One of Che's comrades shot the guide and a dog, but this warned the rest of the approaching column, and it did not fall into the ambush. As the soldiers withdrew down the road, they exchanged shots with a group of the guerrillas. When the shooting stopped, Che sent one of his men to tell this group to withdraw from the area; he learned then that one of his Cuban comrades, Rolando (Eliseo Reyes Rodríguez), had been fatally wounded.

Rolando had joined Castro's guerrilla force in Cuba at the age of sixteen and been promoted to the rank of captain during Che's famous march from the Sierra Maestra to Las Villas. He was a member of the Central Committee of the Cuban Communist Party and one of Che's closest companions. His death was a heavy blow to Che, who had intended placing him in charge of an eventual second front. In his diary, Che wrote that he had lost his best man, one of the pillars of the guerrilla force, and his comrade from the time he had been a messenger in his column in the Sierra Maestra.

Because the army had discovered their location, Che and his men were forced to withdraw from the area where Joaquín's group was supposed to join them. Instead of heading north toward the

Rio Grande, they worked their way back toward the Ñancahuazú River in hopes that they might encounter Joaquín and his companions. Low on food and uncertain of the terrain, they traversed the rugged hills and ravines between El Mesón and the Ñancahuazú. At the end of April, Che wrote in his diary that it had been a month in which "everything was resolved normally," taking into consideration "the necessary eventualities of the guerrilla operation." Yet he also noted that their isolation was complete, that they had lost contact with Joaquín's group, and that they had done nothing to build a base of peasant support. In addition, he had to admit that the capture of Debray and Bustos had cut off his communication with Cuba and ruined his plans for preparing a guerrilla operation in northern Argentina. However, he seems to have been encouraged by radio reports that U.S. military advisers had been sent to help the Bolivian army. He believed that the United States would soon be forced to intervene with its own troops, thereby turning Bolivia into another Vietnam.

During the first week of May, Che and his comrades traversed the area north of their former main base, hoping to encounter Joaquín and the others. On May 7, they arrived at one of the small campsites along the Ñancahuazú, where they had buried some ammunition and supplies. Although it was apparent that the army had visited the campsite sometime before their arrival, their cache had not been discovered. The guerrillas spent the night at the campsite eating the small amount of food they had left. The next morning, they captured four soldiers who stumbled into the area. That same day, a small patrol came down the river, and the guerrillas ambushed them, killing the lieutenant in charge and two soldiers, and capturing six more soldiers. The guerrillas ate what little food they found on the soldiers and supplemented this with some lard they had stored in the supply caves. On the morning of May 9, the guerrillas lectured the soldiers and set them free, minus their shoes and uniforms. Shortly thereafter, Che and his men withdrew from the area and headed upriver. Since they had no other food, they were forced to eat lard soup that night, and many of the men became quite sick.

On May 12, the guerrillas came upon a small farm and feasted on pork, roasted squash, and husked corn, which they obtained from the local peasants. They departed that evening with almost every member of the group sick. The next day, Che made the following entry in his diary: "A day of belching, farting, vomiting, and diarrhea, a veritable organ concert. We remained absolutely immobile trying to digest the pork." On May 16, Che was overcome by an attack of vomiting and diarrhea so violent that he lost consciousness and had to be carried in a hammock. He wrote in his diary that when he awoke he felt quite relieved, but because he had no water to clean himself, his stench extended for at least a full mile. Throughout the next week, Che and his men kept on the move and, apart from capturing a few peasants, did not engage in any military action.

On May 28, Che and his men took control of the small town of Caraguataenda. They stationed themselves at either end of the town and confiscated two vehicles belonging to the government petroleum company and two that were privately owned. That evening, they drove these vehicles to the neighboring town of Ipitacito, where they broke into a store and took some merchandise. As payment for the items they had taken, they left behind five hundred dollars in U.S. currency and a rather ceremonious affidavit. From Ipitacito, they traveled to the town of Espino, which is situated near the railroad line that runs from Santa Cruz south to the Argentine border. Che at first planned to go from Espino toward the Rio Grande, but later changed his mind and decided to follow the road leading north from Espino to the town of Muchiri, where there was plenty of water.

On May 30, the guerrillas started for Muchiri, but they soon discovered that they had chosen the wrong road. Consequently, Che established an ambush along the road and sent out exploring parties to ascertain which direction they should follow. At about three o'clock, a column of soldiers preceded by a truck came toward the ambush. The guerrillas opened fire, forcing them to withdraw. An officer and a soldier were killed, and four were wounded. When Che was sure that the army had retreated, he ordered his men to leave the ambush area.

The guerrillas were forced to abandon all the vehicles confiscated in Caraguataenda, except one jeep; the others had run out of gasoline or water. By urinating into the radiator of the jeep and adding a few canteens of water, they were able to drive it north toward Muchiri. The next day, they discovered that the dusty road they had been following came to an abrupt end. They detained a peasant on a side road and asked him where they could find water and roads out of the area. With the peasant as their guide, Che sent a group of his men out to look for water and food. On the way, they saw two army trucks and hastily established an ambush. They partially destroyed one of the trucks with a grenade and wounded two soldiers. When they reported back to Che, he ordered everyone to resume the march. They advanced another nine miles, but during the course of this march the jeep ran out of gasoline and had to be left behind. That night, Che wrote his summary of the month, in which he indicated that he was encouraged by the military actions of his group but worried about their lack of contact not only with Joaquín's group but with their comrades in La Paz and Cuba as well. He also mentioned that they had as yet failed to incorporate a single peasant into their movement. With Joaquín's group absent, he noted, his force consisted of only twenty-five men.

It is difficult to say with any certainty where Joaquín and his companions were during this period. Che thought they had moved north of the Rio Grande, but it appears that they were well hidden somewhere in the Ñancahuazú area. At any rate, they successfully avoided contact with the army during April, May, and June.

On June 1, several aircraft circled the area through which Che and his men were moving, but they apparently did not see the guerrillas, who continued their march without encountering any soldiers. On June 2, Che and his men reached a farm, where they took a large pig and forced the farmhands to serve as their guides. While they were following an arroyo running alongside a road, an army truck passed carrying two soldiers and some barrels. It was an easy target, but Che let it go by and they continued on their way. They spent the night cooking and eating the pig, and afterward released the peasants, paying them each ten dollars for the inconvenience. The following day, they established an ambush along the road, and the same army truck that they had let pass the preceding day came down the road again. As before, two very cold-looking soldiers wrapped in blankets were riding in the rear of the truck. They looked so pitiful to Che that he let the truck pass through the ambush unmolested. Later, he wrote in his diary that he did not have the heart to shoot at them and didn't think fast enough of the possibility of detaining them. The guerrillas gave up the ambush that evening without having caught a single military vehicle. For the next few days, they hiked overland until they reached the banks of the Rio Grande, just below the village of Puerto Camacho. From there, they slowly worked their way east along the south bank of the river.

Che and his men reached a point along the river on June 9 that required that they either cross to the other bank or leave the river and trek through thickets and ravines. They decided to cross the river. However, their efforts to build a raft failed, and Che sent a small party out to find a boat. A short time later, this group was sighted by a detachment of troops on the other side of the river, who began shooting at the guerrillas with mortars and small arms. The guerrillas exchanged some shots with the soldiers and then returned to where Che and the others were anxiously waiting. Instead of withdrawing from the area, Che ordered his men to establish an ambush if the soldiers attempted to cross the river. Meanwhile, he had a couple of his men cut a trail so that they could get out of the area without crossing the river. The army failed to advance, and Che and his comrades left the area the next day by way of the new trail.

For several days, the guerrillas headed east parallel to the Rio Grande. On June 16, they crossed the river and continued east past the town of Abapo. On the way, they took as prisoners three men they thought were traders. Later, near Abapo, they encountered a peasant boy named Paulino, who informed them that the three prisoners were in fact working for the army. Although Che considered killing the three, he decided to turn them loose with a severe warning and without their pants. Paulino said he was willing to help the guerrillas and promised them he would travel to Cochabamba to deliver several messages for them, including a coded letter to be sent to Cuba. But he was caught by the army shortly after leaving the company of the guerrillas.

Che and his group headed north toward the town of Florida, and on June 26 Che had his men establish an ambush on the road leading to this town. Later in the day, a column of soldiers fell into this trap; when they withdrew, they left behind four of their men dead. Che assumed they would not counterattack, and he did not order his men to evacuate the area. As it grew dark, however, Che and his group came under heavy fire from the returning soldiers and were forced to retreat. In the withdrawal, two of the Cubans, Pombo and Tuma, were wounded. Pombo was only slightly wounded in the leg, but Tuma (Carlos Coello) died a few hours later.

Tuma's death was another great personal loss for Che. He wrote in his diary that Tuma had been his inseparable and loyal comrade throughout the preceding years since the Sierra Maestra campaign, and that he had come to regard him almost like a son. As an expression of his affection for his fallen comrade, Che personally buried Tuma, and he was still grieving over Tuma's death several days later when he called his men together for a general discussion in which he explained what the loss of Tuma meant to him personally. Moreover, in his monthly summary, he noted that the loss of each of his men amounted to a grave defeat, although the army did not realize it.

From the town of Florida, Che and his men continued north toward the main highway that runs between Santa Cruz and Cochabamba. Che's asthma seems to have become a constant source of discomfort during this time. Nevertheless, on the night of July 6, he led his men in the most daring action of the entire guerrilla operation. That night, they stationed themselves along the highway near a place called Peña Colorado. Che's plan was to stop a vehicle coming from the town of Samaipata, a few miles to the west, and find out from the driver how well guarded the town was. But, after waiting in vain for a vehicle to come from the direction of Samaipata, Che had Coco, El Chino, and several of the Cubans stop a truck coming from Santa Cruz and drive it into Samaipata. When they reached the town, they immediately captured two policemen and then took the town's small army post after an exchange of gunfire with one of the soldiers on guard. Having captured the post, they transported the lieutenant in charge, along with the ten soldiers under his command, to a place some distance from the town and left them naked in the dark. They also raided the local pharmacy but failed to bring back the type of medicine that Che needed for his asthma. The entire foray was carried out in view of a large number of spectators, and the news of this raid, so close to the city of Santa Cruz, shocked the country, and particularly the government. After this action, the army began an all-out effort to eliminate the guerrillas.

Following the raid on Samaipata, Che and his men withdrew south, almost retracing the route they had taken from the Rio Grande to Samaipata. During this period, Che's asthma steadily grew worse, and a decision was made to return to the Ñancahuazú area in order to get medicine for him from the supply caves. On July 12, Che heard over the radio that the army had clashed the day before with a group of guerrillas in the Ñancahuazú area, killing one of the guerrillas and taking his body to Lagunillas. The report was based upon an encounter between Joaquín's group and the new army units sent into the Ñancahuazú region as part of the army's "operation Cynthia," the government's answer to the Samaipata raid. On July 9, the hiding place of Joaquín's group had been discovered by the army. Joaquín and his companions managed to flee before they were surrounded, but they were forced to leave behind a large quantity of their supplies and possessions. When the army arrived, it found a number of documents, photographs, a code book, and a list of the members of Joaquín's group. On the following day, the army almost encircled Joaquín's group again and in the encounter killed one of its Bolivian members.

Meanwhile, following the Samaipata raid, Che's group avoided contact with the army until July 27. By then, the guerrillas had moved south, past the town of Florida, on their way to the Rosita River, which runs into the Rio Grande. On this date, they caught a small reconnaissance patrol of eight soldiers in an ambush that they had set up just outside the village of Moroco. Three soldiers were killed, and a fourth was wounded. They continued moving south and, on the night of July 29, camped next to the Suspiro River. Just before dawn the next morning, they were surprised by a company of soldiers, who had stumbled upon their camp. There was general confusion on both sides, and in the darkness Che and his men withdrew across the river. However, in the prevailing confusion, eleven of their knapsacks were left behind, along with some medicine, binoculars, a tape recorder (which they used to record coded messages from Cuba disguised as part of the regular shortwave broadcasts of Radio Havana), and Che's personal copy of Debray's *Revolution in the Revolution?*, containing his own notes. Worse yet, in the withdrawal across the river, three of Che's men were shot. Two of them, the Bolivian called Raúl and the Cuban named Ricardo, were fatally wounded, while the third, Pacho, sustained only a slight wound. The army suffered three dead and six wounded.

Che was very disturbed by this encounter. However, he does not seem to have grieved as much over the loss of Raúl and Ricardo as he did over the earlier death of Tuma and Rolando. In his diary following this encounter with the army, Che referred to Ricardo as the most undisciplined member of the Cuban contingent, but acknowledged that he had been an extraordinary fighter and an old comrade from the campaigns in Cuba and the Congo. Of the Bolivian Raúl, he had little good to say, noting that he was neither much of a fighter nor much of a worker.

On the other hand, the reduction of his force to twenty-two

members, and the fact that three of this number (including himself) were "crippled" (in his case by asthma), was a matter of some concern to Che. He was also upset about the mistakes that members of his group had made in the last encounter with the army, particularly their having been surprised and forced to leave behind a good deal of their equipment and personal possessions. Che knew that the army's capture of these items would give the government a tremendous propaganda victory and greatly increase the morale of their troops. Although he did not state it in so many words, it is obvious from the monthly summary in his diary at the end of July that he recognized the guerrillas' situation had worsened considerably from that of previous months. He noted their failure to make contact with La Paz and Cuba through the peasant boy Paulino, and their continued lack of support from the peasantry. He wrote that their most urgent needs were to reestablish contact with the outside and to recruit more men. In addition, he observed that his most urgent need was to obtain medicine for his asthma.

Chapter 10

THE END NEARS

They will be hounded relentlessly like hunted animals in the areas they have chosen for their operation. They will suffer the constant uneasiness of having enemies at their heels, and they will constantly have to suspect all they encounter, since the frightened peasants will in some instances hand them over to the repressive troops in order to rid themselves of the latter by removing the reason for their presence. Their only alternative will be death or victory, at times when death is a thousand times present and victory is a myth about which only a revolutionary can dream.
        —Che Guevara, *Guerrilla Warfare: A Method* (1963)

Throughout the first week of August, Che's group slowly worked its way southwest toward the Rio Grande. On August 8, deciding he could no longer do without medicine for his asthma, Che sent several men ahead to the supply caves in the Ñancahuazú area to bring some back. That night, he brought all the men together and informed them that in his present condition he was little more than a human carcass and that the situation facing them was one of those in which great deci-

sions have to be made. He then told his comrades that the struggle in which they were involved offered them the opportunity to
convert themselves into true revolutionaries, which he characterized as the highest level of the human species, and the chance to
become men. He made it clear that those who felt they could not
attain either of these states should say so and leave the struggle.
Afterward, Che wrote in his diary that "all the Cubans and some
of the Bolivians stated they would continue until the end." He
also noted that this was followed by a discussion in which several
members of the group criticized one another about petty matters,
and he was forced to end the meeting by telling them that such
bickering took the greatness out of the decision they had made.

Che's condition became so bad after the departure of the group
sent to fetch his medicine that he was forced to ride on one of the
pack mules that had been bought from some peasants several
weeks earlier. (As the days passed, the guerrillas were forced to
eat these mules.) On August 12, Che was disturbed by a radio
announcement claiming that the army had killed a guerrilla and
discovered two deposits of arms and ammunition in the Ñancahuazú area. This report referred to the clash between the army
and Joaquín's group that had taken place on August 10. In this
encounter, the army shot the Bolivian guerrilla called Pedro (a
former university student from the Cochabamba region) while
he was covering the retreat of Joaquín and the others. The army
was extremely proud of its performance in this encounter; it carried off the entire action without a single soldier being killed or
wounded.

Worse news was yet to come. Following this encounter, the
army captured two of the Bolivian members of Joaquín's column, Chingolo and Eusebio. These two prisoners told their captors everything they knew and then led a column of soldiers to

the supply caves where the guerrillas had hidden, among other things, Che's medicine, all kinds of documents, and various rolls of undeveloped film. When Che heard the radio announcement concerning the discovery of these caves, he was terribly shaken. He wrote in his diary, "Now I am condemned to suffer asthma for an indefinite period. They have also taken documents of all types and photographs. It is the hardest blow they have given us; someone talked. Who? This is the mystery."

Since it was too late to send word to the group that had been sent ahead to obtain his medicine, Che and the men with him continued to the Rio Grande, intending to wait there for the others to return. Che's group reached the north bank of the Rio Grande on the evening of August 17, after considerable delay and difficulty. The following day, they crossed the river and headed west along its south bank. That night, Che received the first indication that some of the Bolivian members of his force wanted to resign. Inti informed him that the guerrilla called Camba had told him privately that he wanted to leave the guerrilla band; Camba claimed that his physical condition would not allow him to continue and that, besides, he did not see any future in the struggle. Che wrote in his diary that Camba's case was a typical one of cowardice and that it would be best to let him go. However, since Camba knew of their plans to try and find Joaquín and his group, Che decided that they could not afford to let him leave yet. The next day, Che explained this to Camba and also talked with his companion, Chapaco, who told Che he wanted some hope of being able to leave the guerrilla force within six months to a year. Che noted in his diary that Chapaco did not seem well and that he had talked in a confused manner about a series of disconnected subjects.

On August 24, Che's group was heading west along the north bank of the Rio Grande when it spotted three men on the other side of the river. The group immediately took positions for an ambush, and soon eight soldiers appeared. Che instructed his men to let the soldiers cross the river by way of the ford in front of them and then to shoot them as they approached the ambush. However, the soldiers did not cross the river. Instead, they walked off in the opposite direction. The next day, the same thing happened. Seven soldiers appeared on the opposite bank of the river but did not attempt to cross. Shortly afterward, Che wrote in his diary that Camba had reached the ultimate point of moral degradation, since he had begun to tremble at even the mention of soldiers.

The same seven soldiers returned on August 26, but this time two crossed the river while the remainder stayed on the other side. The Cuban called Antonio (Olo Pantoja), whom Che had placed in charge of the ambush, shot at the two soldiers too soon and missed both of them. They escaped and, together with their comrades, withdrew from the area on the run. Inti and Coco ran after them, but the soldiers took cover and began shooting, forcing them to give up the chase. Meanwhile, Che noticed that bullets coming from the direction of his own men were hitting the area around Coco and Inti. He ran to the ambush and found Eustaquio shooting in their direction because Antonio had failed to give him any orders. Che was so angered by this that he lost control of himself and manhandled Antonio.

In a short time, the soldiers returned with reinforcements, but Che decided to withdraw from the area, and the soldiers did not pursue them. August 27 was spent in a desperate search for a way out of the rugged area into which they had withdrawn. The day was brightened, however, by the appearance of the men Che had sent to the Ñancahuazú supply caves. After a long trek, during which they had barely escaped capture several times, they had heard the shooting between Che's group and the soldiers the day before. They then located Che and his men by following their tracks from the river.

Che and his force spent the remaining days of August slowly making their way through the dense thickets and rugged terrain somewhat to the north of the Rio Grande. Although they had expected to find water in the area, they did not, and on August 29 Che wrote that Chapaco, Eustaquio, and El Chino were on the verge of collapsing from thirst. The next day, he reported that the men he had sent ahead to cut a path through the thickets were suffering from fainting spells and that several of them were drinking their own urine. Later in the day, however, they finally discovered some water, and with renewed strength they spent the final day of the month scaling the last ridge between them and the Rio Grande.

In his summary for August, Che wrote that it had undoubtedly been their worst month since the war began. He concluded by noting that the morale and revolutionary legend of his force had reached a low point and that their most urgent tasks were to reestablish contact with the outside world, to incorporate new members, and to obtain medicine and supplies. The only optimistic note in the diary entry was that the two Bolivians brothers Inti and Coco were becoming increasingly outstanding soldiers and revolutionaries.

Several days later, Che heard news that Joaquín's entire column had been wiped out in an army ambush on August 30. At the time, he did not believe it. In fact, Joaquín's column was ambushed no more than a day's march from where Che and his men were located, although neither group knew it. Apparently, Joaquín and his comrades were heading toward the area where they assumed Che and his group were operating, but their decision to cross the Rio Grande in order to find Che and his men turned out to be a fatal mistake.

In preparation for their journey to find Che's group, Joaquín and his companions had bought a cow from a peasant named Honorato Rojas. They had asked Rojas where the best place was to cross the Rio Grande, and he had told them of a ford, called El Vado del Yeso, where it was possible to wade across the river. Confiding in Rojas was a fatal mistake. The day following the guerrillas' encounter with him, a column of thirty soldiers under the command of Captain Mario Vargas visited Rojas's house. Rojas told Vargas that the guerrillas were probably going to cross the Rio Grande at El Vado del Yeso that very day. Captain Vargas and his column headed immediately in the direction of El Valdo del Yeso. Along the way, they ran into two peasants who had been taken prisoner by Joaquín's group the day before but had managed to escape the guerrillas' camp just a few hours earlier. With the peasants as their guides, Vargas and his men set up an ambush across from where the guerrillas were expected to ford the river.

The soldiers waited impatiently for Joaquín's group to arrive. Finally, at about six o'clock in the evening, the Cuban with the code name of Braulio (Israel Reyes Zayas, who had been with Che in the Congo) appeared out of the brush across the river. As he walked to the bank of the river, some of Captain Vargas's men asked permission to open fire, but the captain told them to hold their fire until all the guerrillas were clearly visible. As the soldiers waited, Braulio signaled to his comrades, and they appeared from the brush one at a time. They began crossing the river in single file, with Joaquín in the lead and Tania at the rear. When the majority of the guerrillas were in the water, Vargas gave the order to commence firing. As the first shots hit the water around the guerrillas, they threw off their knapsacks and tried to escape in the river. They scattered, forcing Vargas and his men to leave their positions. The soldiers ran along the banks of the river shooting at the guerrillas still in the water as well as those trying to escape into the brush. Within twenty minutes, the soldiers had liquidated Joaquín's column, killing everyone but the Bolivian named Paco (whose real name was José Carrillo), who was wounded and later taken prisoner.

Tania was one of the first to fall. Dressed in a white blouse and brown pants, in sharp contrast to her fatigue-clad comrades, she was a perfect target in the evening twilight. She was shot before she ever had a chance to throw off her knapsack or use her rifle. Her body was carried some distance downriver by the current and was not found until several days after the ambush. Meanwhile, the remains of her comrades were taken to the town of Vallegrande, where they were inspected by the press and high military officials. Among the bodies laid out for inspection were those of the former Bolivian miners' union leader Moisés Guevara and the Peruvian called El Negro. Ciro Bustos was taken from his cell in Camiri to a location near El Vado del Yeso so that he could identify certain of the guerrillas.

Several days later, when Tania's body was brought to Vallegrande, President Barrientos was there on an inspection tour of the combat zone. He was clearly pleased by the events of the last few days and told reporters that the remaining guerrillas operating in the region would be promptly exterminated. He also offered amnesty to any Bolivian member of the guerrilla force who was willing to surrender. A few days later, President Barrientos announced that the government would give fifty thousand Bolivian pesos (forty-two thousand U.S. dollars) for the capture of Che Guevara dead or alive.

Although Che had heard a shortwave broadcast by the Voice of America on September 2, announcing that a group of ten guerrillas led by a Cuban called Joaquín had been liquidated by the Bolivian army in "the zone of Camiri" three days earlier, he refused to believe it and similar announcements broadcast subsequently. It was not until the end of September that he finally admitted that the news about Joaquín's group was true. Even then, he still hoped that a few members of Joaquín's column had escaped the ambush and were avoiding contact with the army.

On September 3, at a place near the Rio Grande called Masicuri Bajo, a small group of Che's men clashed with a unit of forty soldiers while they were on a mission to purchase food from the local peasants. The soldiers surrounded the guerrillas, but for some unaccountable reason they then retreated instead of closing in on them. In the confusion, the guerrillas killed one of the soldiers and escaped without any casualties. However, they were forced to return without any food. The next day, Che sent out a second group under the command of Inti, with instructions to obtain food and to capture a soldier if it was possible to do so without risking losses. On September 5, they returned with a mule and some food, but without a prisoner. On the following day, Che had eight of his men establish an ambush along the path by which Inti and the others had returned to the camp, in case the army followed their tracks. Late that night, Che sent a man to tell the ambushers to rejoin the rest of the group. On his way, the messenger ran into an army patrol. The shots fired by the soldiers warned the men in the ambush as well as those with Che. Consequently, in the darkness, both groups were able to link up and withdraw from the area unharmed. As they left, they heard prolonged gunfire behind them, as the soldiers fired aimlessly into the darkness.

On September 7, Che heard over the radio that Paco (the only survivor of Joaquín's group) had given valuable information to the army concerning Che's guerrilla movement and Debray's participation in it. Che was incensed at Paco's conduct and wrote in his diary that "he would have to be punished as an example." How Che thought he could punish Paco is a mystery, and one wonders what state of mind Che was in when he wrote this. The next day, Che heard via the radio that President Barrientos had been present at Tania's burial and that a Communist newspaper in Budapest, Hungary, had criticized Che as a pathetic and irresponsible leftist adventurer. This last announcement prompted Che to write in his diary that he would like to seize power if only to unmask cowards and lackeys of all species and rub their noses in their own dirt.

Following their brush with the army on September 6, Che and his men headed in a northwesterly direction, away from the Rio Grande toward the town of Alto Seco. During the next week, they were forced to climb an almost unending series of rugged hills and ford several swollen streams and small rivers. This march cost them equipment, lost in one of the streams, and weakened them both physically and mentally. On September 15, they were jolted by a radio broadcast announcing that sixteen members of their underground network in La Paz had been arrested, among them Loyola Guzmán. Loyola had visited the guerrillas' main base prior to the outbreak of hostilities and been photographed with Inti and Coco on the film that was discovered in the supply caves near the guerrillas' former main base in the Ñancahuazú area. It was these captured photographs that led the Bolivian authorities to Loyola, and from her to most of the guerrillas' urban underground network of supporters in La Paz.

At Loyola's house, the Bolivian authorities found much valuable information, including a list of all of Che's contacts in La Paz. Loyola tried to commit suicide while she was being interrogated in the Ministry of Interior by jumping out of a third-floor window, but her fall was broken by a cornice of the building, and she was only slightly injured. After the police took her to the hospital, she told the press that she had wanted to kill herself because she did not want to betray her comrades.

The news of Loyola's arrest and the police roundup of suspected guerrilla contacts in La Paz appears to have had a demoralizing effect on many of Che's men. On September 16, there was an altercation between the Bolivian Chapaco and the Cuban Antonio. And that night, the Peruvian Eustaquio accused one of the Bolivians of having eaten an extra portion of their food. Moreover, two days later, Chapaco staged a scene in which he accused Arturo (the Cuban René Tamayo), of having stolen fifteen bullets from his rifle's magazine, and another Cuban, Benigno (Dariel Alarcón Ramírez, who had been with Che in the Congo), of having committed the error of allowing some peasants to see him and then leave the area freely. When Che learned this, he furiously called Benigno's error an act of treason. Che's angry rebuke hurt Benigno deeply, and he broke down crying.

On September 22, Che and his men arrived at the village of Alto Seco, where they discovered that the mayor had learned they were coming and had left to inform the army. Nevertheless, the guerrillas spent the rest of the day there, and that evening Inti Peredo gave a lecture on the objectives of the guerrilla movement to an audience of fifteen dumbfounded villagers in the local schoolhouse. Later that night, after purchasing a considerable quantity of food from the frightened inhabitants of Alto Seco, the guerrillas left, heading toward a nearby ranch at Loma Larga. On September 24, they arrived at the ranch exhausted and sick. Che reported in his diary that all but one of the peasants in the area had fled upon their arrival.

Two mornings later, when Che and his men reached the village of La Higuera, they noticed that something was wrong: all the men were gone, and only a few women were in the village. Coco went to the telegraph office and discovered there a telegram from Vallegrande informing the mayor that the guerrillas were in the zone and that any information about them should be sent to the authorities in Vallegrande. The guerrillas questioned the few people left in the village, who nervously explained that most of the inhabitants were attending a celebration in the nearby town of Jahue.

At one o'clock, Che ordered the vanguard of his force to leave for Jahue, but about half an hour later he heard shots coming from the road they had taken. He ordered the remainder of his men to take up defensive positions in the village. A few minutes later, Benigno arrived, wounded, followed by Aniceto and Pablito, whose foot was in bad shape. They informed Che that they had fallen into an army ambush just outside the village and that Coco Peredo and the Cubans Miguel and Julio had been killed. As for the Bolivian Camba, he had disappeared when the shooting began. Hearing this, Che ordered his group to evacuate the village along a road leading to the Rio Grande. As they withdrew from La Higuera, those in the rear of the column came under heavy fire from the advancing troops. During the confusion, contact was lost with both Inti Peredo and the Bolivian called León. A short time later, Inti reached Che and the others, but León did not appear. With Inti reincorporated into the group, the guerrillas departed from the area by taking one of the ravines leading from the Rio Grande.

The news of the encounter with the guerrillas near La Higuera was received by the Bolivian army's high command and the Barrientos government as a clear sign that victory was almost within their grasp. Word was immediately sent to Vallegrande, where the new Ranger regiment Manchego No. 2 had just arrived after finishing nineteen weeks of special counterinsurgency training from U.S. Army Special Forces personnel. By dawn on September 27, the first unit of this new regiment had already moved into the region around La Higuera. In fact, it was a unit of these U.S.-trained Rangers that captured Camba (his real name was Orlando Jiménez Bazán). Camba's comrade León (whose name was Antonio Rodríguez Flores), who had deserted the guerrilla force on the day of the ambush, turned himself in to the authorities several days later.

In his diary, Che acknowledged that his losses were very great in the La Higuera encounter. He considered Coco the most grievous loss but noted that Miguel and Julio had been magnificent fighters and that the human value of all three was inexpressible. His diary also reveals that the last days of September were tense ones for him and his men. They were forced to move by night and hide during the day, and on more than one occasion they were nearly discovered by the soldiers.

By the end of the month, it was clear to everyone in Che's small force that they were in a desperate position. Not only was the circle of troops closing in around them, but their every move was being reported to the army by the local population. Their tragic plight was summed up by Che in his diary: "Our conditions are the same as last month, except now the army is demonstrating increasing effectiveness in its actions and the campesinos are giving us no support and have turned into informers."

Nevertheless, Che still believed they could continue their mission. He thus noted in his diary, "The most important task is to escape and look for more propitious zones; and then afterwards our contacts, in spite of the fact that the whole apparatus is disrupted in La Paz where they have given us severe blows." In view of the circumstances, however, Che and his comrades had little chance "to escape and look for more propitious zones." They were completely surrounded by thousands of troops and unable to move rapidly across the difficult terrain because of their wounds and fatigue.

These photographs were taken from a roll of film found in the Ñancahuazú camp. The top picture shows Che talking to several of his comrades. The woman standing behind the tree is Tania. Below, Che and some of the other guerrillas at the campsite.

Bustos, El Chino, Che, and Debray in the Ñancahuazú camp.

Some sketches of the guerrillas drawn by Bustos, which were in his possession when he was captured.

The guerrillas' main camp in the Ñancahuazú area shortly after the Bolivian army took possession of it in April 1967.

The adobe shack where Che's body was placed on display in Vallegrande.

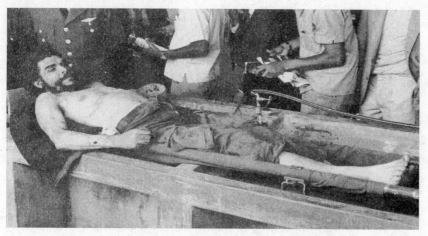

Che's body on display in Vallegrande.

Close-up of Che's face in death.

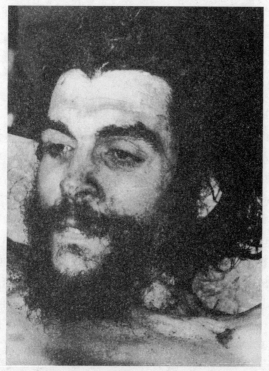

Chapter 11

HOW CHE DIED

Each spilt drop of blood, in any country under whose
flag one has not been born, is an experience passed on
to those who survive, to be added later to the liberation
of his own country.

> —Che Guevara, "Message to the Tricontinental:
> Create Two, Three, Many Vietnams" (1967)

Throughout the first few days of October, Che and his
group, now reduced to sixteen, spent most of the daylight
hours on the crests of the ridges north of La Higuera,
and the nights in the hollows at the base of these ridges. On
the evening of October 3, Che heard a news broadcast concerning Camba and León, and he made the following entry in his
diary: "Both gave abundant information about Fernando [Che's
own code name], his illness and everything else. . . ." Che added
sarcastically, "thus ends the story of two heroic guerrillas." Che
also made a sarcastic comment on a recorded interview that he
had heard between a Bolivian student leader and the imprisoned
Régis Debray. The entry in his diary reads, "I heard an interview
with Debray, very courageous in front of a student provocateur."

On October 4, Che wrote that he had heard a commentary on the radio whose conclusion had been that if he was captured by troops of the Fourth Army Division, he would be tried in Camiri, but if by the Eighth Division, he would be tried in Santa Cruz.

On Saturday, October 7, the last day Che made an entry in his diary, he and his men camped in one of the many ravines near La Higuera. There they encountered an old woman herding goats and attempted to question her about the presence of soldiers in the area, but they were unable to obtain any reliable information. Afterward, fearing that the old woman would report them, Che ordered two of his men to go to her house and pay her fifty pesos to keep quiet. He noted in his diary, however, that he had little hope that she would do as instructed. He began this last entry in his diary with a notation that it had been exactly eleven months since the inauguration of his guerrilla movement.

Apparently, the old woman or someone else who had seen Che and his group pass through the area reported their presence to the army in La Higuera. By the morning of Sunday, October 8, several companies of Rangers were deployed in the zone through which Che's small force was moving. Early that morning Captain Gary Prado and his company of Rangers, all recent graduates of the U.S. Army Special Forces training camp near Santa Cruz, took up positions on the heights of the Quebrada de Yuro, one of the most rugged ravines in the area. Che and his men, after marching the night before, had stopped to rest in this ravine until they could resume marching under cover of darkness.

About noon, a unit from Prado's company made contact with the guerrillas. In this initial encounter, two soldiers were killed and several others wounded. Having located the guerrilla force, the lieutenant in charge of the small probing unit radioed Captain Prado for assistance. The subsequent series of events reads like a scenario out of a U.S. Army counterinsurgency manual. Captain Prado immediately deployed the rest of his troops in a circle around the guerrillas. Meanwhile, Che divided his small force into two groups in an effort to confuse the Rangers and escape. The group led by Che moved toward the closest exit from the ravine. However, the hill commanding this exit was occupied by a sizable number of troops and had been chosen by Captain Prado as the site of his command post. As Che and his group came within shooting range of Prado's men, they found themselves caught in a rain of automatic-weapons fire.

Through his field glasses, Captain Prado watched the guerrillas disperse and run for cover and ordered Sergeant Bernardino Huanca and his men to descend in pursuit. A few minutes later, Sergeant Huanca fired a burst from his submachine gun at a guerrilla moving through a thicket of thorn bushes. One bullet sent the guerrilla's black beret flying off his head, while two others tore into his leg and forced him to the ground. The fallen guerrilla was Che. As he lay helpless, the Rangers began to concentrate their fire on the area where he had fallen. But Willy (Simón Cuba, one of Moisés Guevara's recruits, whom Che had begun to regard as a potential deserter) rushed to his side and helped him get out of the line of fire and up one side of the ravine. As the two scrambled upward, they ran into four Rangers who were positioning a mortar. The Rangers ordered them to surrender, but Che, supporting himself against a tree, fired his carbine in answer. The soldiers returned the fire. A few seconds later, a bullet hit the barrel of Che's carbine, rendering it useless and wounding him in the right forearm. At this point, Che reportedly raised his hands and shouted, "Don't shoot! I'm Che Guevara, and I'm worth more to you alive than dead." A few yards away, Willy threw down his rifle and also surrendered.

It was approximately four in the afternoon when Che and Willy were brought before Captain Prado. The latter immediately ordered his radio operator to signal the divisional headquarters in Vallegrande and tell them that they had captured Che Guevara. When the radio operator established contact with Vallegrande, he shouted, "Hello, Saturno, we have Papa!" (Saturno was the code name for Colonel Joaquín Zenteno, commandant of the Eighth Bolivian Army Division, and Papa was the code named they used for Che.) In disbelief, Colonel Zenteno asked Captain Prado to confirm the message. Following the confirmation, there was general euphoria among Colonel Zenteno's divisional headquarters staff. When the back-patting subsided, Colonel Zenteno radioed Prado to immediately bring Che and any other prisoners to La Higuera.

Since the Rangers had come into the Quebrada de Yuro on foot, Che had to be transported the seven kilometers to La Higuera stretched out in a blanket carried by four soldiers. Willy was forced to walk behind with his hands tied against his back. They arrived in La Higuera shortly after dark. The prisoners were placed in the little town's two-room schoolhouse, Che in one room and Willy in the other. Later the Rangers brought in a third guerrilla, the Cuban Aniceto, who had been taken prisoner near where Che and Willy were captured. He was placed in the classroom with Willy. The bodies of four other guerrillas were also brought to La Higuera that night.

The remaining group of guerrillas, led by Inti Peredo, had gone to the opposite end of the Quebrada when Che ordered the column to separate. They were able to hold out until nightfall and then slip out of the ravine. In subsequent weeks, half the members of this second group were killed by the army. Of those who survived, the three remaining Cubans (Pombo, Benigno, and

Urbano) managed to flee the country via Chile, and the three surviving Bolivians (Inti, Daíro, and Ñato) went into hiding.

During the night of October 8, and the next morning, Che
was interrogated by a number of army officers, including Major
Miguel Ayoroa, Colonel Andrés Selich, Captain Prado, and Colonel Zenteno. He was also questioned by the CIA agent who called
himself Félix Ramos (Félix Rodríguez), one of the Cuban exiles
sent by the CIA to participate in the counterinsurgency campaign
against the guerrillas. Che refused to answer any of their questions, but he did exchange a few words with some of the officers
and soldiers around him. At one point, one of the younger officers
asked Che what he was thinking about. At first, Che ignored him,
but when he overheard the officer say sarcastically to another officer that he (Che) was probably thinking about the immortality of
the burro, Che answered, "No, I'm thinking about the immortality of the revolution." On another occasion, one of the junior
officers, who had drunk too much in celebration of Che's capture,
tried to harass him. Che responded by punching the officer in the
face. Although Che's wounds were painful, they were not serious,
and he remained conscious during this entire period.

In La Paz, President Barrientos and the high command of the
Bolivian armed forces held an emergency meeting to decide what
to do with Che. They ruled out any prospect of prosecuting him
through judicial proceedings, because they reasoned a trial would
focus world attention on him and present the "Communists" with a
propaganda field day. Moreover, since Bolivia did not have the death
penalty, they feared that if Che remained alive as their prisoner,
sympathizers from all over the world would converge on Bolivia in
an effort to save him or carry on his fight. They decided, therefore,
that Che had to be executed immediately and that officially they
would announce he had died from wounds received in battle.

Early on the morning of Monday, October 9, the top-ranking officers in La Higuera received the order from La Paz to execute Che. They in turn instructed the noncommissioned officers present to carry out the order. Since none of the latter were anxious to do so, they chose lots to determine who would execute Che. Several hours before, these noncommissioned officers, as well as the officers and the soldiers on guard around the schoolhouse where Che was being held prisoner, had divided among themselves the money and personal objects taken from Che after his capture. His watches, carbine, compass, Parker fountain pen, two berets (including the one with a bullet hole through it), belt, stainless steel dagger, two pipes, and cigarette holder were the most important pieces of booty distributed among those who had the honor of participating in the capture of the famous guerrilla leader.

Shortly before noon on Monday, October 9, 1967, some twenty-four hours after Che and his men had been discovered in the Quebrada de Yuro, Sergeant Mario Terán walked to the little schoolhouse in La Higuera to carry out the order sent down from the Bolivian government's top leaders in La Paz. He had drawn the shortest straw. When he entered the classroom where his victim was waiting, he found him propped up against one of the walls. Che guessed the nature of Sergeant Terán's mission and calmly asked him to wait a moment until he stood up. Terán was so frightened by the prospect of what he had to do that he began to tremble. He turned and ran from the schoolhouse. But both Colonel Selich and Colonel Zenteno ordered him to go back and shoot Che without further delay. Still trembling, Terán returned to the classroom and, without looking at his victim's face, fired a burst from his carbine. The bullets slammed into Che's chest and side, passed through his body, and made large holes in the soft adobe wall of the classroom. The sergeant had been told not to inflict any wounds in Che's head or heart so that the army could later claim that he had died from wounds received in combat. However, while Terán's carbine was still smoking, several soldiers pushed past him into the classroom. They said that they, too, wanted to shoot Che so that they could boast that they had shot the famous Che Guevara. Sergeant Terán weakly nodded his approval, and they began firing.

When the shooting was over, there were nine bullet wounds in Che's body, two of which were obviously instantaneously fatal. Moments later, Willy and Aniceto were executed by another sergeant in Captain Prado's company. The shooting resounded through the streets of the village, startling the townspeople and causing them to crowd around the little schoolhouse. In a short time, the entire town knew what had taken place there.

Soon after Che and his comrades were shot, the senior army officers and the CIA agent, Félix Rodríguez, left La Higuera by helicopter for the army headquarters in Vallegrande. Che's body was wrapped in a canvas and strapped to the runner of a helicopter bound for Vallegrande. At the Vallegrande airstrip, nearly half the population of the town awaited the arrival of Che's body. Colonel Zenteno had announced several hours earlier that Che was dead and would soon be brought to Vallegrande.

When the helicopter arrived in Vallegrande, it landed on the side of the airstrip away from the waiting crowd of townspeople, reporters, and soldiers. Before the rotor of the helicopter had stopped, Che's body was loaded into the back of a white Chevrolet panel truck (the type used at the time as ambulances throughout most of Latin America) and transported at high speed through Vallegrande's narrow streets to the Señor de Malta hospital.

The body was placed in an adobe laundry shack apart from the main hospital building. In this shack, several officials washed the blood from Che's body, made an incision in his neck for embalming fluid, and took his fingerprints. According to two British journalists who arrived on the scene early, the entire process appeared to be under the supervision of the CIA agent who called himself Dr. Eduardo Gonzales (Gustavo Villoldo). He refused to let the two journalists photograph Che, and when they asked him in English where he was from, he answered sarcastically, "From nowhere!"

Soon General Alfredo Ovando, head of the Bolivian armed forces, and a number of other top military figures came to see the body of the famous guerrilla. By this time, a large crowd had excitedly collected around the shack. The people probably would have broken through the cordon of soldiers trying to hold them back, had it not been for the quick intervention of General Ovando. The general explained that they all had a right to see Che, but that they would have to wait until the doctors and various officials had finished preparing and identifying the body.

Once the doctors and the officials had finished their work, the soldiers allowed the waiting newsmen to enter the shack and take pictures. Afterward, they let the townspeople file past to view the corpse. Throughout the night, a silent file of staring townspeople, peasants from the surrounding area, and soldiers passed by the body. Che's body was on a stretcher that had been placed across the length of a concrete laundry sink. He was nude from the waist up—the officials had removed his jacket during the preceding investigation and preparation. The bullet wounds in his chest and sides were almost inconspicuous. He looked amazingly alive. Not only were his eyes open and brilliant, but there was a haunting smile on his lips. Pictures of this vibrant and serene expression were conveyed around the world by the news media.

Che's body was exhibited in the hospital at Vallegrande for

approximately twenty-four hours. What happened to it afterward was a mystery to the world until almost thirty years later. On October 11, General Ovando first stated that the body had been buried in the Vallegrande area. The next day, however, his office officially announced that the body had been cremated, and President Barrientos said a few days afterward that Che's ashes had been buried in a hidden place somewhere in the Vallegrande region. Almost nine months later, an article in the Peruvian paper *La Prensa* claimed that members of President Barrientos's personal guard had told a high functionary in the Peruvian police, when the Bolivian president visited Lima in July, that Che's body had been taken to the United States by the CIA in order to prevent it from falling into the hands of Marxists intent on sanctifying his remains. A few days later, however, President Barrientos's personal guard publicly denied that any of its members had said anything to anyone about Che's body during the president's visit to Peru.

In any case, the rapid disposal of the body was probably motivated by the impending arrival in La Paz of Che's brother Roberto Guevara, who was intent on claiming the body and taking it back to Argentina. When Roberto, a lawyer, arrived in Bolivia on October 12, he was told that it was impossible for him to see his brother's body, since it had been cremated the day before. Not wanting to believe that his brother had been killed, Roberto asked to see the hands that the Bolivian officials claimed they had cut from the body as proof that it was really Che Guevara whom they had killed. But he was denied even this request and was forced to return to Argentina without having seen any evidence that his brother died in Bolivia. A few days later, however, a team of Argentine police experts arrived in La Paz in response to an invitation by President René Barrientos Ortuño sent to General Onganía, the military dictator ruling Argentina at the time. The Argentine police experts were allowed to examine Che's hands and compare his fingerprints with those in the files of the Argentine federal police. On their departure, they issued an official statement to the effect that the fingerprints were identical and belonged to Ernesto "Che" Guevara.

The contradictions in the official statements given by the Bolivian authorities with regard to the disposition of Che's body were minor compared with those that appeared in statements concerning how and when Che died. On October 13, Dr. José Martínez Casso, who was one of the two doctors at the Señor de Malta hospital who had been asked by the military to conduct an autopsy on Che's body, reported to the press that Che had received two mortal wounds, one in the lungs and the other in the heart. He also stated that on examining the body shortly after it had been brought to the hospital in Vallegrande, he had estimated that Che had died not more than five or six hours earlier. The doctor's statements obviously indicated that he had died from wounds he received shortly before being brought to Vallegrande, not during the battle in the Quebrada de Yuro on the preceding Sunday.

Yet on the same day that Dr. Martínez Casso made his statement, Colonel Zenteno stated before a press conference that although he was not able to say precisely when Che had died, it was "almost immediately after he was wounded in combat." This was contradicted on the same day by General Ovando, who stated that Che had died early Monday morning (October 9) as a consequence of wounds received the preceding afternoon in combat. Although Che could not have lived overnight with a fatal bullet wound in both his heart and lungs, General Ovando denied emphatically and indignantly the suggestion that Che had been shot to death after he was taken prisoner.

The official death certificate emitted by the Hospital Señor de Malta de Vallegrande, stated that on October 9, 1967, at 5:30 P.M., the body of the individual who the military authorities said belonged to Ernesto "Che" Guevara, approximately forty years of age, was brought to the hospital, and that the deceased had died of multiple bullet wounds in his thorax and extremities. Dr. Moisés Abraham Baptista, director of the hospital, as well as the hopital's forensic specialist, Dr. José Martínez, produced a report of the autopsy they preformed on Che's corpse. The report gave a detailed account of the wounds that Che had suffered "in combate." According to this report, Che's body had the following nine bullet wounds:

1. A bullet wound in the left clavicle (collar bone) region, with an exit wound in the scapular (shoulder blade) region on the same side.
2. A bullet wound in the right clavicle (collar bone) region, with a fracture and without an exit wound.
3. A bullet wound in the right costal (ribs) region, without an exit wound.
4. Two bullet wounds in the left lateral costal (ribs) region, with exit wounds in the dorsal (back) region.
5. A bullet wound in the left pectoral (chest) region between ribs 9 and 10, with an exit wound in the same side.
6. A bullet wound in the middle third of the right leg.
7. A bullet wound in the middle third of the left thigh.
8. A bullet wound in the lower third of the right forearm, with a fracture of the ulna (the outer forearm bone).

The report clearly stated that "the cause of death was the wounds in the thorax and the resulting bleeding." There was no possibility Che could have lived twenty-four hours with such wounds, which is what some members of Bolivian military told the media.

The seemingly endless capacity of the Bolivian officials to contradict themselves made it clear not only that Che had been executed but also that the government and military were incapable of discussing the matter without creating confusion and making embarrassing errors. The government's bungling efforts at a later date to sell Che's campaign diary (obtained along with a number of other important items when he was captured in the Quebrada de Yuro), and the incredible circumstances surrounding the clandestine delivery of the diary for free to Cuba by none other than one of the top officials in President Barrientos's cabinet, were further evidence of the weaknesses, both moral and otherwise, in the Bolivian regime. Indeed, the entire episode gave the appearance of a nightmarish comedy of errors. Most of this tragic comedy was occurring when I arrived on the scene.

Chapter 12

THE ABSENCE OF
POPULAR SUPPORT

It is important to emphasize that the guerrilla struggle is a
mass struggle, it is the struggle of a people. . . . The guerrilla fighter therefore relies on the complete support of the
people of the area. This is absolutely indispensable.

—Che Guevara, "The Essence of
Guerrilla Struggle" (1960)

The success of any guerrilla movement depends upon the
degree of support it receives from the civilian population
in its area of operations. Che knew this truth well and
mentioned it frequently in his writings on guerrilla warfare. However, the complete absence of popular support for his guerrilla
operation in Bolivia was one of the main reasons, if not the primary reason, that his mission there failed.

Many professional military experts mistakenly consider that
the outcome of any guerrilla insurrection depends upon the effectiveness of the military tactics used by the counterguerrilla forces,
the nature of the terrain in which the guerrillas operate, whether

or not the guerrillas have a privileged sanctuary (such as the Vietnamese guerrilla fighters possessed in Cambodia and Laos), and the extent of external assistance received by the guerrillas. Some of these experts also attach some importance to the use of political measures that are designed to prevent the local population from supporting the guerrillas, but they tend to regard these measures as secondary in importance to the former considerations.

However, the historical evidence indicates that military factors play a secondary role in determining the success or failure of revolutionary guerrilla movements. The crucial factor is clearly the degree of sympathy and support that the general population gives to the guerrillas. Widespread popular support has been the one characteristic common to every successful guerrilla movement. In fact, it is only through the active assistance and cooperation of the general population that a guerrilla force can survive and go on to defeat the vastly superior forces of the regime it opposes.

Revolutionary guerrilla warfare depends upon, and is a struggle for, the loyalties of the civilian population. Close guerrilla-civilian cooperation enables the guerrillas to develop a superior system of intelligence, extreme mobility, an inexhaustible source of supplies, and the ability to surprise the enemy's forces when they are off guard. Without close ties to the civilian population, the guerrillas cannot develop even the minimal level of capabilities necessary for successful guerrilla warfare.

For example, in the area of intelligence, which is both a military necessity and a major factor contributing to the morale of the guerrillas, the cooperation of the civilian population is of paramount importance. The guerrillas are dependent upon the local population for the information they need in order to know the location of the enemy forces, to discover their points of weakness, and to escape their efforts to trap them. In order to obtain this kind of information on a systematic and continuing basis, the guerrillas must organize a widespread civilian intelligence network. This kind of a civilian spy system gives the guerrillas a great advantage over the enemy forces, since every movement these forces make takes place within a "fishbowl." This intelligence capability, plus the citizenry's provision of food, supplies, and shelter to the guerrillas, also gives the guerrillas greater mobility than the enemy troops have. With the entire population as their logistics and intelligence system, they are able to operate with far greater independence than the enemy's regular forces.

Past instances of guerrilla-led insurrections indicate that a guerrilla movement can obtain widespread popular support only if the general population feels a strong sense of hostility toward the existing political authorities. In this kind of situation, the guerrillas can win the support of the general population by virtue of their fighting against the "enemies of the people." In other words, the population supports the guerrillas not because of their identification with the guerrillas' long-range political objectives or ideological doctrine but because the guerrillas are intent upon removing the existing authorities from power and thereby eliminating the main cause of the local population's grievances.

One of the reasons Che's guerrilla movement failed to obtain any popular support in Bolivia is that the majority of Bolivians at that time believed their country had already undergone its revolution of national liberation. Although Che visited Bolivia shortly after the revolution of 1952, he failed to perceive either then or later how much importance the Bolivians attached to this event. In fact, many Bolivians regarded the revolution of 1952 in much the same way as the Cubans regard their revolution. Because Che did not understand this reality, and because his Bolivian sources of information did not convey it to him, he believed that his guerrilla movement would be able to capitalize on the hostility and discontent that he assumed the Bolivian people felt toward their political rulers.

What Che failed to understand is that the revolution of 1952 gave the Bolivian masses, for the first time in Bolivian history, what they perceived as a real stake in the social order as well as a sense of involvement in the political system and cultural community of their country. Despite the military coup of 1964 and the consequent fall from power of the National Revolutionary Movement (the group that spearheaded the revolution of 1952 and ruled the country until the military coup), the changes set in motion by the revolution still had continuing relevance for most of the Bolivian population in the mid-1960s when Che and his comrades arrived there.

The revolution of 1952 was neither a barracks revolt nor a middle-class rebellion; it was a genuine popular revolution that gave rise to a new sense of Bolivian nationalism. Its goal was nothing less than the dismemberment of the old social, economic, and political order. Consequently, one of the first things the new revolutionary government did was to nationalize the country's three largest tin mines. Since tin was the basis of Bolivia's national economy at the time, the nationalization of these mines was an act of tremendous symbolic importance. On the basis of this act alone, the new government was able to claim that control over the country's national wealth had been taken out of the hands of foreign interests and given to the Bolivian people.

As a result of the revolution of 1952, new legislation was passed that gave to all of Bolivia's adult citizens, whether literate or not, the right to vote. Previous literacy requirements had limited the vote to the country's large landholders and to the small educated middle and upper classes in the cities. The new electoral law enfranchised for the first time Bolivia's rural peasant masses, its miners, and its urban working class. Thus, for the first time in the history of the country, these groups were given the legal rights of full citizenship and a voice in the national political process.

The revolution of 1952 also brought about extensive land reform. However, this land reform was the work not so much of the new revolutionary government as of the peasants themselves who organized and carried out the dismemberment of the country's large, almost feudal estates and the redistribution of these lands. The new government's role was simply to provide the bureaucratic machinery for formalizing the redistribution of land, which had already been carried out by the peasants. The latter, organized into local "agrarian syndicates," or unions, declared war on the large landowners shortly after the revolution began. They killed or chased away their former landlords, expropriated their lands, and confiscated their houses, vehicles, and farm equipment. Thus, it was the peasants themselves who were responsible for the land reform measures associated with the revolution of 1952, and the sense of self-esteem that possession of their own land gave them was one of the most significant consequences of the revolution of 1952.

In this way, the revolution of 1952 liquidated Bolivia's landed aristocracy and produced a newly awakened and politically mobilized peasantry. The agrarian syndicates that were formed to acquire land for the peasants became important political organizations. In the Cochabamba valley alone, these syndicates were capable of mobilizing over 500,000 armed men on relatively short notice. As a result, they emerged as a significant source of political power in Bolivia. In fact, armed peasant militias were used by the government to put down both uprisings in Santa Cruz and miners' strikes on the altiplano. Moreover, for the first time in

Bolivian history, peasants were elected to the national legislature and appointed to such local political posts as mayor and prefect. These developments had a profound impact on the character of Bolivian politics and contributed greatly to the growth of a sense of national consciousness among Bolivia's rural masses.

Che failed to appreciate the importance of this national consciousness and believed that the Bolivian peasantry and the workers would provide a popular base for his revolutionary guerrilla movement in Bolivia and subsequently in the neighboring countries. However, the conditions for creating a successful revolutionary *foco* were obviously missing in Bolivia in the mid-1960s. In the first place, the guerrillas could not hope to win the support of the rural masses by offering to give them land. Since 1952, Bolivia's peasants had controlled the land and the entire countryside. Moreover, they had seen some improvement in their political, social, and economic status and had hopes of further improvement.

This is not to say that the peasants were well off, for their situation was, and still is, one of the worst in Latin America. Nevertheless, they were much better off in the mid-1960s than they had been in the past. Furthermore, they were not isolated from the centers of national political power. Through their local syndicates, they had a significant voice in the country's political affairs, and certain groups, such as the campesinos in the Cochabamba area, even had direct access to President Barrientos. Consequently, the leaders of the syndicates and many of their members did not regard the political authorities as enemies of the people.

In view of their increased involvement in national affairs, the peasants perceived Che's guerrilla movement in terms totally different from what he had expected. Instead of supporting Che's guerrilla movement, they opposed it. For example, at the end of

June 1967, the National Congress of Farm Workers issued a public declaration that denounced the guerrillas as an "anti-national
force, financed from abroad and destined to create nothing but
confusion and disruption." This group further proclaimed its
readiness to cooperate with the armed forces "in totally liquidat-
ing this foreign aggression that is attempting to undermine in a
systematic manner the economic and social development of our
people."

That the Bolivian public viewed the guerrillas as foreigners
seriously handicapped the guerrilla movement. Saddled with
this stigma, they were incapable of winning widespread popular support among the general population. In fact, certain Bolivian observers referred to the foreign character of Che's guerrilla
movement as its "original sin." Since the guerrilla operation was
neither organized nor led by Bolivians, it aroused a nationalistic
reaction among nearly every segment of Bolivian society. Its foreign character also made it possible for President Barrientos and
the Bolivian military to wrap themselves in the Bolivian flag and
play the role of defenders of the Bolivian nation.

Che failed to note that the Barrientos regime was not a typical
right-wing military government. First of all, Barrientos was popularly elected to the presidency in 1966. Afterward, he attempted
to build a broad base of popular support for his regime by court-
ing the peasant syndicates. In addition, he cloaked his regime in
many of the legitimizing symbols of the revolution of 1952 and
promised to extend the social and economic reform measures put
into practice after the revolution. Furthermore, to a degree unpar-
alleled in Bolivian history, Barrientos traveled from one end of
the country to the other to meet with the general public and talk
to local political leaders. His showmanship and his command of
both Aymara and Quechua (the two major languages of Bolivia's

large indigenous population) earned him the respect and support of a large segment of the population. At times, Barrientos displayed a remarkable degree of political flexibility. For example, he appointed four Marxist politicians to his cabinet during the height of the guerrillas' activities. In his reply to the confusion and criticism that followed this move, he indicated that he was not opposed to Marxists per se, so long as they operated within the democratic process and did not engage in illegal activities against the state.

In view of these facts, Che's efforts to establish a revolutionary guerrilla *foco* in Bolivia appear to have violated one of the fundamental precepts of his own theory of revolutionary guerrilla warfare. In his writings on guerrilla warfare, Che made it clear that it is impossible for a guerrilla movement to succeed in a country where the government (1) has risen to power by some form of popular consultation, (2) maintains at least the appearance of constitutional legality, and (3) gives the people some hope that their social and economic status will be improved.

In his introduction to the Cuban edition of Che's diary, Fidel Castro claims that the unresponsiveness of the Bolivian peasantry did not surprise Che. Fidel maintains that Che knew their mentality perfectly and that he therefore knew that it would require prolonged and patient work to win them over to the cause for which he and his men were fighting. However, it is difficult to believe that this would have happened when one considers that Che's diary is filled with bitter remarks about the indifference, suspicion, and betrayal that he and his men encountered in their contacts with the local peasantry.

In the months following the outbreak of hostilities, Che became increasingly preoccupied with his movement's lack of support among the peasantry. He wrote, "The inhabitants of the region are as impenetrable as rocks. You speak to them, but in the depths of their eyes you can see that they do not believe you." Not only did the peasants distrust the guerrillas, but they also continually gave information to the authorities about their movements. On the same day that the Anglo-Chilean reporter George Roth encountered the guerrillas, Che discovered that the two peasants they had bought food from a few days earlier had informed the authorities about his group. It seems that they were motivated to do so by the government's offer of a five-hundred-dollar reward to anyone providing information that would lead to the capture of the guerrillas.

Throughout the first month of hostilities, the guerrillas found that the local peasantry were both frightened and suspicious of them. In his monthly summary at the end of April, Che wrote in his diary that they had as yet failed to build a base of peasant support, but that through "planned terror" they could "neutralize" the peasants and gain their support later. This is surprising, in view of Che's previous opposition to the use of terrorism as a tactic of revolutionary guerrilla warfare, and probably reflects Che's frustration with the local peasantry's attitude toward his guerrilla movement. At any rate, it should be noted that neither he nor his men subsequently committed any acts that could be regarded as terrorism against the peasant population. Apart from detaining campesinos as temporary prisoners when they feared they would give their presence away to government troops close at hand, the guerrillas treated the local peasantry with kid gloves.

During May 1967, Che's group encountered a few peasants who, in their desire to get rid of the guerrillas and avoid any trouble, sold them food and gave them information (mostly about the location of watering places and roads). At the end of the month, Che thus wrote in his diary that there was still a complete absence of peasant support for the movement, but that it appeared that his group was gradually winning the admiration of the peasants and dispelling their fears. He also mentioned that the army had issued an order for the detention of all those who collaborated with his force. He expressed the hope that this marked the beginning of a period in which both sides would exert pressure on the peasants. He made it clear that he anticipated that the army would use methods that would alienate the peasants and turn them toward the guerrillas.

By the end of June, Che was forced to admit that instead of alienating local peasants, the army was successfully turning them against the guerrilla movement. He wrote in his diary that even though the army continued to be ineffective in the military sphere, it was working on the peasants in a manner that should not be underestimated. Through the clever use of fear and deceit, the army was indeed persuading the entire rural population to act as informers against his guerrilla force. These observations were based upon his discovery that the army had been working on the peasants in even the most isolated parts of the area in which the guerrillas were operating. He had also discovered that many of the peasants in the area belonged to a campesino syndicate that supported the Barrientos government.

Probably as a result of his recognition of the unfavorable prospects for obtaining popular support in the local area, Che noted that his group was caught in a vicious circle: in order to obtain peasant support it had to carry out permanent action in a populated area, but in order to do this it had to recruit more men, and this was impossible in the absence of popular support. Between the time that the guerrillas were discovered by the army in March and their defeat some six months later, they were not able to recruit a single person.

Throughout July, August, and September, the guerrillas tried to win the peasantry's confidence by offering them very high prices for food and other items. But this did not allay the fears of the peasants, who did almost everything they could to avoid the guerrillas. For example, on July 7, Che wrote in his diary that a peasant from whom they had bought a pig that day had warned them that there were some two hundred soldiers nearby. But the next day Che learned that no soldiers were in the immediate area and that the peasant had lied to them in order to make them leave his farm. By the end of September, the situation was far more serious, and Che was forced to acknowledge that not only were they not making any gains with the peasantry but that the majority of the peasants had actually turned to informing on them. Indeed, it was a local peasant who gave Captain Prado's Rangers the information which led to Che's capture.

Given the largely foreign composition of Che's guerrilla force, it is not difficult to understand why the local peasantry reacted negatively toward them. But it is difficult to understand how Che could have overlooked this problem. Régis Debray certainly seems to have been aware of it. In both his 1965 article "Castroism: The Long March in Latin America" and his book *Revolution in the Revolution?*, Debray calls attention to the parochialism and distrust of strangers that characterize the rural population in most parts of Latin America. According to him, the mentality of the peasants in these areas makes it extremely difficult for a guerrilla force to win their support and cooperation. Past experience has taught them to distrust the outsider, the white man, and the stranger. For this reason, Debray says, the guerrillas and not the government troops are most likely to be regarded by the local peasantry as the foreigners. Apart from their being strangers without any status in the local area, their presence generates the unpleasant prospect of government repression, bloodshed, and the destruction of property.

Even if Che's group had not been marked with the stigma of "foreign intruders," it seems highly unlikely that it would have been able to establish a base of popular support among the peasants in the southeast of Bolivia. They would not h ave been receptive to any type of armed uprising. That Che and his group were considered foreigners, of course, made it impossible for them to develop any popular support among the local peasantry, and so they found themselves isolated and surrounded on all sides by informers and government sympathizers.

Chapter 13

THE BETRAYAL AND ABANDONMENT OF THE GUERRILLAS

Incompetent leaders who are imposters and manipulators can criminally check the development within the revolutionary framework of men who are completely ready and able to fight.

—Fidel Castro, introduction to Che's *Bolivian Diary* (1968)

I n what is a familiar pattern throughout most of the developing states of Latin America, Asia, and Africa, the left wing of Bolivia's political parties and movements was deeply divided among a number of separate and opposing political factions. Because of the breakup of the international alliance between the Soviet Union and the Peoples Republic of China that took place in the mid-1960s and their subsequent competition for support among the left in the Third World, the Bolivian Communist Party split into two hostile political factions: the Bolivian Communist Party (pro–Soviet Union) and the New Bolivian Communist Party (pro-China). Each claimed that the other had betrayed the Marxist-Leninist cause. The pro-Chinese Communists referred to the pro-Soviet Communists as "revisionists," one of the dirtiest word in the Communist lexicon at the time, and spoke of themselves as the only true Marxist-Leninists in Bolivia. The pro-Soviet Communists, on the other hand, pretended that their party was the only Communist Party in Bolivia, but when forced to speak of the pro-Chinese group, they referred to them contemptuously as "Maoistas" (in reference to Mao Zedong, who was at the time the leader of Communist China).

However, the majority of Bolivia's leftists were not members of either of these two Communist groups. They were dispersed among a variety of leftist political parties, the most important of these being the Trotskyist Workers' Revolutionary Party (which itself was divided into two factions), the Revolutionary Party of the Nationalist Left, the Party of the Revolutionary Left, and the National Revolutionary Movement. Owing to their ideological differences and competition for public support, little love was lost between the supporters of this fractious array of left-wing political parties.

Che's efforts to obtain political support for his guerrilla operation were decisively influenced by the fragmentation of Bolivia's leftists as well as by the conflict between the Soviet Union, the People's Republic of China, and Cuba over who should exercise leadership over the political left in Latin America. It is important to note that the Cuban Communists regarded themselves as a third force, as an alternative to the pro-Soviet and pro-Chinese Communists in Latin America. They advocated the Castro-Guevara doctrine of promoting socialist revolutions in Latin America through the creation of revolutionary guerrilla movements based on the Cuban model. They also argued that the Cuban revolution demonstrated that an insurrectionary guerrilla force could be an effective substitute for the Communist Party, taking the party's place as the revolutionary vanguard of a popular insurrection. They argued that the guerrillas, instead of the party, could best mobilize the masses and lead them in an armed struggle to gain power. Only after power had been seized was a Marxist-Leninist party a necessary condition for the establishment of a socialist society.

Fidel Castro had stated that he was willing to work with all those who wanted to join the revolutionary struggle against U.S. imperialism in Latin America. For example, in March 1967, he publicly stated that Cuba would give its total support to those political parties in Latin America that consistently took a revolutionary position. He also said that in any country where the Communists did not show themselves disposed to carry out their revolutionary duties, Cuba would support those who were true revolutionaries. In sum, Castro and his supporters throughout Latin America claimed that the revolution came first and ideological concerns second, and that in any given country of Latin America a revolutionary guerrilla force could unite all the anti-imperialist and revolutionary groups within the country, regardless of their political labels.

Both the pro-Soviet and the pro-Chinese Communists found it impossible to accept the doctrine that the Communist Party could be replaced in the Latin American setting by a revolutionary guerrilla movement. They firmly believed that their respective parties had to be the sole source of leadership and ideological direction for any leftist revolutionary undertaking. Moreover, they did not accept the Castroist-Guevarist assumption that it was possible for revolutionaries holding different ideological positions to work together in making a popular revolution.

Of the two Bolivian Communist parties, the pro-Chinese Communists had more in common with the Cuban revolutionary position than did the pro-Soviet Communists, since the Maoists agreed that an armed revolutionary struggle was the only way to liberate the masses of Latin America from imperialist exploitation and domestic oppression. However, the pro-Chinese Communists believed that it was first necessary to educate the masses in order to make them politically conscious of their oppressed and exploited condition, whereas the Castroites argued that it was not possible to awaken the revolutionary consciousness of the predominantly rural and illiterate masses of Latin America without first initiating insurrectionary focal points throughout the continent. The pro-Chinese Communists also firmly believed that the revolution required "correct" Marxist-Leninist planning and direction if it was to succeed. They contended, therefore, that the revolution could not be entrusted to those who did not have a sound Marxist-Leninist (that is, pro-Chinese Marxist-Leninist) ideological orientation.

In Bolivia, the pro-Chinese position had been defined by Oscar Zamora, leader of the New Bolivian Communist Party (the Pro-Chinese Communist Party). He made it quite clear on a number of occasions that his party believed that the Bolivian people could be liberated only by a revolutionary force whose leadership was Marxist-Leninist (pro-Chinese) and free of all counterrevolutionary currents, particularly "contemporary revisionism" (that is, pro-Soviet communism). Moreover, Zamora had stressed that the political mobilization of the masses, especially the workers and peasants, was inseparable from any armed struggle, and that this political activity had to be carried out before and during the armed struggle by his party.

In contrast, the pro-Soviet Communists in Bolivia argued that a guerrilla-led insurrection was only one of the many forms of struggle that the masses and their political vanguard, the genuine Communist Party, could adopt in their fight to wrest power from the imperialists and their local lackeys in Bolivia's military regime. In line with the international strategy of the Soviet Union, the pro-Soviet Communists in Bolivia and throughout Latin America were attempting to pursue a policy of peaceful coexistence with the regimes in the region. Consequently, they had restricted most of their efforts to gain power to legal and parliamentary means. Moscow's reasoning was that there was little likelihood that the United States would allow another Cuban type of revolution to succeed anywhere in Latin America. Moscow's strategy thus involved offering the existing Latin American governments gener- ous amounts of economic aid while at the same time assisting the pro-Soviet Communist parties in these countries in their efforts to win popular support through more or less legitimate means.

However, the pro-Soviet Communists in Latin America real- ized that by following this strategy of peaceful coexistence they risked losing much of their support to more revolutionary groups, such as the pro-Chinese Communists and the Castroites, who advocated the immediate change of the existing order through the use of force. Consequently, the pro-Soviet Communists often paid lip service to the idea of an armed revolution when they were in leftist circles. But they argued that the right moment to launch an armed revolution had not yet arrived. Until it arrived, they claimed, their party had to follow a policy that would allow it to operate openly among the masses.

Castro's independent brand of revolutionary Marxism, and particularly Che's attempts to put it into practice, seriously threatened the position of the pro-Soviet Communists in Latin America. It was extremely difficult for these parties to control their more militant members and pursue their policy of "struggle within legality," especially when charismatic individuals like Che Guevara were calling for the immediate establishment of revolutionary guerrilla *focos* throughout Latin America.

After the division of the Bolivian Communist Party into two opposing political groups in early 1965, Fidel Castro, under pressure from Moscow, refused to recognize the pro-Chinese group and thereafter confined his relations to the pro-Soviet Communists. Thus, only the pro-Soviet group was officially invited by the Cubans to send a delegation to the Tricontinental conference held in Havana in January 1966. Much to the surprise of the Cubans, however, the pro-Soviet delegates from Bolivia took a position at the conference that was far more revolutionary than would have been expected from loyal supporters of the Moscow line of struggle within legality. The Bolivian delegates outdid themselves in paying lip service to the need for an armed revolution in Latin America. This was undoubtedly influenced by the fact that most of the other delegates to the conference took a position that was quite revolutionary, and the Bolivians did not want to appear less militant than the others.

The Bolivian delegation did such a good job of acting like zealous revolutionaries that they gave the Cubans the impression that they might be interested in establishing a revolutionary guerrilla *foco* in Bolivia. Consequently, Fidel Castro arranged a secret meeting with the Bolivian delegation to discuss the possibility of such an undertaking. The Bolivians were quite surprised when they discovered that Castro wanted to give them large sums of money to organize a guerrilla operation in Bolivia. While their commitment to the Moscow line obligated them to refrain from engaging in any overt revolutionary action such as guerrilla warfare, the leader of the Bolivian delegation, Mario Monje, pretended that his party was interested in organizing a guerrilla operation in Bolivia—if the Cubans gave them the necessary financial support and training. Monje led Castro to believe that his party in Bolivia was disposed to launch a Cuban type of revolution, and that his party could count upon widespread support among the peasantry and workers for a revolutionary insurrection.

Monje's exaggerated description of conditions in Bolivia and of his party's willingness to take up armed struggle convinced Fidel Castro that Bolivia was the most promising country in Latin America in which to establish a revolutionary guerrilla *foco*. As a result, he promised Monje considerable Cuban support if he would organize a guerrilla force there. At this point, of course, there was no mention of Che's going to Bolivia, since he was still in the Congo. Castro did offer, however, to send a contingent of Cubans to Bolivia to help Monje and his comrades train their guerrilla force. As might be expected, Monje reacted quite nega- tively to this suggestion, insisting that any guerrilla operation in his country would have to be completely Bolivian in composition. Although Castro disagreed with Monje on this point, he did not press the matter at the time. Consequently, Monje came away from the meeting believing he had Castro's promise of financial support.

Following the Tricontinental conference, Castro requested additional information from Monje on conditions in Bolivia, and Monje continued to portray his country as an ideal place to launch a guerrilla-led revolutionary movement. When Che returned to Havana from the Congo and spoke with Fidel about his desire to direct a guerrilla operation in South America, Fidel therefore sug- gested that he consider Bolivia as the base for his operation. This, plus the other considerations discussed earlier, led Che to choose Bolivia as the site for establishing his guerrilla force, which he hoped would be able to operate not only in Bolivia but also in the neighboring countries of Argentina, Peru, Brazil, and Paraguay. The only major drawback with regard to Bolivia was that Monje had previously insisted that any revolutionary struggle launched in Bolivia would have to be wholly Bolivian in composition and under the direct control of his party. Furthermore, Che had been informed by his own contacts in Bolivia that Monje and his group had a habit of working against any leftists who did not adhere to the Moscow line of struggle within legality. Nevertheless, Fidel and Che minimized these considerations and decided that Che should take a handpicked contingent of Cubans to Bolivia to establish the initial base for his continental revolutionary movement there.

Because of Cuba's economic and military dependency upon the Soviet Union and its worsening relations with China, Fidel Castro asked Che not to deal with the pro-Chinese group in Bolivia and to try and obtain the cooperation of Monje and his party once Che was in Bolivia. However, it seems clear that Che never really expected that Monje's party would openly join forces with him. Nor did this possibility discourage him, for his intention was to establish a force devoid of any sectarian spirit, one that would incorporate all those who were willing to fight for the revolutionary liberation of Bolivia and Latin America as a whole from U.S. imperialism, political oppression, and capitalist exploitation.

The primary preparations for the guerrilla operation in Bolivia were entrusted to a small number of Castroite sympathizers within Monje's party. But these individuals, whom Fidel Castro called "valuable and discreet collaborators" in his introduction to the Cuban edition of Che's diary, worked secretly for Che without informing anyone, including Monje and the other party leaders, about what they were doing. As a result, Monje did not learn of Che's presence in Bolivia until after Che arrived in the country.

It was in mid-December that Monje was informed by Havana that Che was in the southeast of Bolivia and that he wanted to meet with Monje to discuss the launching of a guerrilla force in that area. Although he was uncertain about Che's plans, Monje agreed to meet Che at his camp in the Ñancahuazù area. At this point, Monje had no idea that Che planned to stay in Bolivia and that he wanted to launch an armed struggle destined to encompass all of Latin America.

Monje arrived at Che's camp on New Year's Eve. The entry in Che's diary for that date indicates that Monje's reception was cordial but tense. Che noted that the question "Why are you here?" hung in the atmosphere, revealing that when Monje arrived he was still unsure why Che was in Bolivia. This entry in Che's diary, as well as that recorded for the same day in the diary of one of the other guerrillas, reveals that in response to Che's request for his party's support, Monje made it clear that his party could not officially support the guerrilla operation. However, he offered to resign from the party, obtain at least its neutrality, and bring several cadres of men to join those already in training, provided Che agreed to give him both the political and the military command of the entire operation, and a free hand to seek the support of the Communist parties in the other South American countries where Che planned to extend his guerrilla movement.

Monje's conditions for supporting the guerrilla movement were totally unacceptable to Che. He told Monje that he could accept no conditions concerning his leadership of the military operations. He knew that in the kind of revolutionary struggle he was planning, the military leadership of the struggle would have to come from the guerrilla force itself, not from a politician or group of politicians hundreds of miles from the scene of battle. Nor was he about to turn over the command of a movement that, in its final phase, would engulf all of Latin America to a man who lacked both the proper revolutionary vision and the necessary military experience. As for Monje's resigning from his position as leader of the party, Che said that he considered this a tremendous error, since it would accommodate those in his party who should be publicly condemned for their hypocrisy.

Having reached a deadlock in the discussions, Monje told Che he wanted some time to think over the whole matter and asked whether he could talk to the Bolivian members of Che's group. Che agreed and took Monje to the area nearby where most of the group were camped. Monje met with the Bolivians and told them that they could stay with Che and be expelled from the party, or support the party and return with him to La Paz. Much to Monje's surprise, all the Bolivians present said they preferred to stay with Che.

The next morning, Monje announced that he was leaving for La Paz. He claimed that as soon as he returned he was going to resign his position in the party and retire. Che noted sarcastically in his diary that Monje left looking as though he were being led to the gallows. Actually, this was a rather transparent deception on the part of Monje, since he clearly never had any intention of giving up his post as party leader. Che appears to have seen through Monje's subterfuge at the time. He noted in his diary that after Monje discovered from Coco that he (Che) would not compromise on the crucial question of who was to lead the movement, Monje obstinately persisted in his demand for the number one post. Che realized that Monje had disagreed with him over who should command the movement as a pretext to escape any responsibility for working with the guerrillas.

If Monje had accepted the political leadership of the movement (while deferring to Che's military leadership) and had sent members of his party to fight with Che's nuclear group, then the guerrilla operation might not have suffered from the stigma of being directed and organized by foreigners. As it was, the Bolivian government was able to argue convincingly once hostilities began that the guerrillas were foreigners intervening in the domestic affairs of the country.

When Monje learned from Che that he was planning to organize and direct a guerrilla movement designed to turn all of Latin America into another Vietnam, he knew he had no choice but to disassociate himself from the undertaking. First of all, he regarded the operation as totally impractical. Second, he was not willing to break with Moscow and submit to Guevara's (and to some degree Fidel Castro's) strategy of fomenting revolution in Latin America. Finally, for Monje to have involved himself in a guerrilla operation would have been counter to his own personal interests. As leader of the pro-Soviet Communist Party in Bolivia, he enjoyed a comfortable bureaucratic life in La Paz. Joining Che and his guerrillas would have meant giving this up for a life of hardship and danger. Such a sacrifice Monje would not have been willing to make under even the most favorable circumstances.

When Monje returned to La Paz, he called an emergency meeting of his party's Central Committee. He told its members of Che's presence in the country and of his plan to initiate a guerrilla movement that would extend into neighboring countries. It was agreed that Che had presented the party with a very grave problem. If they supported him, they would be acting contrary to Moscow's Latin American strategy and jeopardizing the very survival of their own party. Moreover, they all agreed that there was little chance the operation would succeed. On the other hand, if they didn't support Che, he might actually succeed in overthrowing the existing regime with the help of the pro-Chinese group, or even worse, the Trotskyists. Nevertheless, it was decided that the party could not afford to take the risk of cooperating with the guerrillas.

Following this meeting, Monje sent a letter to Fidel Castro criticizing him for not having respected his position that any guerrilla operation in Bolivia would have to be totally Bolivian in composition. He told Castro that since the guerrilla force was largely Cuban in composition and Che was its leader, it was doomed to failure. He wrote this letter not because he wanted the leadership of the guerrilla movement for himself but because he wanted to justify his refusal to collaborate with Che and his companions.

After Monje left, Che called all the members of his group together and explained to them the substance of his talks with the Communist leader. He told them that the party had refused to support the guerrilla operation, and as a result they were now free to unite with all those who wanted to bring about the revolution. He expressed the belief that while Monje's attitude might hurt the guerrilla movement in the short run, it would contribute to its development in the long run by freeing it of any sectarian political entanglements.

If Che felt this way, why had he asked Monje for his support in the first place? The answer is clear in Fidel Castro's introduction to Che's diary. There Fidel states that it was in deference to his Bolivian comrades who were members of the pro-Soviet Communist Party that Che made an effort to gain Monje's support, even though he distrusted Monje. Che also noted in his diary that one of the Bolivian members of his group, Bigotes, was willing to collaborate with him whatever the party did, but also respected Monje and seemed to care for him. Like Bigotes, most of Che's

Bolivian comrades were members of Monje's party, and they were reluctant to fight for a cause that did not have the backing of their party. In view of this fact, Che's effort to secure Monje's support is understandable.

It is quite clear, however, that Che never expected the pro-Soviet Communists in Bolivia to support his guerrilla operation. For example, on December 12, several weeks before his meeting with Monje, Che noted in his diary that he gave his group a lecture on the realities of war and warned the Bolivians in the group of the responsibility they had undertaken by adopting "another line and violating party discipline." This clearly indicates that Che had recruited the Bolivian members of his force with the expectation that the pro-Soviet Communist Party in Bolivia would most likely not approve of their participation in his guerrilla force. In reality, Che hoped to recruit the most militant and revolutionary members of Monje's party and, with recruits from other leftist groups, to build a nonsectarian revolutionary force.

At the end of January 1967, Che made a reference in his diary to his meeting on New Year's Eve with Monje. He wrote that, as he had expected, Monje's attitude had been at first evasive and later traitorous. He also noted that "the Party was taking up arms against his group" and that he didn't know where this conflict would lead. However, he seems to have viewed these developments optimistically, for he wrote that he was almost certain the party's actions would prove to be beneficial to his cause in the long run.

It is hard to imagine how Che could have believed that the opposition of the pro-Soviet Communist Party would prove to be beneficial to his guerrilla movement. His reluctance to be tied to the pro-Soviet Communists is understandable, but it is difficult to see how he could have failed to realize that their open opposition to his cause would not only deny him the recruits and urban support that he vitally needed but also lead to efforts on their part to sabotage his entire operation. Perhaps Che assumed that they would not dare attempt to sabotage an undertaking that was under his personal leadership and that had Fidel Castro's support. If so, he was gravely mistaken.

Following his meeting with Monje, Che notified Castro that Monje had refused to support the guerrilla operation and that Monje's party appeared to be opposed to the undertaking. Castro then contacted Jorge Kolle, the number two man in the pro-Soviet Communist Party in Bolivia, and Simón Reyes, the pro-Soviet trade union leader. He asked them to come to Havana to discuss Che's guerrilla operation. They arrived in Havana during the first part of February, and, according to the message that Che received from Castro, the latter was quite hard on both of these Communist leaders. But Kolle gave Castro the excuse that he had not been aware of the intended continental magnitude of the guerrilla movement, which of course was a lie. He also told Castro that, as soon as he returned to Bolivia, he would go to see Che in order to discuss with him how the party could help the guerrilla operation.

Kolle returned to Bolivia in mid-February, and although he stated several times over the next four or five months that he supported the guerrillas and was going to the southeast to visit Che, neither his trip to the guerrilla camp nor his promised support ever materialized. In fact, in the March 25 entry in his diary, Che contrasted Kolle's announced intention to come and discuss how he could help the guerrillas with his party's simultaneous expulsion of all the Bolivian members of his force from the party.

Following the army's discovery of the guerrillas in March 1967, and the publicity that ensued, the pro-Soviet party leaders told the members of their party that they supported the guerrillas. The party leaders deemed it necessary to make it appear that they supported the guerrilla operation in order to pacify their party's middle-level leaders and militants who were in sympathy with the guerrillas. As it was, they cleverly deceived their members into believing that the party was giving full support to Che's guerrilla force and had cordial relations with Che and his comrades.

Monje and Kolle were able to prevent the more militant members of their party from going to join the guerrillas by convincing them that Che's force did not need additional recruits just yet. Thus, while the pro-Soviet leaders were making declarations of support for the guerrillas, they were preventing their people from going to join the guerrillas, and in so doing they were sabotaging the operation's chances of success.

In May 1967, when Che's group was totally cut off from contact with both Havana and La Paz, an editorial in the party's newspaper, ironically called *Unidad* (unity), stated that the party's position was one of "support and solidarity with the guerrilla struggle" and that this support was in the areas of organization, logistics, information, and propaganda, in order "to prevent the isolation" of the guerrilla force. The editorial conspicuously avoided any mention of sending contingents to join the guerrillas, and in fact it is clear that the party leadership had no intention of assisting the guerrillas even in the specified areas. Indeed, it was largely because of the pro-Soviet party leaders that Che and his group were isolated and lacked any support at the very time this editorial was written. The same editorial in the party's newspaper also stated that, above all else, the guerrilla movement needed to be supported by the effective work of the party among the masses. Yet the party leadership knew full well that the guerrillas had little chance of obtaining the support of the masses and that they had no intention of using the party apparatus to mobilize popular support in favor of the guerrillas.

When the middle-level leaders and militants of the pro-Soviet party finally realized that their top leaders had not provided the guerrillas with the support that they claimed they were giving them, many of them demanded that they be allowed to go to the southeast and fight with Che. However, by this time it was too late. Che and his battered little group were completely surrounded, and the party leadership was able to argue in a convincing manner that the guerrillas were beyond help.

Even though the party leaders did absolutely nothing to help Che, they did not hesitate to take credit for supporting the guerrilla operation when it seemed in their interest to do so. An example of this occurred at the July 1967 inaugural meeting of the Latin American Organization of Solidarity, the regional subsidiary of the Tricontinental. At the start of the deliberations, held in Havana, Che was proclaimed president in absentia of the meeting by the delegates as a sign of their support for his revolutionary ideals and example. The Bolivian delegation, which was composed largely of representatives from the pro-Soviet Bolivian Communist Party, tried to give all those present the impression that they were working hand in hand with the guerrillas fighting in the southeast of Bolivia. In fact, on August 3, one of the Bolivian delegates went so far as to read a message to the meeting that was supposedly from the guerrillas. On hearing of this later, Che sarcastically noted in his diary that this message must have been the result of "telepathy." Elsewhere, he wrote that the meeting appeared to have been a triumph, but that "the Bolivian delegation was a pile of shit."

In his introduction to Che's diary, Fidel Castro bluntly accused Mario Monje of having sabotaged Che's guerrilla movement.

He stated that Monje himself actually intercepted well-trained Communist militants who were on their way to join the guerrillas and prevented them from leaving La Paz. Castro argued that this demonstrated that there were men in the Communist ranks who had both the desire and the ability to fight, but that their efforts to do so were "criminally frustrated by incapable leaders, charlatans, and tricksters." He went on to say that leaders such as Monje had turned revolutionary ideas into a "dogmatic opium" for the masses, and that they had discredited the revolutionary organization of the people by entering into political deals with both their foreign and domestic exploiters. These were extremely serious accusations for one Communist to level at another. Yet it is interesting to note that Castro condemned Monje the individual, rather than Monje the loyal representative of the Moscow line and leader of the pro-Soviet Communists in Bolivia. Cuba's close relations with the Soviet Union obviously kept him from openly stating this.

What is the full story behind Fidel Castro's accusations? How did Monje betray Che, and why did Monje and the other pro-Soviet Communist leaders sabotage Che's guerrilla movement? The answers to these questions provide a remarkable insight into the nature of the mortal struggle taking place at the time between the different leftist factions in Latin American politics.

It is perhaps best to begin by enumerating the five ways in which Bolivia's pro-Soviet Communist leaders betrayed Che and his guerrilla operation:

1. They gave Havana false information about the political situation in Bolivia and about the determination of their party to launch a guerrilla operation there.
2. They prevented members of the party, who had been trained in

Cuba, from going to join Che's guerrilla force.

3. They promised Che and his companions support that they never gave them.

4. They prevented the militants in their party from providing support to Che and his comrades.

5. They provided the Bolivian authorities and the CIA with important information about Che and his guerrilla force.

Each of these actions was an act of betrayal, and together they ensured the defeat of Che's mission in Bolivia.

The first and perhaps most important act of betrayal committed by the pro-Soviet Communist leaders was the false information they gave Havana about Bolivia's revolutionary potential, for this information was instrumental in bringing Che to Bolivia in the first place. The lies and boasting of the Bolivian delegation at the Tricontinental conference in January 1966 misled the Cubans into believing that a guerrilla-led uprising in Bolivia would be able to count upon the support of a very strong and revolutionary local Communist Party, and that the political conditions in Bolivia favored a Cuban type of revolution.

Monje and his comrades portrayed the Bolivia political system as an anarchic state characterized by tumult, violence, and widespread discontent. They boasted that their party had control over the workers and the peasants, who they said were ready to rise up in arms against the government. They conveyed a picture of Bolivia that was favorable for carrying out a guerrilla-led insurrection. The information provided by the pro-Soviet Communists led Che to believe that once armed actions against the government were started, the peasantry and workers would leave their farms and jobs to go in search of his guerrilla force (as they did during the Cuban revolution). In reality, of course, Che and Fidel

Castro were deceived by some of the best "con artists" in Latin America. Monje and his friends had planned a fraudulent guerrilla operation in order to expand their party treasury at Cuba's expense, and when Fidel and Che tried to establish a guerrilla force in Bolivia largely on their own, Monje paid them back by sabotaging their efforts.

Over thirty years later, Pombo, or Harry Villegas Tamayo, who was Che's Cuban bodyguard and one of the survivors of the Bolivian mission, stated publicly that he firmly believed that Mario Monje engaged in a conscious act of treason against the guerrillas; and Che's widow, Aleida March, contemptuously holds Monje responsible for betraying her husband (Anderson 1997, 705). In view of the information available from various sources, it is hard to come to any other conclusion.

After the failure of Che's guerrilla movement, the pro-Soviet group denied that it ever informed Cuba that the conditions in Bolivia were favorable for a guerrilla-led revolution. Its members claimed in their party newspaper and elsewhere that they indeed warned Havana on a number of occasions that the political situation in Bolivia was not appropriate for an armed struggle such as Che planned. The evidence to the contrary is overwhelming, but this did not deter the pro-Soviet leadership from making such claims.

Once Monje and the other pro-Soviet Communist leaders learned that Che was in Bolivia organizing a guerrilla movement, they consulted Moscow and, with Soviet encouragement, sabotaged the movement. One of their first acts of overt sabotage was reported by Che in his diary only three weeks after his New Year's Eve meeting with Monje. Che's entry indicates that Monje spoke to three young Bolivian Communists who had been sent from Cuba to fight with his group and persuaded them not to join the guerrilla movement. Following this incident, Monje notified Fidel Castro that he would not allow any members of his party to join the guerrillas in the southeast.

Sometime later, Coco Peredo was in La Paz for the purpose of taking several recruits to the guerrilla camp in Ñancahuazù. Much to the surprise of Coco and these recruits, who were all members of the youth wing of the pro-Soviet Bolivian Communist Party, they encountered Monje waiting for them at the bus terminal in La Paz. Monje interposed himself between Coco's group and the door of the bus they were planning to take to the southeast. He forbade the young Communists with Coco to join the guerrilla movement and assured them he would give their names to the authorities if they refused to do as he said. Although Coco reacted violently and threatened to kill Monje the next time he returned to La Paz, he realized he had no choice but to return to the guerrilla camp alone. Under no circumstances could he afford to take the risk that Monje might inform on the guerrillas at that point in their preparations. As things turned out, Coco never returned to La Paz. The guerrillas were discovered by the military soon thereafter, and Coco was never able to leave the combat zone in the southeast. The news of Coco's death six months later was probably received with some relief by Monje, who was reportedly very frightened by Coco's threat to kill him.

As was previously mentioned, the leaders of the pro-Soviet party deceived the rank and file of the party for several months after the initiation of hostilities, leading them to believe that the party was giving sufficient support to the guerrillas. By deceiving their members in this way, they were able to keep the more militant members of the party, who sympathized with the guerrillas, from going to the southeast to fight alongside Che. When the more militant members of the party realized that Che needed help badly, they demanded that their leaders allow them to go fight with the guerrillas. However, at this point the party leaders answered that the guerrilla operation was a hopeless failure and that they could not jeopardize the party by allowing its members to participate in an armed struggle that was certain to fail.

In addition to denying Che valuable recruits for his guerrilla force, the pro-Soviet leaders also prevented the guerrilla movement from receiving any political support. The number two man in the party hierarchy, Kolle, promised Fidel Castro the party's support on several occasions, but, as indicated above, this support never materialized. If the party leaders had not been so intent on sabotaging Che's guerrilla operation, they could have greatly assisted the guerrillas in the urban areas by serving as a source of propaganda, supplies, and information for them. Che's diary indicates that his lack of contact with the cities was a serious shortcoming after the outbreak of hostilities. Within a month after the hostilities began, Che and his men were totally cut off from the outside. The failure of the pro-Soviet group to give the guerrillas the promised logistical, organizational, informational, and propaganda support greatly contributed to their isolation.

The pro-Soviet leaders not only abandoned Che and his men to their tragic fate; they also insidiously worked to ensure their quick demise. I learned from reliable sources in Bolivia that a full month and a half before the guerrillas were discovered by the army, several middle-level leaders of the pro-Soviet party attempted to sell the CIA and the Bolivian intelligence service information about Che's presence in Bolivia and his preparation of a guerrilla force in the southeast of the country. Convinced that this was just another attempt to sell false information, a common political pastime in Bolivia, both the CIA and the Bolivian authorities rejected the information as absurd and not worthy of further attention. However, shortly after the initiation of hostilities, when the CIA and the Bolivian authorities realized that they had rejected reliable information about the guerrillas almost two months earlier, they reestablished contact with the pro-Soviet Communists. This time, the Communist leaders provided them with valuable information about the guerrilla operation, such as its true size, composition, strategy, location, and sources of support. In other words, there is evidence that the pro-Soviet leaders engaged in the worst kind of treachery in order to sabotage Che's guerrilla force.

In fact, Oscar Zamora, the leader of the pro-Chinese Communists in Bolivia, told me during a long conversation about the guerrilla episode that Jorge Kolle himself worked with the Barrientos regime and the CIA to help defeat the guerrillas. The character of Bolivian politics being what it is, this is entirely possible. Kolle's brother was head of the Bolivian air force, and he had the mysterious ability to travel freely, while other Communist leaders, especially the pro-Chinese leaders, had to remain almost continuously in hiding and could travel only clandestinely. Kolle was even able to obtain permission from the government to travel to the Soviet Union. As Zamora suggested, it may well be that Kolle served as the connecting link between the Bolivian regime and Washington, on the one hand, and the Pro-Soviet Communists and Moscow, on the other. If this is so, his actions with regard to Che's guerrilla movement take on an even greater significance and reveal that the leaders of the pro-Soviet party were working secretly with the Bolivian regime to make sure Che's guerrilla force was defeated.

However, leaving aside the question of whether or not Kolle worked with the Barrientos regime and the CIA, it is important to consider the motives behind Monje's and Kolle's efforts to sabotage Che's guerrilla operation. Why were these two Communist leaders so determined to ensure the defeat of Che's force? What were they afraid of? In the first place, it seems clear that Monje and Kolle were acting in accordance with encouragement from Moscow. The moment Moscow learned that Che was preparing a guerrilla movement in Bolivia and that he planned to extend this movement into the neighboring countries, Moscow advised the leadership of the pro-Soviet group in Bolivia to do nothing that would contribute to the success of the guerrilla operation.

The Soviet leaders regarded Che's operation in Bolivia as a threat to their Latin American strategy. If Che succeeded in turning Bolivia into another Vietnam, or even another Congo, the Soviet Union's relations with the existing regimes in Latin America, as well as with the United States, would be seriously threatened. Not only would the Soviet Union's policy of promoting closer relations and establishing economic ties with the existing regimes in Latin America be undermined, the situation could even provoke a direct confrontation between the Soviet Union and the United States. Moreover, Moscow was afraid the Chinese would be the ones to profit from such a situation. Che's sympathy for the Maoist political line was well known. Therefore, the Soviet leaders, as well as Monje and Kolle, were afraid that Che might seek the support of Bolivia's Maoists and perhaps even place himself at the service of the Chinese. Consequently, Moscow instructed Monje and Kolle to refuse Che the cooperation he requested, to prevent him from obtaining recruits, and to do nothing that would assist the operation.

Furthermore, both Moscow and the pro-Soviet party leaders in Bolivia saw the situation as an excellent opportunity to demonstrate to the Bolivian people and the rest of Latin America that efforts to liberate the masses through armed struggle were impractical and that there was no other alternative than the position advocated by the pro-Soviet Communists—that is, to struggle within legal bounds. In other words, they reasoned that if the famous Che Guevara himself failed to liberate the Bolivian people by means of a guerrilla movement, then the people of Latin America would have decisive proof that an armed revolution was not the answer to their problems. Evidence that this consideration motivated Monje and Kolle was revealed in some of the articles that appeared in their party's newspaper following the announcement of Che's capture and death. In these articles, the party's leadership used Che's death and the failure of his guerrilla *foco* to emphasize these points.

In evaluating the death of Che and the defeat of his guerrilla operation, these articles stated that even though the party leaders had supported the guerrilla movement, they had regarded it from the beginning as an effort that was dramatically divorced from the reality of prevailing conditions in Bolivia. And one particular article, after elaborating on the idea that Che's undertaking was based on a misconception of existing realities, actually admitted that the party leaders had decided at the outset of the guerrilla operation that they believed it would "demonstrate what was the best way for the Bolivians to follow in order to achieve a revolutionary victory."

In addition to the factors mentioned above, it is important to note that neither Monje nor Kolle was willing to take the personal risks or make the sacrifices that involvement in an armed struggle would have entailed. The leaders of the pro-Soviet Communists in Bolivia were leading a rather bourgeois lifestyle at the time. They talked a great deal about the misery, hunger, and poverty of the masses, but they themselves had never known any of these. The funds they received from Moscow allowed them to live very comfortably, and they enjoyed their comfortable existence too well to want to give it up for the dangerous life of revolutionary guerrilla fighters.

Che's brand of revolutionary internationalism was not shared by the leaders of most of the pro-Soviet Communist parties in Latin America or, for that matter, by the leadership of the Soviet Union. The Soviet leaders regarded Che's "leftist adventurism" to be contrary to their own strategy. However, there also appears to have been some sympathy for him among the Soviet leaders, especially since his influence had been decisive in persuading Fidel Castro to align Cuba with the Soviets shortly after the revolutionary triumph in Cuba.

According to Feder Burlatsky, a former adviser to Soviet Premier Nikita Khrushchev, the Soviet leaders disliked Che's revolutionary adventurism and were afraid his example would lead the Cubans and other leftist adventurers in Latin America into taking actions that would provoke a confrontation between the Soviet Union and the United States (Anderson 1997, 581). But in an interview that Burlatsky gave to the journalist Jon Lee Anderson in 1995, he claimed, "Even though Che was against our interests, there was still some sympathy for him. . . . There was a romantic aura around him; he reminded people of the Russian Revolution" (Anderson 1997, 581).

Anderson also conducted interviews with Nikolai Metutsov, who was responsible for maintaining relations between the Communist Party of the Soviet Union and the Communist parties in the non-European socialist states such as Cuba and Vietnam. Metutov told Anderson that he "fell in love" with Che upon meeting him, because of his " very beautiful eyes," because his stare was "so generous, so honest," and because he was impressed by the way he spoke with such impetus, "as if his words were squeezing you" (Anderson 1997, 585). According to Anderson, Metutsov's appraisal was that Che's views could not be easily classified.

> Externally one could truly say that, yes, Che Guevara was contaminated by Maoism because of his Maoist slogan that the rifle can create power. And certainly he can be considered a Trotskyite because he went to Latin America to stimulate the revolutionary movement . . . but in any case I think these are external signs, superficial ones, and that deep down, what was most profound in him was his aspiration to help man on the basis of Marxism-Leninism. (Anderson 1997, 585)

Metutsov told Anderson that he thought Che's personal commitment to the cause of revolution was his "peculiarity." He said Che's dedication to armed struggle, while a source of worry for some members of the Central Committee of the Soviet Communist Party, was not perceived by the Soviet leadership to be a cause of significant concern.

Che was committed to both fomenting revolution on a truly international scale and personally putting into practice his thesis that it was possible for a small, but committed, guerrilla force to ignite a full-scale popular revolution in countries that were under the control of oppressive regimes backed by U.S. imperialism. His "peculiar" commitment to these beliefs was shared by most of his closest friends and comrades as well as by many admirers and sympathizers around the world. However, this so-called peculiar commitment threatened the positions of the orthodox, pro-Soviet Communists and of certain other leftist parties and groups.

Apart from the pro-Soviet Communists, the other left-wing groups in Bolivia knew little or nothing about Che's guerrilla operation until the news broke at the end of March that the army had discovered a guerrilla force in the southeast of the country. In the months that followed, nearly all these groups expressed their solidarity with the guerrillas. However, none of them provided Che with any tangible support.

The pro-Chinese Communists did not know anything about the guerrillas until they were discovered by the army. In fact, the principal leaders of the pro-Chinese group were in prison at the time and could not have come to Che's assistance even if they had wanted to do so. Oscar Zamora, the top leader of the pro-Chinese party, had been imprisoned in the "leprosarium" at Puerto Moreno for several months when he learned of the guerrillas and the possibility that their leader might be Che Guevara. He told me that if he had not been imprisoned at the time and if Che had contacted him personally to ask for his aid, he probably would have supported the guerrilla operation. As it was, though, members of the pro-Chinese group remained little more than spectators throughout the entire episode.

They made several pronouncements of moral support for the guerrillas after the fighting began, but they also clearly felt that the guerrillas lacked the necessary ideological direction. They even declared on several occasions that the guerrillas faced the prospect of being annihilated because of their ideological confusion. One document in particular warned the guerrillas that in a revolution there cannot be any type of opportunism, and that the correct political ideology must command the gun rather than the gun commanding the ideology of a revolutionary movement.

There does appear to have been some belated communication regarding the guerrilla operation between Havana and two of Bolivia's leftist groups: Juan Lechín's Revolutionary Party of the Nationalist Left and Hugo Gonzales's Trotskyist Workers Revolutionary Party. On March 23, 1967, Castro sent Che a message stating that Lechín was in Cuba. Castro indicated that he had informed Lechín about the strategic objectives of the Bolivian guerrilla operation and about Che's personal direction of it. According to Castro, Lechín was very enthusiastic about the undertaking and promised to give his support in the form of both men and public declarations. The message said that he would secretly reenter Bolivia within the next month to meet with Che. However, Lechín never returned to Bolivia. A few months later, he was arrested in Chile while traveling under a false Argentine passport. From the safety of Chilean soil, he issued a statement saying that the guerrillas were fighting to liberate his country from the foreign yoke imposed on it by the traitorous Barrientos regime.

Lechín's motives and behavior were unclear. Perhaps he intended to use Che's guerrilla operation to his own advantage in a bid to seize power. On the other hand, Antonio Arguedas, the high Bolivian official who sent Che's diary to Castro, has stated that the CIA asked Arguedas early in 1967 to provide Lechín (who was wanted by the government at the time) with a passport so that he could travel overseas. Arguedas, who was then minister of internal affairs in the Barrientos government, claims he refused the request since Lechín was an avowed enemy of the regime. But why did the CIA want to help Lechín travel overseas? Could it have been that he was working for them, or did they want him out of the country?

The situation is further complicated by the fact that the pro-Soviet Communist leader Jorge Kolle, in an interview with a *New York Times* correspondent in May 1967, claimed that the guerrilla force in the southeast of Bolivia was composed of militants from both Lechín's party, the Trotskyist Workers' Revolutionary Party, and Zamora's pro-Chinese group. However, Kolle was most likely lying about the association of these groups with the guerrillas in an effort to bring the wrath of the government down upon these other parties, and thus make life more difficult for his party's major left-wing rivals.

A message from Fidel Castro to Che dated July 4, 1967, reveals that one of Castro's agents in La Paz had contacted the "section of the Workers' Revolutionary Party led by Hugo Gonzales and learned that this faction of the Trotskyists was predisposed to help the guerrillas." The same message also indicates that certain elements within the more centrist National Revolutionary Movement were interested in going to Cuba for guerrilla training. However, in the final analysis, neither of these two groups participated in Che's guerrilla operation. They were contacted when it was already too late, and it seems unlikely that their leaders ever had any serious intention of doing anything more than expressing their moral support for the guerrillas. The leaders of these groups, as well as those of other left-wing groups in Bolivia, hoped that the guerrilla operation would create a situation that would lead to the collapse of the Barrientos regime. Consequently, they expressed support for the guerrilla movement not particularly because they identified with its revolutionary objectives, but because they regarded the guerrilla operation as something that would help promote their own objectives, which included toppling the Barrientos regime.

Che's failure to obtain the positive support of Lechín's followers, Gonzales's Trotskyists, or the militant elements within the Nationalist Revolutionary Movement—as well as the support of the country's two Communist parties—ensured the total political isolation of his movement. Che preferred to overlook the fact that he was surrounded on all sides by opportunists, charlatans, and cowards. However, Che was betrayed by the pro-Soviet Communists and abandoned by those leftist parties who loudly acclaimed their revolutionary ideals but did not put them into practice. His single-minded determination and devotion to his ideals provided a sharp contrast to the opportunism and posturing of the left-wing opportunists and impostors that were an important part of Bolivia's political scenery at the time.

This leaves the question of whether Fidel Castro and the Cuban government did everything they could to assist Che and his comrades, especially when it became clear that they were isolated and surrounded by the Bolivian army. Some have even suggested that the Cubans betrayed Che's guerrilla force because they did not send help to rescue them. However, there is absolutely no evidence that supports this line of reasoning. In 1987, twenty years after Che's death, an Italian journalist asked Fidel whether there was anything he and the Cuban government could have done to help Che in the final stage of his Bolivian operation. His reply was there was nothing that they could do, especially after the entire underground network of support for Che's force within Bolivia had been destroyed (Deutschmann 1994, 128). In fact, there was nothing the Cubans could have done. They did not have the military capability to rescue Che and his force inside of Bolivia, thousands of miles from Cuba. Moreover, since Bolivia's borders were sealed by the military and police after the guerrilla operation was discovered, it was impossible for the Cubans secretly to insert a sizable number of combatants into the country. Even if they had somehow succeeded in doing so, they would not have gotten past the large number of troops in the region where Che and his battered force were isolated and surrounded.

Che's Bolivian mission could never have been conceived or launched without the support of Fidel Castro and the Cuban government. The Cuban government financed and supplied the logistical support for the mission, provided and trained the main core of the combatants, and placed its intelligence service and clandestine political network in Latin America at their disposal. Indeed, Castro and the Cuban government took a great political risk in supporting Che's mission, since it placed Cuba in the position of being castigated by the United States and its allies in Latin America for breaking international laws, violating the national sovereignty of Bolivia, and attempting to overthrow its government by armed intervention. It also strained Cuba's relations with its main ally and protector, the Soviet Union, which strongly opposed such an adventurist course of action, especially within an area considered by the United States to be its core sphere of influence.

A declassified CIA intelligence information cable dated October 17, 1967, supports this conclusion. This cable summarizes intelligence that was gathered from September 1966 through June 1967 and focuses on the disagreement between the Soviet Union and Cuba over Che's mission to Bolivia. It provides specific information on the Soviet leader Leonid Brezhnev's objections to Castro about the "the dispatch of Ernesto Che Guevara to Bolivia" and reveals that Brezhnev sent Soviet Premier Aleksei Kosygin to Cuba in June 1967 to discuss the Kremlin's opposition to Castro's support of Third World revolutionary operations such as Che's mission in Bolivia. The CIA sources summarized in the cable reported that Kosygin accused Castro of "harming the communist cause through his sponsorship of guerrilla activity . . . and through providing support to various anti-government groups, which although they claimed to be 'socialist' or communist, were engaged in disputes with the 'legitimate' Latin American communist parties . . . favored by the USSR." In reply, the cable indicates that Castro argued that Cuba would support the "right of every

Latin American to contribute to the liberation of his country" and supposedly "accused the USSR of having turned its back upon its own revolutionary tradition and of having moved to a point where it would refuse to support any revolutionary movement unless the actions of the latter contributed to the achievement of Soviet objectives . . ." (Kornbluh 2007).

Chapter 14

U.S. INVOLVEMENT IN
THE GUERRILLA EPISODE

Mr. President, This tentative information that the Bolivians got Che Guevara will interest you. It is not yet confirmed. The Bolivian unit engaged is the one we have
been training for some time and has just entered the
field of action.

—Walter Rostow, memorandum to
President Lyndon Johnson (October 9, 1967)

U.S. political and economic involvement in Bolivia was
extensive at the time of Che's revolutionary mission
there. In fact, the Bolivian economy was largely controlled by U.S. interests. The United States was the largest buyer
of Bolivia's tin, which was the country's economic mainstay. In
addition, U.S. investments were the main sources of foreign
capital investment in Bolivia, and the majority of Bolivia's private mining enterprises and its largest oil development scheme
were controlled by U.S. corporations. Furthermore, the Bolivian
government was dependent upon the financial assistance of the

U.S. government, which annually provided the regime with direct budgetary support in the form of outright grants and low-interest, long-term loans. This financial support, plus a large number of technical assistance and economic development programs, made Bolivia the recipient of one of the largest U.S. aid programs in Latin America during the late 1960s.

After the 1952 revolution, the U.S. government gave Bolivia over $400 million in aid. The motivation behind this extensive amount of foreign aid was largely political, as is evident in the following statement from a U.S. Senate report published in 1956: "The Department of State, which constantly appraises political, social, and economic developments, has concluded that the Bolivian government is Marxist rather than Communist and has advocated United States support of this regime on the same premise that it advocated support of the preceding military junta—to prevent displacement by more radical elements." As this statement indicates, once the U.S. government determined that the postrevolutionary political leadership in Bolivia was leftist and nationalist rather than Communist and pro-Soviet (a distinction that American officials usually found difficult to make during the Cold War), it decided to support the Bolivian regime—in particular, the more moderate elements in the ruling National Revolutionary Movement. The primary motive was to stabilize the political situation in Bolivia and prevent any further movement to the left, but equally important was the desire to protect the U.S. economic interests in Bolivia.

The American presence in Bolivia increased notably in the 1960s. This was particularly true in the southeast, where over $100 million was invested by the U.S. government alone, not to mention the amounts invested by Gulf Oil and other U.S.-owned firms interested in opening up the area. These investments went

into the construction of the Cochabamba–Santa Cruz highway
(the only paved, all-weather road in Bolivia at the time) and the
Santa Cruz–Corumba railway (which links Santa Cruz with
southern Brazil), as well as into sugar mills, oil wells, agricultural
improvement projects, farm credit programs, school construction
projects, and the like.

The American presence was also visible in the form of hundreds of American missionaries, Peace Corps volunteers, and
civilian advisers of one kind or another. It is interesting in this
regard to note that Régis Debray paid tribute to the importance
of this pervasive American presence in the rural areas of Latin
America by asserting that it made the establishment of guerrilla
movements there more difficult. For example, in his book *Revolution in the Revolution?* Debray stated,

> As for American imperialism, it has increased its forces in the
> field, and is making every effort to present itself, not in repres-
> sive guise, but in the shape of social and technical assistance. . . .
> Thousands of Peace Corpsmen have succeeded in integrating
> themselves in rural areas—some of them by dint of hard work,
> patience, and at times real sacrifice—where they profit by the
> lack of political work by left-wing organizations. Even the most
> remote regions are today teeming with Catholic, Evangelical,
> Methodist, and Seventh Day Adventist missionaries. In a word,
> all these close-knit networks of control strengthen the national
> machinery of domination, and without exaggerating the depth
> or scope of their penetration, we can say that they have indeed
> changed the scene. (Debray 1967, 53)

There is little doubt that the increased American presence in
countries like Bolivia made life more difficult for revolution-

ary guerrilla movements such as Che's. But as important as the extensive American political and economic involvement was the American military assistance in these countries.

During the late 1960s, U.S. military assistance to Latin America increased enormously. The United States spent over one billion dollars in equipping and training the armies of thirteen countries in Latin America. One very important by-product of this massive program of military assistance was the increased influence of the local military elites in Latin American politics. It was no accident, therefore, that over two-thirds of the countries that received U.S. military aid during the sixties ended up with military dictatorships or military-backed regimes during the 1960s and 1970s.

The main emphasis of American military aid was placed on increasing the "internal security" capability of the Latin American countries. The U.S. government was not concerned that Latin America was threatened by external aggression. American military assistance, therefore, was directed not toward promoting hemispheric defense against foreign aggression but rather toward the suppression of internal "Communist subversion" and popular insurrections within the Latin American countries. In accordance with this objective, the police and armed forces of most of the Latin American countries were trained and equipped by the United States to handle anything from student protests to large-scale popular revolts.

Latin American army officers and soldiers were taught the latest U.S. counterinsurgency tactics (which had been developed for use in Vietnam) and given instruction in the administration of "civic action" programs designed to improve the military's public image among the population. In fact, close to twenty thousand Latin American officers and soldiers received special counterinsurgency training from the U.S. Army at Fort Gulick, in the Panama Canal Zone, and many others were trained by American military advisory teams stationed in their countries.

In the case of Bolivia, the armed forces, particularly the officer corps, were greatly influenced by American military assistance and training. In fact, the Bolivian military establishment was created by the Bolivian president Paz Estenssoro of the MNR with American advice and equipment in order to serve as a counterweight to the miners' and peasants' militias, which had destroyed the traditional army in the 1952 revolution. Under American guidance, the new Bolivian army became the first in Latin America to launch a civic action program aimed at "winning the hearts and minds" (referred to as "WHAMing") of the general population. This program, involving the construction of schools and roads in the rural areas, was undertaken at the suggestion of and with the help of the U.S. Military Assistance and Advisory Group (MAAG) in Bolivia. Evidently, the "civic consciousness" resulting from the introduction of such programs partly explains why the new, American-advised army ousted the elected civilian government in 1964 and placed in power the senior officer most closely associated with the American military advisers, General René Barrientos.

Although a number of journalistic accounts have exaggerated the role played by the U.S. government and American personnel in the defeat of Che's guerrilla operation in Bolivia, a dispassionate analysis of the evidence available reveals that *direct* American involvement in the entire episode was minimal but not insignificant. Far from pushing the panic button when word was first received of the guerrilla operation in the southeast of Bolivia, the Washington policy makers responded to the situation in a very uncharacteristic manner for the times—they played it cool.

Perhaps this response was a result of their determination to avoid another Vietnam-like involvement, since they were encountering increasing popular resistance to the Vietnam War at home. At any rate, early in the game the decision was made to restrict American assistance to the Bolivians to the areas of military supplies, training, and intelligence. Moreover, the U.S. government persuaded the military government of the Argentine strongman General Juan Carlos Onganía that there was no need for Argentina to intervene in the Bolivian guerrilla operation. It seems the Argentine military regime was worried about the ineffectiveness of the Bolivian army and the proximity of the guerrilla operation to Argentina's northern border. As a result of American assurances, the Argentine government merely moved some troops to Argentina's frontier with Bolivia and sent a shipment of arms and ammunition to the Bolivian army. Shortly thereafter, the Peruvian and Brazilian governments did essentially the same thing.

President Barrientos's first response to the discovery of the guerrilla operation in his country was to call immediately upon the U.S. government for additional military aid. However, the U.S. ambassador to Bolivia, Douglas Henderson, was more concerned about the possible overreaction of the Barrientos government to the situation than about the guerrilla threat itself. Among other things, he and his advisers were afraid the Bolivians would indiscriminately start bombing the zone of guerrilla operations and thereby alienate the local civilian population. Washington was anxious not to repeat its mistakes in Vietnam by giving napalm and additional aircraft to the Bolivians. On the other hand, something obviously had to be done, for if the Bolivian army failed to respond effectively to the guerrilla threat, the guerrillas might succeed in winning popular support, or the Barrientos regime might be toppled by elements within the military eager to find a scapegoat for their failures. Consequently, Washington decided that the Bolivian army should be given only certain kinds of military equipment and special training in counterguerrilla warfare to improve its combat effectiveness.

On April 1, 1967, the first installment of American military equipment arrived in Santa Cruz aboard a U.S. Air Force C-130 cargo plane. Subsequent shipments increased the amount of material assistance, but this aid was restricted to light arms, ammunition, communications equipment, and helicopters. Meanwhile, the U.S. government persuaded the Bolivians that their most important need was in the realm of training. Consequently, by mid-April plans had already been made for the establishment of a special training camp in Bolivia where U.S. advisers would train a new elite counterinsurgency force.

By the end of April, this special training camp was opened at the site of a former sugar mill, named La Esperanza, near Santa Cruz. The training staff sent to organize this camp consisted of fifteen U.S. Special Forces "Green Berets" under the command of Major "Pappy" Shelton. Members of this group, most of whom had served in Vietnam, were from the special forces garrison in the U.S.-controlled Panama Canal Zone. Their mission was to train in the shortest time possible a new, crack regiment of 640 Bolivian Rangers who would be capable of carrying out an effective antiguerrilla campaign against Che and his small force.

The members of this new regiment were specially recruited from the tropical areas of Bolivia in order to obtain individuals whose prior conditioning would allow them to adapt quickly to the climatic and geographic conditions of the southeast. In addition, the Bolivian officers selected to lead this new regiment had been chosen because of their past training in counterinsurgency at Fort Gulick. One of the most capable officers in the Bolivian army, Colonel José Gallardo, was placed in command of the new regiment and the training camp at La Esperanza.

Major Shelton's orders were to mold an effective counterinsurgency unit out of his raw Bolivian recruits in nineteen weeks, and keep all U.S. military personnel clear of the combat zone at all times. They were to have everything they might need in the way of supplies and equipment. The training program that Major Shelton and his team set up for the new Ranger unit was modeled on that of the Green Berets. However, certain special exercises were tailored to the particular needs of their Bolivian trainees. Working on the assumption that the Bolivian army was one of the worst armies in Latin America, and that this opinion was shared by many Bolivians themselves, Major Shelton and his staff concluded that one of their most important objectives was to develop a high degree of esprit de corps and self-confidence among the Bolivian recruits. Thus, in addition to intensive training in the techniques of counterinsurgency warfare, the Bolivian recruits were also exposed to a number of morale-boosting programs. These included periods during which they spent hours shouting "I'm the toughest" and "I'm the best." Although this may seem somewhat ridiculous, it appears to have been necessary in order to overcome the inbred sense of inferiority and lack of confidence suffered by most of Bolivia's indigenous, nonwhite population.

The new Ranger regiment, called Manchego No. 2, completed its special training program in mid-September, less than five months after its formation. Evaluating the caliber of the military unit that passed in review before them at the ceremony marking the termination of their training, Major Shelton and his staff could take pride in having worked a true miracle in military training. The troops who passed before them, wearing green berets and marching smartly with their heads high, were far better equipped and trained than any other unit in the Bolivian armed forces. Unlike their less fortunate comrades already in the field, they were both properly trained and equipped to fight under the conditions of guerrilla warfare. Among the speeches at the passing out ceremony for Manchego No. 2, Colonel Gallardo, the regimental commander, thanked the U.S. advisers for their invaluable assistance and credited them with having created "the new personality" possessed by his troops. This assistance, more than anything else, seems to have been the main U.S. contribution to the military defeat suffered by Che's guerrilla force. Following their training at La Esperanza, the Rangers of Manchego No. 2 were sent into the Vallegrande–La Higuera area, where they rapidly proceeded to eliminate the handful of guerrillas left under Che's command.

While Major Shelton and his team were training the Rangers, the CIA made a determined effort to improve the intelligence capabilities of the Bolivian army and civilian intelligence service. Pressure was placed on the minister of interior, Antonio Arguedas, to accept several CIA agents as "advisers" on security and intelligence matters in his ministry. Additional agents were attached to the military high command, and two Cuban American special agents, who used the names Eduardo Gonzales and Félix Ramos were assigned to the southeast to collect firsthand information on the guerrilla operation and work closely with the troops in the field. Félix Ramos's real name was Félix Ismael Rodríguez, and he subsequently wrote a book (Rodríguez 1989) about his involvement in Che's death as well as his other exploits as a CIA operative. Eduardo Gonzales, or "Dr. Gonzales," as he called himself, was placed in charge of the CIA team. His real name was Gustavo Villoldo. He had been assigned by the CIA to find Che after he left Cuba, and he followed him to the Congo and then Bolivia

(Tamayo 1997). Rodríguez and Villoldo became part of a CIA task force in Bolivia that included the case officer for the operation, "Jim," another Cuban American, Mario Osiris Riveron, and two agents in charge of communications in Santa Cruz.

Because Washington was anxious not to have Anglo-Americans present in the combat zone and because they naïvely assumed that U.S. agents of Cuban origin would be less conspicuous in Bolivia than Anglo-Americans, all of the operatives assigned to the guerrilla situation were Cuban exiles with a history of involvement in anti-Castro operations. However, their Cuban accents and phony-sounding names made them as conspicuous as any of the gringo advisers in the Bolivian government.

Gustavo Villoldo, or Dr. Gonzales, appears to have been responsible for interrogating all the prisoners taken in association with the guerrilla operation. He was the CIA agent who questioned Régis Debray and to whom Debray appears to have given information about Che and the guerrilla operation. In fact, Villoldo claims that "he talked through his elbows," which is a Cuban expression for someone who confesses everything (Tamayo 1997). Villoldo also interrogated the deserters and the guerrillas taken prisoner during the last months of the guerrilla operation. Moreover, he went to La Paz to question Loyola Guzmán and the other members of the guerrilla urban underground who were arrested in September 1967. Finally, he claims to have been the person in charge of secretly burying Che's body near the airport in Vallegrande.

Félix Ismael Rodríguez (code name Félix Ramos) was assigned to work with the Bolivian troops in the field (Kornbluh 2007). A trained radio operator, he was responsible for combat intelligence and for collecting as much information as possible on the guerrilla operation. Ramos visited every skirmish site and campsite of the guerrillas, questioned peasants and soldiers who had been taken prisoner by them, and carefully compiled a comprehensive and detailed dossier on the entire operation. On the basis of his interrogation of one of the captured guerrillas, he advised the Second Ranger Battalion to focus on the Villagrande region. According to those who had occasion to meet him, he was much more talkative and friendly than Villoldo, who spoke very little and avoided contact with just about everyone.

Sensationalist claims about how "the CIA got Che" have no factual foundation at all. To be sure, the CIA was ever present during the entire episode; it certainly was determined to see that Che was defeated and, if possible, captured. However, it was not responsible for the failure of Che's guerrilla operation or his execution. In fact, the U.S. government and the CIA appear to have opposed the idea of executing Che. Purely for professional reasons, they wanted to keep him alive. This appears to have been the position of the U.S. government, from the highest levels down to the two CIA agents on the scene. Thus, in his (now declassified) memorandum to President Lydon Johnson confirming the death of Che Guevara, Walt Rostow (who was the president's special assistant for national security affairs) told the president,

> CIA tells us that the latest information is that Guevara was taken alive. After a short interrogation to establish his identity, General Ovando—Chief of the Bolivian Armed Forces—ordered him shot. I regard this as stupid, but it is understandable from a Bolivian standpoint, given the problems which the sparing of French communist and Castro courier Regis Debray has caused them.

Rostow also provides in this memorandum his analysis of the "significant implications" of Che's death. He said,

- It marks the passing of another of the aggressive, romantic revolutionaries like Sukarno, Nkrumah, Ben Bella—and reinforces this trend.
- In the Latin American context, it will have a strong impact in discouraging would-be guerrillas.
- It shows the soundness of our "preventive medicine" assistance to countries facing incipient insurgency—it was the Bolivian 2nd Ranger Battalion, trained by our Green Berets from June–September of this year that cornered him and got him.

Rostow closed the memorandum with the comment that he had "put these points across to several newsmen" (Rostow 1967).

According to the former CIA agent Rodríguez, who later became the president of the militant Cuban-exile organization Brigade 2506, "the order came from the Bolivian government to shoot him. I tried in all my power to stop them because of my instructions to take him to Panama for the CIA." However, even though Rodríguez has claimed repeatedly he was under CIA instructions to "do everything possible to keep him alive," Rodríguez has also admitted he transmitted the order to execute Guevara that came by radio from the Bolivian high command to the soldiers at La Higuera. He also claims he directed them not to shoot Guevara in the face so that his wounds would appear to be combat related (*Miami's Cuban Connection* 2006).

Rodríguez contends he personally informed Che that he would be killed. He also claims he shook Che's hand and embraced him before he was executed. He told *Miami's Cuban Connection* in a 2006 interview, "I walked in and gave the order to untie him. Che had asked if we could untie him and let him sit down. . . . Later, the order came from the Bolivian government to shoot him.

I tried in all my power to stop them because of my instructions to take him to Panama for the CIA. . . . At the end, I asked him if he wanted me to do something for his family. He said 'Tell my wife to marry again and try to be happy.' We shook hands, hugged. I left the room and someone came in and shot him." Later in this interview, he said it was Mario Terán who shot Che (*Miami's Cuban Connection* 2006). After Che was executed, Rodríguez claims, he took Che's Rolex watch, which he has proudly shown reporters over the years. As for the other agent, Gustavo Villoldo, he claims, "At no time did I or the CIA have a say in executing Che . . . that was a Bolivian decision" (Tamayo 1997).

If the CIA agents advised the Bolivians to keep Che alive, their advice was clearly rejected by the Bolivian government's top leaders, who felt they could not afford to allow the famous revolutionary to live. Bolivia had no death penalty, so they were afraid if they imprisoned Che he would become a cause célèbre that would attract leftists to the country from around the world. Moreover, if they turned him over to the CIA, they would give the world and the Bolivian people the impression that the U.S. government was running things in Bolivia. They felt they had no other choice politically but to execute Che. They also decided to cover this up by claiming that he died after capture from wounds received in battle.

After Che's body was displayed in Vallegrande, it disappeared from public view without any official word about its disposal. Since the Bolivian military refused to give any information to the public about this subject, there was considerable speculation about what had happened to it. Some people believed that the CIA had taken Che's body back to the United States, others that his body had been cremated and his ashes spread over the jungle by air, and some that he was buried in a secret location. It now appears that the CIA agent Gustavo Villoldo was responsible for burying Che's body in an unmarked grave near the Vallegrande airport along with six of Che's former companions in arms. At least this is where his bones were uncovered in July 1997.

Exaggerated claims about U.S. involvement in the defeat of Che's guerrilla force have also been made with regard to the use of infrared aerial cameras by U.S. planes that supposedly used these cameras to detect and locate the guerrillas. One journalist, in particular, asserted that the mud ovens used by the guerrillas made it possible for the U.S. Air Force to pinpoint their location at all times by using new, highly sensitive heat-detecting cameras in an around-the-clock aerial surveillance of the combat zone. However, after leaving their main camp in the Ñancahuazú area, where they did have a mud oven, the guerrillas never stayed anywhere long enough to build another one. In fact, they rarely even built fires.

Furthermore, the Bolivian authorities knew at least the general location of the guerrillas throughout the entire period from their initial discovery to their elimination in October. They did not have to rely upon such sophisticated American gimmickry as heat-sensing infrared cameras. For one thing, during the first four months of operations, Che's column clashed with the army on a fairly frequent basis, and it was possible to ascertain simply from these encounters the general location of the guerrillas. Moreover, the army constantly received information about them from the local peasantry. The irony of the situation is that the Bolivian military knew far more about the guerrillas than the latter knew about the army—the exact reverse of the usual situation in guerrilla warfare.

In sum, the U.S. involvement in Bolivian affairs was extensive, but the U.S. contribution to the military defeat of Che's guerrilla operation was minimal and then only at the end. To be sure, the U.S. trained the Rangers of Manchego No. 2, who were responsible for capturing Che and almost completely eliminating his small force in October 1967. However, Che's guerrilla operation was already defeated prior to the arrival on the scene of the U.S.-trained Rangers. His force had lost over half of its original members and had failed to win any popular support. Moreover, the hostility of the pro-Soviet Communist Party leaders and the indifference of the other leftist groups in Bolivia, together with the capture of the guerrillas' urban contacts in La Paz, had left Che and the tattered remnants of his original force completely and hopelessly isolated by the time the Rangers entered into combat against them.

Chapter 15

THE PUBLICATION OF CHE'S DIARY

> We cannot, for the time being, reveal how this diary fell into our hands; it is enough to say that we did not have to pay anyone for it.
>
> —Fidel Castro, introduction to
> Che's *Bolivian Diary* (1968)

P erhaps the most incredible aspect of the story surrounding Che's guerrilla operation involves the publication of his campaign diary. Following his capture and execution, the Barrientos government decided to sell Che's diary to the publisher willing to pay the highest price. However, while the Bolivians were negotiating the sale of the diary, the Cuban government mysteriously obtained a copy and released it through a series of publishing houses in Latin America, Europe, and the United States. By publishing the diary before the Bolivians could sell it, the Cuban government was able to score a significant propaganda victory and greatly embarrass the Barrientos regime. Moreover, the question of how the Cubans managed to get a copy of the diary gave rise to serious doubts in Bolivia about the integrity of the government and the armed forces. Clearly, someone in either the government or the military had placed a copy of the "top-secret" diary in Cuban hands.

On July 1, 1968, while I was in La Paz, Che's diary was made public in Havana, and within a few days it was distributed by leftist publishers in Chile, Mexico, France, Italy, West Germany, and the United States. A few weeks later, on July 17, Antonio Arguedas, minister of internal affairs in the Barrientos government and a close friend of President Barrientos, fled to Chile and was denounced by General Ovando as the traitor who had provided the Cuban government with photostatic copies of Che's diary. The Bolivian public was stunned by the news, and most of the population regarded Arguedas's actions as a national disgrace.

Since Arguedas had been Barrientos's right-hand man, the whole affair seriously undermined the public's confidence in the Barrientos regime and within twenty-four hours plunged the country into a grave political crisis that broke apart the coalition of parties that had previously supported Barrientos. At the same time, the three main opposition parties (the right-wing Socialist Falange, the centrist National Revolutionary Movement, and the Trotskyist Revolutionary Party of the Nationalist Left) issued a manifesto calling upon the Barrientos government to resign. They also called a mass demonstration in the capital on July 20, which resulted in a violent clash with the police and the death of a captain of the civil guard.

The leaders of the demonstration were arrested, and Barrientos declared a nationwide state of emergency. He also called upon the peasant syndicates in the Cochabamba region to come to his assistance, and some five thousand armed campesinos from the Cochabamba valley were mobilized and moved to the outskirts of La Paz. This appears to have been the turning point in the crisis; soon thereafter Barrientos received expressions of public support from the various military garrisons throughout the country, as well as several important political groups. Ironically, the crisis arising from the publication of Che's diary, and particularly Arguedas's part in the whole affair, almost toppled the Barrientos regime—something that the guerrilla operation had never come close to achieving while Che was alive.

But the Arguedas affair did not end there. Much to everyone's surprise, approximately a month after his flight from the country, Antonio Arguedas voluntarily returned to Bolivia to stand trial for his actions. In Chile, Arguedas had publicly declared that he wanted to return to Bolivia to clear his name. However, most Bolivians assumed he had received a large sum of money from the Cubans in return for Che's diary, so no one took seriously his announced intention to return home. This made it all the more surprising when he did return to Bolivia, following a monthlong odyssey that took him to Buenos Aires, Madrid, London, New York, and Lima, before arriving back in La Paz.

On August 17, the day of his return to Bolivia, Arguedas was met at the airport outside La Paz by a heavy police guard and a large crowd of Bolivian and international correspondents. When his plane landed, the reporters attempted to move onto the concrete taxiing strip where the plane was due to halt, but they were stopped by the police. However, two officials of the U.S. embassy, carrying cameras, were allowed to pass through the police cordon, and this obvious discrimination gave rise to heated protests from the assembled reporters, who were finally allowed to move closer.

As the plane came to a halt and the portable stairways were wheeled into position at the forward and rear doors, a rented car, escorted by several police motorcycles and a jeep, pulled up in front of the forward stairway. After the other passengers on the plane had disembarked via the rear door, Arguedas was escorted out of the front door and down the stairs into the waiting car by two police officials. He was followed by a large number of foreign correspondents who had flown with him from Lima. Arguedas was taken to the Bolivian national airline building, where he was allowed to meet with his wife and one of his sons and then, surprisingly, to talk with the waiting crowd of reporters.

The press conference at the airport lasted exactly seventeen minutes before it was abruptly terminated by the director of the Criminal Investigations Division. Arguedas had begun to reveal some of the activities of the CIA in Bolivia and his former ties with this U.S. spy organization, when the director suspended the conference on the grounds that there were public disturbances in the city and that it was therefore necessary to transport the prisoner to safety immediately. Then, amid protests from both the reporters and Arguedas, the latter was forcibly removed to another room in the building.

About five minutes later, a security agent wearing Arguedas's clothing was hurriedly rushed into a car and driven away in the wake of a motorcycle escort. However, the deception failed, and the reporters waited outside the building for Arguedas to reappear. Approximately half an hour later, the director of information for the presidency appeared and admitted to the press that Arguedas was still in the building, but that he was prohibited for the time being from making any public declarations. Shortly thereafter, a police jeep arrived, and Arguedas was taken to it under heavy guard. As he reached the jeep, he shouted at the reporters, "I demand that the press conference be continued in order to expose the CIA." He was cut short by a violent effort on the part of his guards to push him into the jeep. They succeeded in forcing him into it, and, together with another police vehicle, it immediately sped away in the direction of the center of the city.

Later in the day, Arguedas was taken to the Ministry of Internal Affairs, and upon instructions from President Barrientos, he was permitted to meet with the press a second time. This time, he was allowed to answer approximately thirty questions during the course of an hour and a half. Afterward, he was returned to his cell in the Criminal Investigations Division and not allowed to meet with the press again.

Arguedas revealed to the press that his association with the CIA had begun in 1964, shortly after the MNR government of Paz Estenssoro was overthrown by the military. At that time, Arguedas was appointed to a high-level administrative post in the Ministry of Internal Affairs. But two months after his appointment, Colonel Edward Fox, the U.S. Air Force attaché in the U.S. embassy, informed Arguedas that if he continued in office, the U.S. government would suspend all economic assistance to Bolivia and take drastic measures against its government. The reason given was Arguedas's past membership in the Bolivian Communist Party. In order to avoid any trouble, Arguedas resigned.

Several weeks later, however, he was again contacted by Colonel Fox, who told him the U.S. government might reconsider its opposition to him if he would meet with a certain U.S. diplomat in Bolivia. Arguedas agreed, and Colonel Fox introduced him to Larry Sterfield, then the head of the CIA team in Bolivia. Sterfield suggested to Arguedas that he voluntarily undergo interrogation outside of Bolivia so that it could be determined whether or not he had been a militant member of the Bolivian Communist Party and whether the party had instructed him to infiltrate the new military regime.

In order to clear himself with the Americans, Arguedas agreed to go to Lima, Peru, for several days of intensive interrogation by the CIA. In Lima, he was exposed to three days of interviews and interrogation with the use of a lie detector. On the fourth day, he was interrogated while under the influence of drugs. When he recovered, the CIA people told him they were convinced he had not been a militant member of the Communist Party, or been instructed by the party to infiltrate the new government in Bolivia. As far as they were concerned, he was free to resume his duties in the Ministry of Internal Affairs.

Arguedas returned to La Paz and was reappointed to his post in the ministry. However, as time went by, the CIA men asked him to provide them with various kinds of information to which he had access in his position. Later on, they told him that they would see to it that he became the next minister of internal affairs. They promised to praise him in all the right circles and to present him as the ideal person for this important post. Soon articles began appearing in the newspapers concerning the marvelous job Arguedas was doing. In addition, the U.S. officials and advisers around President Barrientos began praising Arguedas.

Evidently, the president assumed that Arguedas had become friends with the U.S. officials through his work in the ministry, and largely because they thought so highly of Arguedas, Barrientos appointed him minister of internal affairs. After his appointment, the CIA invited Arguedas to visit Washington and gave him $6,500 (a lot of money at that time) for traveling expenses. In Washington, he was briefed on the policies of the various Latin American countries and about the revolutionary activities and shortcomings of Fidel Castro's regime in Cuba. Evidently, the CIA wanted to ensure that his outlook on Latin American affairs conformed with the agency's.

After Arguedas became minister of internal affairs, his relations with the CIA assumed a totally different character. According to Arguedas, under the threat of blackmail, it forced him to carry out a variety of activities that served its interests. Through him, he claimed, the CIA took control of the most important operations in his ministry—in particular the state intelligence service. This in turn allowed the CIA to infiltrate agents into many of Bolivia's political parties and to control the information presented to the president and the cabinet on matters of internal security. Naturally, this arrangement also gave the CIA access to all of Bolivia's state secrets.

Arguedas also revealed that the CIA gave him money to corrupt various Bolivian leaders. He told the press of an instance in which the CIA gave him $2,500 to obtain information from an important union leader about the contacts he had made on a recent trip to China and various other socialist countries. On that particular occasion, the individual concerned refused to be bought. However, Arguedas made it clear that a good many other individuals were compromised in this manner. Arguedas also claimed that the CIA had charged him with the task of destroying the reputation of the codirector of Bolivia's best and most independent newspaper, *Presencia*. The newspaperman in question (one of my most important informants) had organized a civic group to carry out a campaign of community development in the rural areas. Because the newspaperman was one of the most prominent critics of the Barrientos government, this greatly alarmed the head of the CIA in Bolivia, and he gave Arguedas money to employ people to paint on the walls around La Paz signs that gave the impression that the newspaperman was organizing his own political party instead of a civic group. The CIA also gave Arguedas money to further discredit the newspaperman by involving him in *"un escandalo de faldas"* (a scandal of skirts).

According to Arguedas, during the time he was in office, the CIA intervened extensively in Bolivian affairs. It spread information that undermined the government's attempts to negotiate credit in France. It recruited agents from, and infiltrated, nearly all of the major political parties and government agencies in the country. It also gave assistance to the military and political careers of those persons whom it was interested in advancing. Moreover, as was previously mentioned, the head of the CIA mission in Bolivia asked Arguedas to give Juan Lechín (the outlawed popular leader of the Trotskyist Revolutionary Party of the Nationalist Left) a passport under a false name so that he could leave the country and travel abroad. Although Arguedas did not say why the CIA wanted Lechín to leave the country, it clearly did want him out of the country.

Because Lechín was an enemy of the Barrientos regime and a wanted man, Arguedas refused to give the CIA the passport. His obstinacy created friction between him and the CIA chief, which increased as time went by. Apparently, his relations with the CIA were further estranged when, under his orders, the Bolivian police broke up an underground spy network that they thought was being run by the pro-Chinese Communists in Bolivia. Following the announcement by Arguedas that the government had uncovered a pro-Chinese spy network, he was angrily informed by Hugo Murray, the CIA agent who worked most closely with him, that the network actually belonged to the CIA. The CIA, not content with controlling the Bolivian intelligence apparatus, had organized its own intelligence network under the camouflage that it was a pro-Chinese operation.

According to Arguedas, when Che's guerrillas were discovered in the southeast of Bolivia, the head of the CIA mission in Bolivia called Arguedas and informed him that he was sending him some "advisers." The CIA chief told him that their presence was required because of the ineffectiveness of Bolivia's security agents. A few days later, four Cuban exiles arrived and assumed "advisory" positions in Arguedas's ministry. Within a short time, the Bolivian officials in the ministry began to refer to these Cubans as *gusanos* (worms), the derogatory name commonly used in Cuba to refer to the exiled opponents of the revolutionary regime.

Arguedas claimed that one of these *gusanos*, who went by the name of Gabriel Garcia Garcia (Julio Garcia), proceeded to operate completely on his own. Without consulting Arguedas, he set up two houses of interrogation where Bolivians suspected of working with the guerrillas were brought for questioning. Arguedas did not find out about this until he received reports that Bolivian citizens were being interrogated and in some cases tortured by foreign agents at both places. He became furious and notified the CIA that he would not permit this sort of thing to continue.

According to Arguedas, the situation grew worse a few months later, when the CIA asked him to influence the outcome of a lawsuit brought against a U.S. mining company by the state-owned Bolivian Mining Corporation. Arguedas claims the CIA told him it was necessary, in order to guarantee private initiative in Bolivia, that the court decide in favor of the U.S. mining firm. However, it seems that Arguedas had received specific instructions from the president to ensure that the court's decision was correct. As a result, Arguedas informed the public prosecutor that if any irregularities occurred in the suit against the U.S. firm, he would bring charges against the prosecutor before the Supreme Court. In the end, the court's decision went against the U.S. company.

According to Arguedas, this incident indicated to the CIA that he was escaping from its control.

The event that led to Arguedas's deciding to turn against the CIA occurred on June 13, 1968, when Arguedas was celebrating his birthday. Arguedas said that he received a call from the head of the CIA mission in Bolivia, who told him to come to his house so that he could congratulate him. This offended Arguedas; he considered the call an affront and did not go to the house of the CIA chief. However, the next day, one of the CIA agents came to Arguedas and told him that his chief was upset that Arguedas had failed to visit him. He said that his superior had a present for Arguedas sent from the United States and that he should go to receive it. Reluctantly, Arguedas decided to go in order to avoid any more friction with the Americans.

Arguedas received the present, chatted for a while with his host, and then returned to the ministry, where he opened the package. It contained a pistol, a belt and holster, and three photographs. One of the photographs was of Fidel Castro, the second was of Che Guevara, and the third was a photograph of Raúl Castro receiving ammunition from a Cuban guerrilla. Arguedas interpreted these items as a threat. He believed this was the CIA's way of telling him that it considered him to be a Castroite and that he had better watch his step.

This "gift" infuriated Arguedas, and in the heat of the moment he resolved to take vengeance against the CIA. He initially claimed that he had sent Che's diary to Cuba because under the glass top on his desk was a European address that had been found on one of the guerrillas killed in La Higuera. This address had been used by them as a terminus from which communications could be sent to Cuba. Arguedas claimed that he wrote this address on a large manila envelope and placed inside a set of photographic copies of Che's diary (made by the CIA agent Félix Rodríguez) that the CIA gave him. He said that he inserted a brief note to Fidel Castro in the envelope saying that he was a friend of the Cuban revolution and that he was sending him copies of Che Guevara's diary as a present. He told Fidel, he said, that he could publish the diary whenever he pleased and that he did not want any financial compensation.

Many years later, in a book about Arguedas (Cuevas Ramírez 2000), the author quotes what Arguedas said were his reasons for giving his copies of Che's diary to a friend, Víctor Zannier, a Bolivian lawyer and journalist, to arrange for it to be given to Fidel Castro as a gift from Arguedas. In this book, he is quoted as saying he gave the diary to Fidel because he "was bored in his position in the ministry and under pressure from his family because his wife did not want him to work in the ministry and she and his son who was in high school at the time were both openly in favor of the guerrillas." In addition, Arguedas said, "I was disillusioned by the extensive corruption I saw in the government: the Minister of Public Works was robbing the money for roads, the Director of Road Services was making money from construction contracts, the Ministry of the Economy was making scandalous deals selling wheat and so on, all of which made me absolutely uncomfortable, and to this was added the campaign that the Americans had initiated against me."

Arguedas's friend Zannier contacted the Chilean journalist Hernán Uribe to ask for his help in getting the diary to Fidel Castro in Cuba. Out of this contact emerged what became known as Operación Tía Victoria (Operation Aunt Victoria), which involved various journalists and lawyers who were tied to the Chilean leftist periodical *Punto Final*. Members of this group met with Zannier and afterward communicated with their contacts in Cuba.

Once they had done this, Zannier took the copies of Che's diary given to him by Arguedas to Chile, and from there it was transported to Havana by a Chilean journalist named Mario Díaz. On June 29, 1968, the Cuban newspaper *Granma* announced on its front page that the Instituto del Libro (the Book Institute) was preparing Che's Bolivian diary for publication and that it would be distributed the following Monday. *Granma* indicated a number of publishing houses in Latin America and Europe that were also in the process of preparing the diary for immediate distribution in French, English, Spanish, and other languages. In Chile, *Punto Final* published the diary as a special issue. In the prologue of this first published version of Che's Bolivian diary, Fidel Castro wrote, "From a revolutionary point of view there is no other alternative than to publish Che's diary and with regard to how it was possible to obtain it I simply say that one day this will be known."

After he arranged for the diary to be sent to Fidel Castro, Arguedas informed President Barrientos of the disturbing present he had received from the CIA chief. He asked Barrientos to relieve him of his duties in order to avoid any further difficulties with the Americans. However, Barrientos refused to accept Arguedas's resignation and promised to look into the matter personally. The following day, Arguedas called the head of the CIA mission and demanded an explanation about the photographs and the other items he had been given. On the phone, the CIA chief told him that it was all a "joke." The pistol was intended as a present, and the photographs were meant to be used as targets.

A little over two weeks after Arguedas had sent off his copy of Che's diary to Fidel Castro, the photographer who had been employed by Arguedas many months earlier to make a photographic copy of the diary came to him and said that he knew Arguedas was the one who had given Castro a copy of Che's diary.

The photographer had just seen the Cuban edition of Che's diary, which contained photographs of several pages of the diary, and he had recognized these photographs as the copies of the ones he had made for Arguedas.

Later the same day, Arguedas received an urgent telephone call from the CIA agent named Garcia Garcia, who said that he had some very important information to give Arguedas and told him to meet him immediately at a certain bridge in La Paz. However, Arguedas was suspicious. He concluded that the CIA had discovered he had given Castro a copy of Che's diary, and that it was now intent upon having him gunned down in the streets and then placing the blame on leftist terrorists or one of the opposition parties. Since he had no intention of dying this way, he did the only thing left for him to do—he fled the country.

Arguedas escaped to Chile with the help of his brother by driving a jeep overland across the altiplano to the Chilean border. There he asked the Chilean authorities for political asylum (Chile and Bolivia did not have diplomatic relations at the time) and informed them that the CIA was intent upon eliminating him. The Chilean police immediately placed Arguedas under guard and took him to Santiago. However, much to Arguedas's surprise, he discovered that the Chilean police and the CIA were working hand in hand.

In Santiago, he was questioned by a Chilean police official named Señor Zuñiga and a CIA agent named Nicolas Leondiris (one of the agents who had interrogated Arguedas in Lima four years earlier). According to Arguedas, Zuñiga told him that no one would believe his story about the CIA and that he could make a sizable fortune if he publicly accused General Ovando of having sold Che's diary to Cuba. Zuñiga also told Arguedas that there had been a coup d'état in Bolivia and that the new president was General Marcos Vasquez. (It is interesting that about a month later General Vasquez did make an unsuccessful attempt to seize power from Barrientos.) Unless Arguedas denounced Ovando, Zuñiga assured him, they would turn him over to General Vasquez, who would surely have him shot. However, Arguedas refused to believe that a coup d'état had taken place in Bolivia, and he refused to denounce anyone. He told Zuñiga and Leondiris that he was determined to follow Che Guevara's example and live by the truth.

Leondiris then told Arguedas that if he went ahead with his plans to expose the CIA's activities in Bolivia, the CIA would in fact engineer a coup d'état in Bolivia and see that his house and family were attacked. These threats frightened Arguedas, but he still refused to slander any of the Bolivian leaders. Instead, according to Arguedas, he made a deal with the CIA. In return for not exposing the CIA's activities in Bolivia, Arguedas exacted a guarantee from Leondiris that the CIA would take no action against his family or the Bolivian government. Arguedas also demanded that the CIA withdraw from Bolivia all of its agents, as well as the U.S. advisory personnel in the various ministries of the Bolivian government.

According to Arguedas, the CIA agents never had any intention of carrying out their end of the bargain, and he knew it. They were merely playing along with him until they could either buy him off, discredit him, or eliminate him. On the other hand, he said he was playing for time and the opportunity to return to Bolivia. As for the Chileans, they wanted Arguedas to leave Chile as soon as possible.

Zuñiga told Arguedas that Chile needed U.S. aid and that the Chilean government was afraid to permit him to stay in Chile because he might explode at any moment and publicly accuse the

United States of all kinds of barbarities, thereby placing Chile in an embarrassing position vis-à-vis the U.S. government. As a result, both Zuñiga and Leondiris suggested to Arguedas that he go to Cuba or France. Arguedas, however, knew that if he went to either of these countries, whatever he might later say about the CIA could easily be dismissed as anti-American propaganda. Therefore, he insisted on going to New York and finally got Leondiris to obtain a visa for him. Arguedas assumed that New York would be the safest place for him to go because he thought the CIA would not dare assassinate him in the United States. Leondiris, on the other hand, made arrangements for himself and Arguedas to fly to New York via London, probably in the hope of persuading Arguedas to go from London to either France or Cuba.

Arguedas reached London escorted by Leondiris and a Chilean police agent named Oscar Pizarro. At the London airport, they were isolated from the waiting reporters and television cameras and kept incommunicado for several hours by the British immigration authorities. According to Arguedas, he asked Leondiris why they were being detained and why, if their agreement was to go to New York, they could not simply take the next flight to New York. At this point, Arguedas claims, Leondiris told him that even the CIA had its problems. A short time later, a British official handed Arguedas a note in Spanish stating that he had entered the country illegally and could stay for only three days. Then his passport was stamped, and he and his two escorts were led to a taxi waiting outside. The taxi took the three of them to the Apollo Hotel, where they registered under their middle names rather than their surnames. Arguedas could not speak English and was completely disoriented. He knew something was up and decided to play the situation by ear. It was not long before Leondiris again approached him about going to France. He refused, fearing that he would have difficulty returning to Bolivia once he was in France, and insisted that they take him to New York as originally planned. Meanwhile, there was increasing pressure in the British House of Commons for Arguedas to be brought out of hiding and allowed to speak to the press.

Leondiris was afraid Arguedas might tell the British press and the public about the CIA's activities in Bolivia, in spite of the threats he had made earlier to keep Arguedas from talking in Chile. With both the British Foreign Office and the Cuban embassy demanding to speak with Arguedas, Leondiris insisted that Arguedas give him proof that he could be trusted not to break their earlier agreement. Because Arguedas wanted to return to Bolivia, he gave Leondiris his assurances that he would carry out his end of the bargain. As proof of his good intentions, he told Leondiris where he had hidden a complete account of Che's death given to him by Sergeant Mario Terán, the soldier who had killed Che. Once this was verified, Leondiris allowed Arguedas to speak by phone with the British Foreign Office and the Cuban and Bolivian embassies. To all three, Arguedas made it clear that he was irrevocably determined to return to Bolivia immediately in order to stand trial for his actions.

Although Arguedas wanted to return to Bolivia directly from London, he claims the CIA prevailed upon him to go to New York first. Apparently, the CIA still believed it could persuade Arguedas to give up his plan to return to Bolivia. According to Arguedas, he encouraged the CIA in this hope in order to keep it from taking drastic action against him. It is not clear what took place once Arguedas reached New York. He spent several days there and then managed to board a flight to Lima, Peru.

Evidently, he deceived the CIA into believing he was going to stay in Lima or it would never have allowed him to go there. On the other hand, perhaps by this time the CIA was no longer that worried about what he might say. It had by now withdrawn its advisers from the Bolivian Ministry of Internal Affairs and replaced all the CIA personnel in Bolivia known to Arguedas. Moreover, it had successfully planted a considerable amount of information in the Bolivian and Latin American press that depicted Arguedas as either a traitor or a madman. Thus, the CIA probably assumed that anything Arguedas might say about its activities in Bolivia would be rejected by the general public as the lies of a disreputable politician. At any rate, Arguedas managed to reach Lima, and much to everyone's surprise he proceeded with his announced intention to return to Bolivia.

When Arguedas reached Lima, he says, he discovered for the first time what the CIA had been doing to blacken his image since his departure from Bolivia a month earlier. He found that the Latin American press was presenting him as an incoherent, half-crazy politician who had received a large sum of money from the Cuban government for Che's diary. Arguedas also learned from reading some Bolivian newspapers that the CIA had not fulfilled its part of the agreement. That is, he discovered that there had not been any withdrawal of the many U.S. advisory personnel in the various ministries of the Bolivian government. At this point, Arguedas apparently called a CIA contact in Lima and told him that because the CIA had not fulfilled its agreement with him, he felt free to expose publicly its activities in his country. He then informed the Bolivian embassy and the press that he was returning to La Paz within the next few days. From this point on, Arguedas was under constant guard by the Peruvian police and was followed everywhere he went by a growing throng of reporters.

Shortly before his departure from Lima, Arguedas held a press conference in which he denied having received any compensation for sending Che's diary to the Cubans. He also denounced the CIA. He said that he had kept quiet until this point because he had made an agreement with the CIA in which it was to leave his country in return for his silence. He said that he had also demanded that all the U.S. advisory personnel in Bolivia be withdrawn and that, in the future, if the Americans wanted to aid the Bolivian government, they should do so on a government-to-government basis. Since the CIA had failed to comply with these conditions, Arguedas told the reporters that he was determined to return to Bolivia and tell the truth about the CIA's involvement in Bolivian affairs.

When he arrived in Bolivia, Arguedas further elaborated on his reasons for returning home. He told the press that he had returned in order to clear his conscience and face the consequences of his past actions. His exact words to the Bolivian press were these:

I am not looking for publicity. I only want to tell the truth about everything that occurred in my career as a subsecretary and minister of government, and alert not only the present government of Bolivia, but all the governments of Latin America, as to how North American imperialism undermines their intelligence services in order to introduce errors, to distort, to present a completely different picture of reality, to obstruct their economic relations with other states, and finally to keep them under its control.

He said he had returned in order to regain his personal dignity by telling the truth at the moment when it was most appropriate to do so. In this regard, he reminded the reporters that he had been the favorite of both the Americans and the most reactionary political elements in Bolivia prior to his sending Che's diary to Fidel Castro, and that he had given up a promising political career because of his disgust over the way in which American political and economic interests had undermined Bolivia's national sovereignty.

At the press conference following his return to Bolivia, Arguedas refuted the suggestion that he had given a copy of Che's diary to Castro because he was a Castroite or because he was a Communist. He denied being either a Castroite or a Communist and declared that he was a nationalist first and a Marxist second. With regard to the accusation that he had received a large sum of money for the diary, Arguedas angrily retorted that this was another of the CIA's insidious attempts to discredit him by slander. He argued that if it had been money he was after, it would have been unnecessary for him to sell Che's diary to the Cubans. He pointed out that as minister of internal affairs he could have made a fortune in bribes from the Americans if he had wanted to do so. He said he had documents hidden outside the country that proved, among other things, that a U.S. engineering firm (which he named) had offered him a bribe of $1.5 million to see to it that it was awarded a government contract for the construction of two new highways. In other words, he argued that he had rejected bribes of much greater amounts than the $500,000 it was rumored he had received from the Cubans for the diary.

Asked whether he was not afraid that the CIA would have him assassinated, Arguedas answered that if the CIA wanted to send some "patriot" to shoot him in his cell, it was welcome to do it. However, he said that he expected it to continue its efforts to discredit him, and that there was nothing that could be done to stop the machinery it had set in motion to do this. In support of this assertion, he recounted how he had planted an article for the CIA in the Bolivian press that falsely reported that Tania had been a Soviet spy operating under orders to sabotage Che's guerrilla operation. He predicted that articles slandering him would continue to appear in the Latin American press. Nevertheless, he said that he was content with having told the truth even if no one believed him.

Arguedas expressed the opinion that among nearly all the political groups in Bolivia there was a growing awareness of the insidious role being played by the United States in the political and economic life of the country. Moreover, the disgrace of Bolivia's dependence upon the United States was contributing to increasing anti-American feeling, he said, and the moment would come when the national conscience would no longer tolerate U.S. interference in Bolivia's internal affairs. In fact, Latin America would turn into another Vietnam if the United States continued to manipulate the governments, officials, and institutions of the Latin American countries in accordance with its own selfish interests.

Several times during his discussions with the press, Arguedas expressed his faith in the young leaders of Bolivia's small Christian Democratic Party, whom he characterized as the hope of the country. He exhorted all Bolivians to listen to these young leaders and to unite behind them in defending Bolivia's national dignity and sovereignty. However, he made it quite clear that he was opposed to a forcible overthrow of the current regime. He added that coups lend themselves to CIA manipulation and that the group that brings off a coup usually ends up being more dependent upon the CIA than its predecessor. For this reason, the only alternative was a general election administered by an impartial and autonomous commission composed of honest and respected civic leaders, but even this was no guarantee against CIA interference. Arguedas said that the CIA had manipulated many elections in Latin America and that several CIA agents had even bragged to him about the CIA's influence over the national elections in the United States itself.

The Arguedas affair was one consequence of Che's guerrilla operation that Che himself could never have foreseen. Arguedas's actions shook the Barrientos regime to the core, whereas Che's guerrilla activities, at least before the Arguedas affair, had the effect of strengthening the Barrientos regime and the Bolivian military. By calling into question the integrity of the government and the armed forces, Arguedas's actions weakened the Barrientos regime and the public's confidence in the existing political system. Moreover, Arguedas's return to Bolivia and his revelations about the nature of the CIA's interference in Bolivian affairs called into question the role of the United States in that country. In fact, the Arguedas affair provides shocking evidence of the U.S. government's involvement in the domestic affairs of the Latin America countries.

The significance of Arguedas's statements about the CIA's involvement in Bolivia and Latin America has to be comprehended in terms of the U.S. government's professed foreign policy goals of advancing democracy and democratic ideals throughout the world. If what Arguedas said was true—and most informed Bolivians believed much, if not all, of what he said in 1968—then the U.S. government was not contributing to the advancing of democracy Bolivia, and there was sufficient justification for labeling the United States an imperialist power. However, the sordid picture that Arguedas gave of the CIA's mafia-like intimidation, blackmail, and subversion of high officials in supposedly friendly governments is not one the average U.S. citizen wants to believe. To do so would require facing up to the fact that the United States is not the great and noble force in the world that it claims it to be.

Following his press conference in the Ministry of Internal Affairs the day of his return to Bolivia, Arguedas was placed in strict confinement and not allowed to make any further statements to the press. However, within a few months he was released from prison, thanks to the Bolivian high court's decision that it did not have the authority to try him. According to the high court, the Bolivian legislature was the only body competent to try a former minister of state for acts of treason committed while in office. The court's decision released Arguedas from prison, pending action by the legislature.

He kept a low profile after his release, but within a short time several attempts were made on his life. Twice bombs were thrown at him, and on June 6, 1969, he and a Spanish journalist accompanying him were machine-gunned while walking on the street in La Paz. Both Arguedas and the journalist escaped with minor wounds. However, Arguedas was hospitalized for almost a month, and following his release from the hospital, he immediately sought asylum in the Mexican embassy.

In a statement to the press at the time, he explained that his intentions were to leave Bolivia and go to Mexico. He said that he had decided to leave Bolivia because of the increasing political instability in the country following the death of President Barrientos (who was mysteriously killed in the crash of his personal helicopter), and because of the recent attempts upon his life. He gave as an additional reason the failure of the government to take any action whatsoever against the agents of U.S. imperialism who were at work undermining Bolivia's national sovereignty.

During this time, Arguedas was the author of yet another incredible episode. He secretly arranged for a glass container with Che's hands in a formaldehyde solution and a plaster mask of his face (made in Vallegrande) to be sent to Cuba much as he had arranged for the copies of Che's diary to be sent there. In this case, though, the existence and transfer of these items to Cuba were not discovered until many years later. In fact, to this day, the story of Che's hands and his death mask is not widely known.

The odyssey of these two items is more complex and more difficult to follow than the story of Che's diary. The man who cut off Che's hands and made his death mask out of plaster was Roberto "Toto" Quintanilla, an official in Arguedas's Ministry of Internal Affairs. Like many of the other figures associated with Che's death, he was killed under unusual circumstances in November 1970. An unknown woman gunned him down with an automatic weapon in his office in Hamburg, Germany, where he was serving as the Bolivian consul. Nothing more is known about him than this. According to Arguedas, Che's hands and his death mask were given to him by General Ovando after they had been inspected by the team of Argentine criminal investigators who were sent to Bolivia to verify Che's fingerprints.

Ovando instructed Arguedas to dispose of both items immediately and to leave no traces of them. However, he chose to ignore Ovando's orders and gave them for safekeeping to a close friend named Jorge Suarez, a Bolivian writer and the editor of the daily newspaper *Jornada*. In a little-known interview that Suarez gave the Argentine journalist Uki Goñi in 1995, he claimed that Arguedas asked him to come to his office seven or eight days after Che's death. Arguedas told him he wanted to discuss something very personal and urgent. When Suarez went to his office, Arguedas produced a glass container and a translucent bag the contents of which Suarez could not at first see clearly. After Arguedas motioned for him to come closer and examine the two objects, Suarez saw two hands floating in the glass container and a white plaster mask in the bag. As he studied the mask closely, he saw that it was an extraordinarily good replica of Che's face with his eyes open. He could even see the details of his beard. It did not appear to be the face of someone dead, rather of someone very much alive. Suarez told Goñi he would never forget that face (Goñi 1995).

Arguedas explained to Suarez that General Ovando had given him strict instructions to incinerate the hands and the mask and then scatter the ashes in a river, but that he had decided not to follow these orders. He asked Suarez to take the items with him and hide them in his home. Although he was shocked and frightened, Suarez agreed to do so. According to Suarez, Arguedas said that he was an "admirer" of Che and that the top levels of the military and the U.S. embassy as well as certain other influential people did not trust him. In fact, the U.S. embassy suspected him of being a revolutionary and a possible contact for the guerrillas. By not destroying the death mask and Che's hands, he was running the risk of losing his life. Suarez considered this decision by Arguedas, regardless of what opinion one might have of him, to be an extremely courageous decision.

Suarez made a sort of sarcophagus or stone coffin for the items under the floor of his bedroom and hid them there. Although his house was searched several times by the Bolivian secret police while Arguedas was in prison, Che's hands and death mask were not discovered. They stayed under the floor in his bedroom until Suarez had to leave Bolivia in 1969, as the new ambassador to Mexico appointed by the military government of none other than General Ovando. Suarez told Goñi (1995) that the Bolivian intelligence services and the CIA concluded afterward that he had probably carried Che's hands and death mask out of the country in his diplomatic pouch, so they stopped looking for them. However, he left them hidden in the floor of his bedroom.

At the time, Arguedas had sought exile in the Mexican embassy and was staying there until he could get out of the country. When he learned that Suarez had left the country for Mexico, he asked his journalist friend Víctor Zannier in July 1969 to arrange for the two items to be sent to Cuba. Zannier in turn delegated the mission to Jorge Sattori and Juan Coronel. Although they were members of the pro-Moscow Bolivian Community Party, Zannier felt they could be trusted and could use the party's international connections to get out of the country and travel to Cuba. Coronel kept the glass container with Che's hands and the bag with his death mask wrapped up in old newspapers under his bed for five months while he and Sattori made their arrangements to leave the country and go to Cuba by way of Europe and the Soviet Union.

According to Coronel, the glass container was cylindrical, about 25 centimeters high and 18 centimeters in diameter, and was sealed with red wax. Inside were two hands floating in a brownish liquid. They appeared to be robust, and to have belonged to someone who had been quite strong. Coronel said they were covered in a beautiful film (most likely the ink used to record Che's fingerprints), seemingly amputated from Che's wrists with an inadequate instrument that left the cut in a very irregular manner just before the wrists. Coronel's description of the way the hands were amputated matches exactly the shocking close-up photographs of Che's hands that were taken by the Argentine criminal investigators sent to Bolivia to prove that the Bolivian military had indeed captured and killed the famous Che Guevara. Their story and their photos were not released until years later (De Carlos 2006). In their photographs, Che's hands are seen palms up on a newspaper page with the curled fingers covered in ink and the ink bottle and pad near the edge of the page. Coronel said he was struck by how much the death mask revealed Che's features. According to

Coronel, both the hands and the mask left a tremendous impression on Sattori and him.

Coronel left Bolivia by himself at the end of December 1969 for Santiago, Chile, and flew from there to Madrid. He took only one small carry-on bag, which contained Che's hands and death mask along with a few items of Coronel's clothing (De Carlos 2006). In Madrid, he changed planes for Paris, where he took another flight to Budapest. His bag was not inspected by customs officials at any of these stops. From Hungary, which had a pro-Soviet regime at the time, he flew to Moscow. In Moscow, he met Víctor Zannier, who had flown there by another route, as originally planned. Zannier and Coronel went to the Cuban embassy to make the arrangements for their trip to Havana. The embassy officials heard their story and told Coronel and Zannier they would have to consult with their superiors in the Ministry of Foreign Affairs in Havana before they could give the two Bolivians visas and arrange for their travel to Cuba.

Later that same day, the embassy informed Zannier that the foreign ministry in Havana had authorized Zannier, but not Coronel, to travel to Cuba. According to Coronel (De Carlos 2006), the Cuban authorities refused to allow him to travel to Cuba because he was a militant of the Bolivian Communist Party, which they accused of having betrayed Che Guevara. Coronel was astonished that he had been denied a visa, especially after the difficult voyage he had made and the risks he had taken.

In a 2006 interview with the journalist Carmen De Carlos, Coronel said he didn't know what to do. He had brought Che's hands and death mask with him because the Bolivian Communist Party had charged him with delivering them to Havana. Although offended by the Cuban government's refusal to grant him a visa to travel to Havana, he didn't feel he had the right to keep Che's hands and mask from reaching Cuba, where Che was loved so much. He therefore gave them to Zannier, and they left with Zannier and a Cuban diplomat on a flight for Havana on January 5, 1970. As far as Coronel knows, Zannier and the Cuban diplomate delivered these invaluable objects to President Fidel Castro upon their arrival in Cuba.

The Mexican embassy arranged for Arguedas to leave Bolivia and go to Mexico in 1969, where I met him briefly at a conference in Cuernavaca. He appeared to be quite happy in Mexico. Still, he left Mexico to live in Cuba, where he was celebrated for his actions (Anderson 1997, 745) and lived for nine years. While in Havana, he was visited several times by Antonio Peredo (Estellano 2000), the oldest brother of Coco, Inti, and Chato. Antonio Peredo is a well-known Bolivian journalist, political activist, and university professor. (He was elected to the Bolivian parliament in 2006 and chosen to lead the parliamentary delegation of the Movimiento al Socialismo—the Movement toward Socialism, or MAS, which is the party of President Evo Morales.) According to Peredo, Arguedas lived a very disciplined and studious existence while in Cuba and regularly spent ten-hour days doing research in libraries.

In 1979, Arguedas returned to Bolivia and disappeared from public view for a while. In the mid-1980s, however, he was accused of being involved in an armed group that kidnapped a wealthy businessman. Although his involvement in this affair was never proven conclusively, he remained in prison from 1986 to 1989. After his release, he dropped out of sight again and did not surface until 1997, the year that the search for Che's body reached a climax and became a highly publicized international effort. During this period, the media and some of the people involved in the search for Che's remains tried to locate Arguedas to see whether he could tell them where Che's body was buried. But the police found Arguedas first and arrested him for allegedly leading a gang that was planning to kidnap businessmen in order to extract ransom money from their families and business associates. Released by the police while awaiting trial, he immediately went into hiding. When he failed to appear in court on the date of his trial, he was declared a fugitive from justice.

During this time, he told Antonio Peredo that he had in his possession the names of everyone involved in the drug trade in Bolivia and that many people knew this. For this reason, he told Peredo, "I'm a dangerous man" (Estellano 2000). He made these declarations a few months after the Bolivian police had launched a campaign to find him. The police were trying to link him to a series of bombings in La Paz that had not caused any serious damage but had created a great deal of concern. They arrested three men who they said belonged to a terrorist group led by Arguedas, but they were unable to present any serious proof that he was involved in this group. Although still in hiding at this point, he told Marcos Domic, the head of the Communist Party of Bolivia, that he was writing his memoirs. Paradoxically, Domic was the target of two of the bombings that the police attributed to Arguedas. Arguedas knew Marcos Domic and Antonio Peredo well since the three of them had joined the Bolivian Communist Party as young men in 1951.

Since the 1980s, Arguedas had dedicated himself to compiling information on the structure and functioning of the mafias involved in the Bolivian drug trade. His was the most complete archive on this subject in the country. As a result, he and his assistants were invited to create the Consejo Nacional de Lucha contra el Narcotráfico (the National Council of Struggle against the Drug Trade, or CONALID) by none other than President Víctor

Paz Estenssoro, following his fourth election to the presidency, in 1985 (some twenty years after he and his MNR government had been overthrown by the military under the command of General Alfredo Ovando and René Barrientos, Paz's vice president at the time). Thus, in a strange twist of fate, in 1985 Antonio Arguedas, Barrientos's former right-hand man, agreed to work for the newly elected Paz Estenssoro in his fourth term in office. Moreover, he worked as head of CONALID without pay or consulting fees and in close association with the U.S. embassy in La Paz.

Arguedas and his team at CONALID reportedly discovered that a diverse array of political and business leaders, most of whom moved in the highest circles of power, were secretly involved in the international drug trade. He was deeply engaged in this project when he tried in 1986 to expose what he called the "Lebanese Connection," a drug ring consisting of several mafia families that had made their fortunes in the Bolivian cocaine trade. For the purpose of publicly exposing this drug ring, he appears to have organized the kidnapping of Antonio Curi Curi, a Bolivian businessman of Lebanese ancestry. The plan backfired, and on May 23, 1986, Arguedas was arrested for kidnapping Curi Curi. Although he was not convicted, he was kept in prison for three years. After he was released on October 16, 1989, he dedicated himself to various public activities as a practicing lawyer. Nevertheless, according to what he told Antonio Peredo during these years (Estellano 2000), he offered to give the names of the principal figures engaged in the drug trade to anyone who would deliver these individuals to the U.S. judicial system. Apparently, he had no confidence in the Bolivian legal system but felt that the U.S. drug enforcement authorities would prosecute and punish the people involved.

In 1997, as has already been mentioned, he was accused of being implicated in another kidnapping ring, which the police characterized as a criminal action designed purely to obtain ransom money. Arguedas was arrested, released while waiting trial, and then allowed to disappear. Between November 20 and December 16, 1999, there were six bombings in random locations around La Paz that made no sense and were never explained by the police. The police accused Antonio Arguedas of being responsible for the bombings, which claimed the lives of several people. He did not turn himself in to the authorities and remained in hiding.

His name did not surface again in Bolivia until February 2000. The police reported that he was killed in La Paz when a bomb he was carrying exploded. The police said he belonged to a right-wing group called C-4, which had declared war against Castroism, drugs, and corruption in Bolivia. Arguedas's family members and local political observers expressed serious doubts about the police account of his death (Estellano 2000). It remains unclear whether his death was accidental or intentional. One newspaper account suggested that the police's explanation of Arguedas's death provided an ironic metaphor for his zigzagging political life. According to this account, Arguedas was killed by the bomb he was carrying because he made a fatal mistake: instead of moving the detonator on the bomb to the right to start the timer, he moved it to the contact point on the left, and the bomb instantly blew up in his hands (Clarin.com 2000). There is no hard evidence that he in fact did blow himself up, and it is more likely he was murdered. We may never know the true story of his death.

Chapter 16

CHE BECOMES AN ICON OF POPULAR CULTURE

If we want a model of a person that does not belong to our time but to the future, I say from the depths of my heart that such a model, without a single stain on his conduct, on his actions, or his behavior, is Che!

—Fidel Castro, public tribute to Che
following his death (1967)

For years after his death, posters displaying Che's portrait and the slogan "Che lives" appeared in almost every major city in the world. The Che on these posters and placards was a heroic figure, with the unmistakable beard, beret, and piercing eyes that have come to be associated with this legendary revolutionary. In many of these mass-produced portraits of Che, the face that peers out from them somehow seems to combine in one human countenance all the races of mankind. His eyes and mustache appear Asiatic, while the darkness of his complexion seems Negroid, and the shape of his nose and cheeks are distinctively European. Perhaps this partially explains why he has become an icon for radical political activists, guerrillas, rebels, students, and intellectuals in every continent, and why, for example, his face is often the only "white" one to appear alongside those of nonwhite revolutionary heroes in Africa, Asia, and Latin America.

In the forty years that have passed since his death, Che has become a revolutionary hero and a symbol of rebellion on a worldwide scale. In a sense, his romantic image and revolutionary example have taken on an almost mystical quality. The reasons for this are of considerable importance, for they tell us a great deal about the global significance of Che's legacy.

In the late 1960s and throughout the 1970s, leftist students and revolutionary movements around the world constantly quoted Che's famous dictum "The duty of every revolutionary is to make the revolution." They believed, as did Che, that revolutions are made by people who are willing to act, not by those who are waiting for the appropriate "objective conditions" or for orders from the Soviet Union or China. It is interesting in this regard to note that the official Communist press in the Soviet Union, Eastern Europe, and the People's Republic of China often referred to the young leftists in these radical student and political movements as "Guevarist hippies" and "left-wing adventurers." However, such attacks were of little importance to these movements, since they regarded Guevara's activist revolutionary ideas as an alternative to the overly dogmatic and bureaucratic party lines of the more orthodox Communists who were in power in the Soviet Union and China, and to the tepid reformism of the moderate socialist and social democratic parties in Western Europe and elsewhere.

Because of his undaunted and fiercely independent revolutionary idealism, Che became the idol of the New Left in the United States and Great Britain, the bulwarks of capitalism and bourgeois democracy. For a time, students at the London School of Economics and Political Science, one of the most hallowed of Britain's institutions of higher education, greeted each other with the salutation "Che." In the United States, buttons, shirts, placards, and posters with Che's face were present at nearly every antiwar demonstration during the Vietnam War years. In Latin America, where Che gave his life fighting for ideals, his name became a battle cry among leftist students, intellectuals, and workers during the 1970s and 1980s. His death at the hands of the Bolivian army made him an instant martyr for all those who were opposed to the ruling elites and the glaring social injustices that plague this troubled region of the world.

Today, many Latin Americans remember and admire him for his uncompromising revolutionary idealism, his sensitivity to the plight of Latin America's impoverished masses, the rapid world-wide fame he acquired as one of the top leaders of the Cuban government during the heady days following the Cuban revolu-tion, and his willingness to die fighting for the realization of his ideals of social justice, anti-imperialism, and socialism. Che truly belongs in the pantheon of the region's most famous revolutionary leaders—José Martí, Augusto César Sandino, Emiliano Zapata, Pancho Villa, Camilo Torres, and Fidel Castro.

In Cuba, Che holds one of the highest positions in Cuba's pan-theon of revolutionary heroes and martyrs. Less than a week after Fidel Castro acknowledged that Che had indeed been killed by the Bolivians, hundreds of thousands of Cubans silently filled Havana's Plaza de la Revolución to listen tearfully to Fidel as he told dozens of anecdotes about Che and praised his intellectual and military virtues. Backed by a huge portrait of Che and flanked by Cuban flags, the Cuban leader gave notice of the importance the Cuban regime would give in the future to Che's revolutionary example. Near the end of his tribute to his fallen comrade, Fidel said,

If we ask ourselves how we want our revolutionary fighters, our militants, and our people to be, then we must answer without any hesitation: let them be like Che! If we wish to express how we want the people of future generations to be, we must say: let them be like Che! If we ask how we desire to educate our children, we should say without hesitation: we want our children to be educated in the spirit of Che! If we want a model of person that does not belong to our time but to the future, I say from the depths of my heart that such a model, without a single stain on his conduct, on his actions, or his behavior, is Che! If we wish to express what we want our children to be, we must say from our very hearts as ardent revolutionaries: we want them to be like Che! (Deutschmann 1994, 78)

Today, the Cuban regime continues to educate the youth of the country about Che. His picture is in every Cuban school, and Cuba's schoolchildren learn by heart passages from his writings and his letters. All know the hymn "Seremos como el Che" (We will be like Che).

Several generations of Cubans also know this famous paragraph from Che's farewell letter to his children:

Grow up as good revolutionaries. Study hard so that you will have command of the techniques that permit the domination of nature. Remember that the revolution is what is most important and that each one of us, alone, is worth nothing. Above all, always remain capable of feeling deeply whatever injustice is committed against anyone in any part of the world. This is the finest quality of a revolutionary. (Deutschmann 1997, 349)

For a regime that wishes to instill a revolutionary tradition in its young, no better example could be chosen than Che. The revolutionary ideals and example of Che have become part of the social consciousness of several generations of Cubans. And he remains the Cuban model of "the twenty-first-century man."

However, Che has also become a "pop hero" in the United States and Western Europe. His image has become commercialized through the marketing of shirts, handkerchiefs, music albums, CD covers, posters, beer, ashtrays, jeans, watches, and towels imprinted with his picture and/or name. As a pop or commercialized hero figure, Che is often depicted in a sardonic or satirical manner. As a commercialized icon, he is not the heroic revolutionary figure that the Cuban leaders put forward as the model of the twenty-first-century human being. For those who admire Che as a heroic revolutionary, the use of his famous image to market products is just as denigrating as the image of Che held by his avowed enemies, who regard him as a fanatical killer and a sinister Communist renegade.

The actor, producer, and director Robert Redford made a popular film version of Che's *Motorcycle Diaries* that was shown in cinemas around the world during 2004 and 2005. The film provides a moving account of Che's journey with his friend Alberto Granado through Latin America and offers insights into the early stirrings of the twenty-three-year-old Che's social conscience. It stars the popular Mexican actor Gael García Bernal as the young Ernesto. After making the film, García Bernal reportedly said of Che, "He's a person that changed the world and he has really forced me to change who I am." Redford traveled to Havana to obtain the right to Che's motorcycle diaries from Aleida March, his widow. After the film was completed, he returned to Cuba to host a special screening of it, which was attended by Aleida, eighty-four-year-old Alberto Granado, Che's children, his former comrades, and people who had worked closely with him during the early years of the Cuban revolution. According to Redford, the film was well received by this audience, and he later said, "I could have probably died there in the seat had I not felt—when I heard people sniffing and crying and I thought, either they're so upset with me I'm not gonna get out of here, or they liked the film. And they did" (Smiley 2004).

As the popularity of this film reveals, Che remains, in one way or another, a popular figure on a worldwide scale, and for many he is a heroic figure. The phenomenon of hero worship and the process by which individuals become popular heroes has always been something of a mystery. In all times and places, there appears to be a need for heroes. In times of great change such as these, this need seems greatest. People around the globe see their societies and humanity as a whole undergoing far-reaching changes. Many are frightened about the future that these changes may bring, while others hope that it will bring significant improvements in society and their own lives. Both groups appear to need the assurance that human beings can control their fate and shape the future according to their desires. They sometimes find this assurance in the words and deeds of an exceptional individual whose courage and efforts to shape the future according to his or her ideals, even if seemingly unsuccessful, give them inspiration. This seems to be one of the reasons Che continues to be a popular hero.

Che had the courage to act in accordance with his ideals. He gave his life fighting for a better, new world that he believed he could help bring into being. It is little wonder that he is admired for this. As a Latin American priest whom I met in Bolivia said shortly after Che's death, "To pass one's life in the jungle, ill clothed and starving, with a price on his head, confronting the military power of imperialism, and on top of that, sick with asthma, exposing himself to death by suffocation if the bullets did not cut him down first, a man, who could have lived regally, with money, amusements, friends, women, and vices in any of the great cities of sin; this is heroism, true heroism, no matter how confused or wrong his ideas might have been. Not to recognize this is not only reactionary, but stupid."

Che's exceptional devotion to the realization of his ideals was truly heroic, and it would indeed be foolish not to recognize this. Those who recognize the heroism in his character and actions cannot help admiring Che, whether or not they agree with his revolutionary politics and utopian idealism. Che continues to be a hero for all those who admire and are inspired by his idealism and his exceptional courage.

Chapter 17

CHE'S LEGACY

■

Each and every one of us punctually pays his share of
sacrifice, aware of being rewarded by the satisfaction
of fulfilling our duty, aware of advancing with everyone
toward the new human being who is to be glimpsed on
the horizon. . . .
  —Che Guevara, "Socialism and Man in Cuba" (1964)

What is Che's legacy? How have his death and the
failure of his Bolivian mission affected subsequent
events and developments? Did he die in vain? There
are those on both the political left and the political right who
argue that the failure of Che's guerrilla operation in Bolivia
and the failure of similar armed revolutionary movements that
followed his death clearly indicate that all efforts to carry out
a successful armed revolution in the current era are futile—
particularly since the collapse of the Soviet Union and the much
celebrated triumph of global capitalism. They also claim that the
failure of Che's mission in Bolivia refutes his theory of revolutionary guerrilla warfare and that his death marked the beginning of
the end for revolutionary movements around the world.

We can begin to appreciate the significance of Che's legacy if we focus on the less problematic aspects of both Che's death and the failure of his mission in Bolivia. For example, Che's operation in Bolivia exposed the true nature of the pro-Soviet Communists and their role not in fomenting revolution throughout the world but in actually preventing or hindering it. It is clear from a critical analysis of the failure of Che's mission in Bolivia that for both the pro-Soviet and the pro-Chinese Communists the promotion of the interests and aims of their parties was their primary goal, and not revolution. It is also clear that the fragmentation of the left and the sectarian in-fighting between leftist factions were (and still are) major obstacles to bringing about a successful popular revolution in Latin America and elsewhere in the world. The publication of Che's Bolivian diary revealed the extent of duplicity and treachery that the leaders of leftist parties and groups were willing to employ to advance their own narrow interests.

Che's diary, along with the prologue written by Fidel Castro, unmasked the true character of the pro-Soviet Communist leaders in Bolivia. This revelation caused quite an uproar in leftist circles. For example, after the publication of Che's diary, Oscar Zamora, the leader of the pro-Chinese Communist Party in Bolivia, publicly condemned the actions of the pro-Soviet Communists. In an open letter published in both of Bolivia's leading newspapers, Zamora said, "The publication of Che's campaign diary confirms once again and definitively what our party has sustained all along, accusing, as it does, the Creole revisionists, led by Mario Monje and Jorge Kolle, of being the direct authors of the most repugnant betrayal in the history of our country's social struggle." Of course, Zamora did not mention that his party had done nothing at all to help Che and his comrades.

In Bolivia and elsewhere in Latin America, the publication

of Che's diary led to the open condemnation of the pro-Soviet Communists by more militant leftists. Thus, the Bolivian episode focused attention on the counterrevolutionary position taken by most Communists who adhered to the Soviet political line. Che's death and the publication of his diary made it clear that any group determined to bring about an armed revolution in Latin America should consider the orthodox or official Communist parties to be almost as great a threat to their effort as the repressive armed forces and police of the ruling regimes. Che's betrayal by the pro-Moscow Communists in Bolivia demonstrated that they were as interested in preventing revolutionary insurrections as the ruling elites. Subsequent events revealed that the center of orthodox communism—the Soviet Union itself—could not even maintain the pretense of being a revolutionary force in the world. And it ultimately succumbed to capitalism, as Che predicted, only a little more than two decades after his death.

Régis Debray for a time after Che's death claimed that he had the answer to the question of the significance of his death and the defeat of his guerrilla operation in Bolivia (Debray, 1975). In his book *Revolution in the Revolution?*—written shortly before Che died—he wrote that "for a revolutionary, failure is a springboard" and that "as a source of theory it is richer than victory [since] it accumulates experience and knowledge" (Debray 1967, 23). In this regard, it is important to note that the defeat of Che's operation in Bolivia led many leftists and subsequent revolutionaries to conclude that Guevara's "*foco* theory" of revolutionary warfare and Debray's early writings about the same subject were no longer valid and required significant revision. A few years later, after he was released from prison in Bolivia in 1970, Debray went to Chile, where he wrote about the "peaceful revolution" being pursued by the democratically elected socialist government of President Salvador Allende (Cooper 2003). At the time, Debray still believed that a bona fide revolutionary had to be committed to armed struggle like Che Guevara. In his lengthy interviews with Allende, Debray found it difficult to accept that Allende's Popular Unity government, which was elected because of its mass base of support, was committed to expanding democracy while pursuing a peaceful transition to socialism in Chile.

One of the most important lessons to be learned from the failure of Che's guerrilla mission in Bolivia was that an isolated guerrilla force without a mass base of support, no matter how determined and well trained the guerrillas might be, cannot survive against the armed forces of even the weakest country. Fidel Castro's revolutionary guerrilla movement could not have succeeded without the organized and widespread support of militant groups in Cuba's cities, universities, towns, and sugar plantations. The failure of Che's guerrilla operation in Bolivia clearly revealed that without political support in the urban areas and a broad base of mass support among the rural population, a revolutionary movement can only expect to be isolated and defeated.

The defeat of Che's guerrilla operation and the main flaw in Che's strategy as well as Debray's theorizing about revolutionary guerrilla warfare in his book *Revolution in the Revolution?* stem from what might be called a kind of military vanguardism. By reducing popular revolution to a special form of guerrilla warfare, Che's strategy and Debray's early writings overemphasized the military aspects of initiating a revolutionary struggle against an unjust regime. And they underemphasized the political dimension of organizing the base of popular support needed for a successful revolutionary struggle.

In fact, Debray ultimately acknowledged this important lesson in his writings following Che's death and the Chilean military's overthrow of Allende's government, while at the same time heap-ing praise upon Che and Allende for their convictions and the sac-rifices they made (Debray 1975, 135–39). Following the election in 1981 of the socialist president François Mitterrand in France, Debray became a foreign policy adviser to Mitterrand and then held various government posts until the mid-1990s. However, in his subsequent writings, Debray has ceased to be a sympathetic critic and admirer of Che and instead has harshly criticized him, Fidel Castro, and contemporary Cuba (Vilas 1996).

It is important to recognize that the ideological cornerstone of Che's revolutionary theory and practice was not guerrilla war-fare but his concept of *el hombre nuevo* (the new man), and this almost spiritual ideal of the new socialist human being of the twenty-first century was an important source of inspiration for him and for those who followed his example (Siles de Valle 1996, 47–92). Che was dedicated to living his life in accordance with his concept of the new kind of human being that would come into existence in the revolutionary struggle to build a new socialist world order for humanity. Che believed that this new type would arise out of the revolutionary struggle to liberate humanity from the egoistic individualism, dehumanizing exploitation, and social alienation of capitalism.

Che felt that the struggle against capitalism and the construc-tion of a new socialist order required a new type of human being who would be committed to making personal sacrifices for the good of others. Nowhere is this concept of *el hombre nuevo* pre-sented more explicitly than in Che's essay "Socialism and Man in Cuba," written early in 1965 while he was traveling as a Cuban statesman in Africa. What follows are some brief excerpts from this essay (taken from Gerassi 1968, 398–400):

Let me say, at the risk of appearing ridiculous, that the true revolutionary is guided by strong feelings of love. It is impossible to think of a true revolutionary without this quality. . . .

There is no life outside the revolution. In these conditions the revolutionary leaders must have a large dose of humanity, a large dose of a sense of justice and truth, to avoid falling into dogmatic extremes, into cold scholasticism, into isolation from the masses . . .

Each and every one of us punctually pays his share of sacrifice, aware of being rewarded by the satisfaction of fulfilling our duty, aware of advancing with everyone toward the new human being who is to be glimpsed on the horizon. . . . The road is long and in part unknown; we are aware of our limitations. We will make the twenty-first century human being, we ourselves!

Che's vision of *el hombre nuevo* inspired him and his comrades as well as the young Bolivian revolutionaries who followed in his footsteps a few years later.

After escaping the Bolivian military's efforts to hunt down the last survivors of Che's guerrilla force, Inti Peredo and Darío (the Bolivian whose real name was David Adriazola) went to the jungles of northern Bolivia. From there, they organized another guerrilla force to continue the struggle initiated by Che (Siles del Valle 1996, 38–40). However, this guerrilla force was short-lived, and in 1969 both Inti and Darío were caught and killed in La Paz. Thus, they too sacrificed their lives fighting, like Che and their former comrades, for a new society and a new kind of human being.

During this period, Che's ideal vision of *el hombre nuevo* and his revolutionary convictions found sympathy among many of the adherents of an unorthodox Christian body of theory and practice know as Liberation Theology (Boff and Boff 1988). In the 1960s and 1970s, this body of socially concerned and unorthodox religious views gained significant support among the more progressive elements of the Catholic Church in Latin America. Many of the adherents of this new theology established close links with popular revolutionary movements in the region. And in some cases the most progressive sectors of the church, influenced by the ideals of Liberation Theology, joined radical Marxist and neo-Marxist political movements in Bolivia and in other countries, such as Chile, Peru, Brazil, Nicaragua, El Salvador, and Guatemala.

After the death of Inti Peredo and Darío, this convergence of views led to the participation of younger members of the Christian Democratic Party in a revolutionary guerrilla movement called the Ejército de Liberación Nacional (National Liberation Army), which was led by Osvaldo "Chato" Peredo, the younger brother of Inti and Coco Peredo (Siles de Valle 1996, 40–43). In 1970, this movement attempted to establish a guerrilla *foco* or base of operations around the mining town of Teoponte, north of the capital of La Paz. They were quickly surrounded and defeated by the Bolivian army. And in a totally unnecessary act of brutality, many of them were massacred by the army after they offered to surrender. Only a few survived, largely as a result of the intervention of the Catholic Church. Chato Peredo, who is now a psychotherapist in La Paz, was one of the few survivors (Anderson 1997, 745).

After the massacre by the Bolivian army of most of the young participants in the Teoponte guerrilla *foco*, an important change began to take place in Bolivian popular culture and politics. Although the idea of guerrilla warfare was rejected as a viable form of resistance to the military regime, important elements within Bolivian society began to idealize and even venerate Che and the other fallen guerrillas as martyrs (Siles de Valle 1996, 44–45). Che's death, his concept of the new human being, the ideals of Liberation Theology, the deaths of so many idealistic young Bolivians in the revolutionary movements inspired by Che and his comrades—all these elements have combined to exert a major influence on Bolivian popular culture, literature, and politics. It is even possible to speak today of the sanctification of the guerrillas in the minds of many people.

Moreover, Che's influence on modern Bolivian culture and politics as well as his continued worldwide popular appeal have been renewed in recent years by the search for and the discovery of his remains. In July 1997, thirty years after his death and following an almost two-year search, a team of Cuban and Argentine experts found his remains with those of six of his comrades in an unmarked grave at the edge of the Vallegrande airport. The Cuban-Argentine team conclusively identified one of the skeletons as being Che's remains on the basis of its facial bone structure, teeth, and its absence of hands (Associated Press July 7, 1997). It was also found with a jacket and did not have any socks. This was consistent with the last photographs taken of Che after he was killed, which showed him lying on a jacket and without socks.

The search for and discovery of Che's remains in Bolivia adds yet another page to the remarkable story of his life and death, and reveals that his legacy continues to take on new dimensions as time passes. On November 26, 1995, the *New York Times* published an article on the statements of the retired army officer Mario Vargas Salinas (who led the unit that wiped out Joaquín's column), indicating that Che's body had been buried under the landing strip at the Vallegrande airport (Castañeda 1997, 404–5). In fact, the widow of Colonel Andrés Selich told the journalist Jon Lee Anderson, who was collecting information for his biography of Che Guevara, that her husband and a couple of other Bolivian army officers (including Vargas) had buried Che's body and the bodies of six of his comrades in two unmarked graves dug by a bulldozer near the Vallegrande airport (Anderson 1997, 742). When Anderson questioned Vargas (who wrote a book in 1988 about Che's Bolivian operation), Vargas told him that all the bodies had been buried in one unmarked grave near the edge of the airport. The reporting of these details of Che's death, especially in the *New York Times* by Thomas Lipscomb (November 26, 1995, 3), caused a political uproar in Bolivia. It also stirred a great deal of interest in the international media and released a flood of new information about Che's death and his fatal Bolivian mission.

Under pressure from both the national and international press, the president of Bolivia ordered the army to recover the bodies of Che and his comrades. What followed was a rather bizarre and highly publicized search for their bodies by an odd assortment of Bolivians, Cubans, and Argentines, which attracted many onlookers and reporters (Anderson 1997, xv). The whole affair turned out to be a source of considerable embarrassment for the Bolivian government and military, since it resurrected a controversial chapter in Bolivia's political history. For his part in the whole affair, Vargas was placed under house arrest for revealing state secrets.

The little town of Vallegrande, with a population of approximately 8,000 people, was in the news again, but this time because of the presence of Cuban forensic anthropologists and geologists. At first, they managed to locate the remains of five of the guerrillas, only a small fraction of the 32 guerrillas who were killed in the area and buried in unmarked graves. But for sixteen months there was no sign of Che's body.

Meanwhile, Vallegrande's municipal government leaders declared Che's remains to be a "national patrimony" and imposed a moratorium on the search until mid-June 1997. Someone in the town also started promoting a $70-per-day walking tour of the route taken by Che and his comrades before they were caught and killed, and there was talk of creating a museum. Loyola Guzmán, who had been the treasurer of the clandestine urban network that supported Che's guerrilla force before she and the others were arrested and imprisoned by the Bolivian authorities, stated publicly that Che's remains should rightfully remain in Bolivian soil. She argued that "his life was an example of heroic internationalism that no single country should monopolize." Following her release from prison, Guzmán returned to leftist activism and was very much involved in the campaign for the defense of human rights in Bolivia. In 2006, she was elected to the Constituent Assembly in Bolivia as one of the representatives of the Movimiento al Socialismo (Movement toward Socialism, or MAS). In his diary, Che noted, "Loyola made a very good impression on me. She is very young and sweet, but one notes a strong determination."

The Cuban team met until four on the morning of June 28, 1997, to decide where to focus their day of digging, according to Alejandro Inchaurregui, one of a team of Argentine forensic anthropologists who were called in to help the Cubans (Tamayo 1997). Ground radar surveys made by the Cuban-Argentine search team earlier in 1997 had discovered a dozen spots of disturbed earth that they thought could be grave sites. Three of these sites appeared to be man-made, and they decided to concentrate on these sites by means of a bulldozer—not the preferred tool of forensic specialists. However, time was running out for the Cuban-Argentine team because of changing political circumstances in Bolivia.

The experts set the blade of the bulldozer to remove four inches of dirt with each pass of the blade. They found nothing at the first site, but at the second site, after eighteen passes, the bulldozer blade uncovered the remains of a human skeleton. As they continued to dig, they found the remains of a total of seven bodies in two groups, separated by two and a half feet. The bodies were buried in a pit between the edge of Vallegrande's old dirt airstrip and a nearby cemetery. The searchers were overcome with emotion when they examined the remains of the second body that was in the middle of the first group of three skeletons. The skeleton had no hands. Since they knew that Che's hands had been amputated after his death, they were almost certain they had finally found his remains. The American author Jon Lee Anderson was present during the digging on this day, and he said: "Just seeing the genuine excitement, the genuine euphoria on the face of the Cubans there [made] me certain this was Che's remains . . . they were simply overcome, crying and hugging each other" (Tamayo 1997).

However, they still had to prove to the Bolivian government that the remains were those of Che and obtain permission to send them to Cuba. According to the Argentine forensic anthropologist Inchaurregui, the Bolivian Ministry of Internal Affairs officials had warned them they needed to move fast, since the inauguration of Bolivia's newly elected right-wing president and former military dictator, Hugo Banzer, was rapidly approaching, and they assumed he would probably block the removal of Che's remains. Thus, on the night of July 5, 1997, a convoy of vehicles with the remains of the guerrillas made the 150-mile trip at full speed along the dangerous mountain roads between Vallegrande and the provincial capital of Santa Cruz.

In Santa Cruz, Che's remains were quickly identified. The

team of examiners was composed of experts from the Institute of Forensic Medicine in Havana, the director of Che's personal archive, María del Carmen Ariet, and the Argentine forensic anthropologists. They matched the evidence of bullet wounds in the bones of Skeleton no. 2 with the historical facts of Che's death. The excavated teeth of Skeleton no. 2 matched a plaster mold of Che's teeth made in Cuba before he left for the Congo. The mold had been made in the event he died in combat and his body had to be identified. Other evidence also supported the conclusion that the remains were those of Che Guevara.

For example, the retired Bolivian air force general Jaime Niño de Guzmán, the helicopter pilot who flew Che's body and the bodies of the other guerrillas killed in or near La Higuera to Vallegrande, spoke with Che in La Higuera shortly before he was killed. He recalled that Che was shot in his right calf, his hair was matted and dirty, his clothes were shredded, and his feet were covered in rough hand-made sandals. According to General Niño de Guzmán, Che kept his head high, looked everyone in the eye, and asked only for something to smoke. The general told a reporter, "I took pity, [since] he looked so terrible, and gave him my small bag of imported tobacco for his pipe. He smiled and thanked me" (Tamayo 1997). When the Argentine anthropologist Inchaurregui inspected the jacket dug up next to Che's remains, he found a small bag of pipe tobacco in the inside pocket that had apparently been missed by the soldiers who searched Che's body after he was killed in La Higuera. General Niño de Guzmán acknowleged that this was irrefutable evidence that the remains were indeed Che's. He told a reporter, "I must tell you I had serious doubts at the beginning. I thought the Cubans would just find any old bones and call it Che. But after hearing about the tobacco pouch, I have no doubts" (Tamayo 1997).

The Bolivian government gave the Cubans permission to take Che's remains to Cuba, along with those of all the other guerrillas who were found buried in unmarked graves in Bolivia, including the bones of Tania and Joaquín. Thus, on October 11, 1997, almost thirty years exactly after Che's death, his remains and those of the other six fallen comrades found buried with him were placed on display in flag-draped caskets inside the monument to Jose Martí in Havana (*Los Angeles Times* October 12, 1997, A1). With a huge, fifty-foot mural of Che overlooking the Plaza of the Revolution, hundreds of thousands of Cubans waited in line to pay their respects. After seven days of official morning and national homage to Che's life and ideals, the caskets were taken to the city of Santa Clara, where Che had led the guerrilla column that scored a decisive victory in the Cuban revolution. In Santa Clara, Che's coffin was placed in a newly constructed mausoleum at the base of a large statue of him holding a rifle in his hand.

At the quasi-religious ceremony held in Santa Clara, and in the presence of Che's widow, Aleida March, his two daughters, and two sons, Fidel Castro praised Che's qualities as the ideal revolutionary. He closed his homage to Che before the assembled crowd with the following words: "Thank you, Che, for your history, your life and your example. Thank you for coming to reinforce us in the difficult struggle in which we are engaged today to preserve the ideas for which you fought so hard" (*New York Times* October 18, 1997, 10).

In the midst of this massive public veneration of Che, his daughter Aleida Guevara, who is a doctor, like her father, told a press conference that her father always shunned public adulation when he was an important public figure in Cuba and that he probably would have been embarrassed by all the celebrations in his honor. She also said that it hurt to see the image of her father marketed for commercial purposes on ashtrays, beer bottles, and jeans, but that she hoped some young people would see beyond this commercialism and search for the ideals that her father stood for, especially in a globalized society that is losing all its values (*Los Angeles Times* October 12, 1997, A12). Like his older sister, Che's son Camilo Guevara, a lawyer in the Cuban Ministry of Fisheries, is protective of his father's memory and image. He also has criticized what he characterizes as "the bad intentions" of some of the authors of the books published about his father.

Interestingly, in many of the articles published by U.S. newspapers on the return of Che's remains to Cuba and the celebrations that were held in his honor, the reporters used the opportunity to criticize Cuba's socialist system and Che Guevara's ideas on revolution. They characterized them as anachronistic and no longer relevant in the contemporary period. However, the defeat of Che's guerrilla operation in Bolivia does not indicate that an armed revolution is impossible in Latin America. As long as the existing political and economic elites in the region continue to postpone badly needed social and economic reforms and the gap between the rich and the poor continues to increase, popular insurrection will remain on the agenda in Latin America and in other parts of the world with similar conditions. Moreover, the use of repressive and undemocratic measures by those in power to block peaceful and legal efforts to bring about basic reforms invariably provokes the use of nonpeaceful and extralegal means by those who see that they have no other options if they want to create a more just social order.

Since the 1960s, the U.S. government has pursued a variety of policies aimed supposedly at supporting social, economic, and political reforms as peaceful alternatives to violent revolution in Latin America. Today, it and most of the ruling elites in

Latin America claim that they support political democracy and socioeconomic reforms that will benefit the poor as well as the rich. However, the evidence indicates that poverty has actually increased and that extreme forms of political, social, and economic inequality continue to characterize this region of the world (Harris 1999). Apart from strengthening Latin America's military forces, most of the assistance that the United States has given to Latin America since Che's death has been used to refinance the international debts of the Latin American countries and to open up their economies to U.S. foreign investments, corporations, and trade.

Very few reforms have been undertaken that address the growing gap between the rich and the poor or the inequities and injustices that exist in this region. The neoliberal reforms introduced by the Latin American governments starting in the 1980s, at the urging of the United States and the major international financial institutions, have promoted the interests of the rich and powerful at the expense of the poor and powerless. Consequently, the gap between the rich and the poor has continued to widen.

Moreover, the death of Che Guevara and the failure of his guerrilla operation in Bolivia have not stopped attempts to bring about meaningful change in the region through armed revolution. In fact, Che's failure helped to clarify what is needed to organize a successful armed insurrection against an unjust and inequitable social order. Subsequent revolutionary movements have appeared in Latin America and in other parts of the world since Che's death, and in most cases they have recognized the importance of mobilizing mass political support for their movements in both the rural and the urban areas. The revolutionary movements that appeared in Central America during the late 1970s and 1980s were founded upon this approach. Since the

1990s, the Zapatista revolutionary movement in southern Mexico and the Bolivarian Revolution in Venezuela have been based on mass political support, and they pay frequent homage to Che's revolutionary legacy.

Che's failed mission in Bolivia proved, among other things, that a well-trained and committed revolutionary guerrilla force is not sufficient to detonate a successful revolution. His Bolivian operation demonstrated that unless an armed movement is combined with the mobilization of popular support among the rural population as well as the middle and working classes in the urban areas, it will be isolated and wiped out by government troops using what are now commonly understood counterinsurgency tactics. In other words, the creation of a popular-based, multiclass revolutionary movement is widely regard today as the basic prerequisite for a successful popular revolution. This type of multiclass, popular revolutionary movement is, of course, far more difficult to create than a guerrilla *foco* in a relatively isolated rural area, but it is not outside the realm of possibility in the present global order. In fact, a popular-based revolutionary movement of this kind has emerged in recent years in various parts of the world (in Latin America, the Middle East, Africa, and Asia) and will surely occur again in the near future.

As the preceding discussion has sought to make clear, Che's death and the failure of his guerrilla operation in Bolivia has enriched the pool of revolutionary theory and practice. His failure has led many revolutionary or rebellious political and social groups around the world to develop more successful strategies for gaining power. Moreover, as a result of his death, Che has become a universal model of revolutionary courage and commitment, and his example continues to inspire new generations of revolutionaries.

Forty years have passed since Che Guevara was killed in the little village of La Higuera in Bolivia. However, the social injustices against which he fought—first in the Cuban revolution, then in the Congo, and finally in Bolivia—are very much in existence today. For this reason, Che's revolutionary life and death continue to inspire those who struggle against these injustices, particularly in Latin America. Che's revolutionary legacy can be found in the words and deeds of workers, peasants, middle-class university students, intellectuals, shantytown dwellers, the leaders of indigenous communities, and the landless and the homeless—from the tip of Argentina to the Mexican border with the United States, from the Andean valleys of Peru and Bolivia to the cities and vast Amazon region of Brazil, and of course everywhere in Cuba. Che is the focus of hundreds of books and articles, as well as films, paintings, sculptures, and murals in Europe, North America, South America, Africa, and Asia. Today his name is known throughout the world, and his revolutionary legacy has an enduring global significance. When and where a new revolutionary movement will be created in the world cannot be predicted, but that one will emerge is almost a certainty, and when it does, the legacy of Che Guevara will be partially responsible for it.

EPILOGUE

■

Above all, always remain capable of feeling deeply whatever injustice is committed against anyone in any part of the world. This is the finest quality of a revolutionary.
—Che Guevara, farewell letter to his children (1965)

Forty years have passed, and Che Guevara remains as politically important today as he was when he died in Bolivia four decades ago. Perhaps he is even more important now. Recent years have seen a dramatic shift to the left in the politics of Latin America. This shift in the political orientation of this important region of the world has given rise to renewed interest in Che Guevara's ideals of Pan-American unity, anti-imperialism, and humanist socialism. The rather remarkable change of direction in the region's politics has occurred largely in response to the failure of the neoliberal agenda of "free-market" and "free trade" capitalism pursued by the U.S. government, the International Monetary Fund, the World Bank, the Inter-American Bank, and most of the governments of the region since the 1980s. The neoliberal economic and social policies associated with the so-called

Washington Consensus have widened the gap between the rich and the poor, while they have denationalized the economies and privatized the governments of most of the countries in the region. The tidal wave of popular opposition to those neoliberal policies and to the adverse effects of the accompanying capitalist "globalization" of these societies have generated new political movements and new populist leaders who openly identify with Che Guevara's ideals and his revolutionary struggle.

There is no better example than Bolivia. After suffering decades under U.S.-backed right-wing governments, which imposed neoliberal policies that adversely impacted the majority of the population, the country's largely indigenous population has risen up in opposition and found its political voice. The political mobilization of the poor majority of the country led to the election in the fall of 2005 of Bolivia's leftist president Juan Evo Morales, who won with some 54 percent of the votes. Popularly known as Evo, he is of indigenous descent (Aymara) and is the leader of the Movimiento al Socialismo (Movement toward Socialism, or MAS). As was previously mentioned, both Antonio Peredo—the oldest brother of Coco, Inti, and Chato Peredo—and Loyola Guzmán, who helped Che's guerrilla force in Bolivia, are prominent members of MAS, as are many other leftist intellectuals, workers, and peasants in Bolivia.

Evo is the first person from Bolivia's indigenous majority to head the country since the Spanish conquest subjugated the indigenous population five hundred years ago. He and the other leaders of MAS are outspoken admirers of Che Guevara. They have placed photos of Che in the national parliament building and a portrait of Che made from local coca leaves in the presidential offices. The MAS-led government has initiated a constitutional revision of the country's governmental system, an agrarian reform program, and the nationalization of the country's mining and natural gas industries. Thus, the Morales government is reversing the direction of Bolivia's economic, social, and political development. Instead of the privatization of public services and the denationalization of the economy, the country's new leadership is committed to regaining national control over the country's mining and natural gas industries and using the revenues from these industries to finance a people-centered, equitable, and environmentally sustainable program of social and economic development.

Before his official inauguration as president of Bolivia, on January 22, 2006, Evo went to the archaeological site and spiritual center of Tiwanaku, the capital of one of the most ancient cultures in the world, where he was crowned the honorary supreme leader of the Aymara and given gifts from representatives of indigenous peoples from all over the Americas. In the speech that he gave at the Door of the Sun, which is the gateway into the ancient temple of Kalasasaya, Morales said, "The struggle that Che Guevara left uncompleted, we shall complete" (*Granma* January 23, 2006). Afterward, in the speech he gave at his official inauguration, he included Che among the fallen heroes in the five-hundred-year struggle of his people for their freedom.

Even more significant is the fact that Evo went to La Higuera, where Che was killed, to celebrate Che's seventy-eighth birthday, on June 14, 2006. He is the first Bolivian head of state ever to have visited the village, and he chose this date to pay tribute to Che, to open officially the medical center the government of Cuba donated to the village, and to congratulate the local graduates of the literacy program called "Yes I Can," which has been advised and equipped by the Cuban government. Che's son Camilo Guevara was present, as well as the Cuban ambassador to Bolivia and a number of Cuban doctors in their white coats. Evo pledged

Bolivia's solidarity with Cuba and Venezuela and said he would be willing to take up arms to defend them if they were attacked by the United States (Delacour 2006). Hugo Moldiz, a journalist who is the coordinator of the political front of some thirty different popular organizations that supports Evo's government, told the press that the medical clinic and the literacy program demonstrated the relevance of Che's revolutionary struggle, since one of the reasons he gave his life fighting in Bolivia was to ensure that the Bolivian people had access to adequate health care and education (*Prensa Latina* June 14, 2006).

Accompanied by Bolivian government officials and the Cuban ambassador, President Morales also went to inaugurate the installation of modern medical equipment at the Vallegrande hospital—the same hospital where Che was last seen before his body was secretly buried near the airstrip in Vallegrande. Today, the laundry building where Che's body was laid out for examination and where the last photos of him were taken has become a shrine in his memory. Evo's visit to La Higuera and Vallegrande as the Bolivian head of state marked the first time that any high government official in Bolivia has paid tribute to Che Guevara and his guerrilla mission in Bolivia. Moldiz, who has close ties to Cuba, told the press that Evo's tribute to Che was consistent with the path of Morales's own struggle and the identification of his government with the ideals of the guerrilla.

Venezuela offers another excellent example of the shift to the left in Latin American politics and the renewed importance given to Che's vision of a socialist future and his ideas about how to get there. Venezuela's flamboyant leftist president, Hugo Chávez, who has close ties with Presidents Evo Morales in Bolivia and Fidel Castro in Cuba, has addressed his audiences in a Che shirt and frequently refers to Che in his speeches. As an example of his support for Evo's government in Bolivia and his admiration for Che and his ideals, Chávez told the international attendees at the World Social Forum in Caracas in January 2006, "We have to create two, three, many Bolivias in Latin America" (Hernández Navarro 2006). This was a reference to Che's famous 1967 Tricontinental speech, in which he called for the creation of "two, three, many Vietnams" in Latin America.

President Chávez has frequently called U.S. President George Bush "Mr. Danger," and he referred to him repeatedly as "the devil" in a speech he gave at the opening of the United Nations General Assembly in September 2006. In return, U.S. Secretary of Defense Donald Rumsfeld likened Chávez to Adolf Hitler. Chávez has accused the U.S. government of wanting to overthrow him in order to keep control over Venezuela's oil. Chávez frequently states that "Venezuela will never again be a colony of the United States" and, like Che, has called for the formation of an international anti-imperialist front to oppose the imperialist domination of the United States in Latin America and around the world (Hernández Navarro 2006).

He claims that the twenty-first century is the defining century for humanity, and it will be decided during this century whether or not humanity survives. For instance, he told the World Social Forum in January 2006,

> There is nothing beyond the 21st century if we do not change. The choice is socialism or death, but death of the human species. Capitalism is destroying life on this planet. It is now or never. Tomorrow could be too late. That is why I am at this forum crying out for the formation of a global front that is expressly anti-imperialist and socialist. (Hernández Navarro 2006)

Anything with Che on it was in high demand at the forum, both as an item of clothing to be worn there and as a souvenir to be taken home by the participants.

In Venezuela today, it is common to see posters of Chávez flanked on one side by Simon Bolívar, the region's great liberator from Spanish colonial rule, and by Che Guevara on the other side. Che's image is everywhere, particularly on banners and flags at the frequent mass demonstrations that are held in Caracas to express support for what Chávez and his supporters call the Bolivarian Revolution and in the many popular assemblies that are held across the country. Moreover, Chávez regularly refers to Che's anti-imperialist and anticapitalist ideas to help explain the aims of the Bolivarian Revolution in Venezuela and the kind of twenty-first-century human beings and socialist society it seeks to create.

Under Chávez's leadership, the Bolivarian Revolution has become a radical political process that is making profound political and social transformations in Venezuelan society. Chávez and his closest supporters argue that this revolution is a life-and-death struggle to do away with poverty and to create a system of popular power in which the country's poor majority will be able to exercise real control over the day-to-day governance of the society (Munckton 2007). The majority of the Venezuelan people live in poverty, even though Venezuela is the fifth-largest supplier of oil in the world and the United States depends on Venezuela for 11 percent of its oil imports. Chávez frequently mentions in his speeches that when he was first elected to the presidency, in 1998, some 80 percent of the population was living below the poverty line although Venezuela is an oil- and resource-rich nation.

Since 1998, he has consistently said that the Bolivarian Revolution is committed to creating a society of equals that excludes no one and that will be based on social justice and direct democracy. His government has organized citizen committees and popular assemblies to exercise popular control at the municipal and community levels. Under his presidency, health clinics have been established throughout the country in the poorest neighborhoods and rural villages, more than three thousand new schools have been opened, and illiteracy has been eradicated. In addition, more than two million people have gained access to fresh water for the first time in their lives, more homes have been built for the poor than in the preceding twenty years combined, and hundreds of thousands of previously landless peasants have been given titles to farmland. There has also been close collaboration between the Venezuelan and the Cuban governments since Chávez has been president. One very visible result is the presence of some fifteen thousand Cuban doctors who are serving in the health clinics that the government has established (Munckton 2005). This would have pleased Che greatly. When he was alive, there were very few governments in Latin America that had friendly relations with Cuba.

The Bolivarian Revolution in Venezuela has so far taken place without a bloody civil war, public executions, or the suppression of civil liberties. In fact, Chávez had been repeatedly sustained in power by a series of democratic election victories in which he and his political allies have won a large majority of the votes. These democratic elections have undermined the vociferous opposition of the country's privileged classes and the Bush administration's efforts to discredit and bring about the downfall of Chávez. The country's oil wealth, which Chávez has increasingly brought under government control, has permitted his government to do what Che in the early 1960s declared that the Soviet Union and other socialist countries should do for the Third World countries—engage in trade that is based on human needs rather than profits. Consequently, Chávez has signed trade agreements with Argentina, Bolivia, Cuba, and many of the Caribbean countries that provide them with oil at relatively low, subsidized prices they can afford. He has also taken the lead in building an integrated regional economic community among the South American countries as an alternative to the proposed Free Trade Area of the Americas promoted by Washington.

Chávez has been described as "a kind of Latin American Robin Hood, raking in tanker-loads of petrodollars in order to bankroll massive social programs and regional integration schemes" (Mirnoff 2006). But his government has earned a great deal of support within the region for providing oil at subsidized rates to poor countries in the Caribbean, especially at a time when oil prices on the world market have soared to their highest levels. In addition, as an act of solidarity with the American people, the Venezuelan state-owned oil company CITGO has offered cheap heating oil to low-income communities in the Bronx, Boston, and other parts of the United States—much to the chagrin of the Bush administration.

Under Chávez, Che's image in Venezuela takes second place only to the country's national hero Simon Bolívar, and Chávez regularly refers to Che and his ideals in his speeches. Thus, when asked, on a recent visit to Spain, to speak to a mass meeting of Spanish workers in Madrid, he emphasized the inspiration that Che Guevara had given to him and the supporters of the Bolivarian Revolution. He mentioned his imprisonment during the U.S.-supported 2002 military coup against him and how he was saved by the soldiers who were assigned to kill him. He said, "There, facing the death squad, I thought of Che . . . how men die" (Munckton 2005).

If the Chávez government's confrontation with Washington worsens, the supporters of his Bolivarian Revolution may find it necessary to refer to Che's ideas on fighting U.S. imperialism and armed revolution. In fact, this appears to have already begun. At a recent Peasant Conference in Defense of National Sovereignty and for Agrarian Revolution, the participants "discussed the need for armed self-defence as well as the possibility of guerrilla warfare if there is a US invasion" (Munckton 2005). Che's ideas about opposing U.S. imperialism are particularly relevant to defending the aims of the Bolivarian Revolution, including his call for a continental alliance against U.S. imperialism. As a result, Chávez has made frequent references to this aspect of Che's revolutionary legacy.

For example, Chávez gave a speech in which he referred to Che as "that Argentine doctor that travelled through the continent on a motorcycle and who was a witness to the US invasion of Guatemala in 1955, one of the many invasions of the US empire in this continent," and then he cited Che when he declared "capitalism can't be transcended from within capitalism itself, but through socialism" (Munckton 2005). He has also referred to Che in arguing for a humanist socialism in contrast to the bureaucratic dictatorial system that was called socialism in the Soviet Union. In this regard, he has stated, "We must reclaim socialism as a thesis, a project and a path, a new type of socialism, a humanist one, which puts humans and not machines or the state ahead of everything." This view of socialism is very similar to the one Che put forward in his essay "Socialism and Man in Cuba."

Che's ideas about the need to create new human beings guided by socialist morality and his critique of bureaucratism have found particular resonance in Venezuela today (Munckton 2007). The Chávez regime has widely distributed copies of the critical essay on bureaucratism that Che wrote while he was a minister in the Cuban government. Although Chávez has pointed to Cuba as an important source of inspiration, he has emphasized that Venezuela will have to create its own form of socialism that fits its particular history and conditions. The emphasis upon direct democracy in Venezuela is consistent with this perspective, and Chávez contends that the only way to overcome poverty is to give power to the poor. Thus, he and his supporters contend that the Bolivarian Revolution will create "a democratic, humanist socialism" rather than the bureaucratic, authoritarian style of so-called socialism that existed in the Soviet Union. It is in this context that Che's revolutionary legacy has found the most fertile soil in Venezuela and Bolivia today. His writings, his deeds in the Cuban revolution, and his personal sacrifice in the struggle for human liberation and social justice are sources of great inspiration and guidance to the Venezuelans and Bolivians who are struggling for these same ideals today.

In this regard, it is significant to note that Che's daughter Aleida Guevara has published a book and made a documentary video based on her interviews with Hugo Chávez. They are both entitled *Chávez: Venezuela and the New Latin America* (Chávez et al. 2004). Aleida traveled to Venezuela in February 2004 to observe the Bolivarian Revolution firsthand. She interviewed Chávez, his supporters, Cuban doctors serving in Venezuela (Aleida is a pediatrician), and others. The documentary footage begins with inspiring images of pro-Chávez demonstrators, mostly poor and working-class people of color, converging in the thousands to proclaim their support for the advances made by the Bolivarian Revolution. Many of them have Che T-shirts or banners. Their chants of "Chávez no se va!" (Chávez will not go!) are an emotional affirmation of their support for Chávez and their determination to prevent Washington or the opposing elites in their country from overthrowing Chávez and stopping the Bolivarian Revolution.

Aleida has followed in her father's footsteps in more ways than one. Not only has she studied and practiced medicine; she has also been active in international campaigns to advance the same ideals as her father. As a pediatrician she served in Angola, in Nicaragua during the revolutionary Sandinista regime, and in Ecuador. She has appeared with President Chávez in Europe as part of the international "Hands off Venezuela" campaign, which is aimed at generating support among Europeans, particularly the youth, for the Chávez regime and the Bolivarian Revolution.

Aleida believes that the U.S. response to the policies of Chávez's government is what other resource-rich Third World countries can expect if they challenge U.S. domination (Hearman 2003). She contends that attempts to channel the earnings from these countries' exports to the benefit of their working people, as the Chávez government has done with its oil revenues, will be viewed by the U.S. government as a revolutionary threat to U.S. business interests. In her book and documentary on Venezuela, she says, "Chavez just wants to get Venezuelan oil into the hands of the Venezuelan people. What is wrong with that?" (Hearman 2003). Washington's response, however, has been to back two unsuccessful plots to depose Chávez. Aleida argues that this shows the hypocrisy of the U.S. government. Its rulers have ignored the fact that Chávez was popularly elected, and she says, "They have no respect for the outcome of the elections, because the elections have produced a leader who challenges their interests." She sounds very much like her father.

She is proud that her father, forty years after his death, is a key inspirational figure for political movements and parties throughout Latin America today. Indeed, this is true for a broad political spectrum of movements and groups, including the Colombian leftist guerrilla movement, the FARC; the Zapatista National Liberation Movement in southern Mexico; and the Sandinistas in Nicaragua, who were supported by Che and influenced in their formative stage by his ideas about revolutionary guerrilla warfare. The leader of the Sandinista movement, Daniel Ortega, was reelected to the presidency of Nicaragua in November 2006 after being out of office for sixteen years. Ortega's supporters wore Che T-Shirts during the victory celebrations for his reelection.

In Ecuador, Che is also held in high esteem. Much like Chávez and Morales, the country's new leftist president, Rafael Correa Delgado, laced his acceptance speech on January 15, 2007, with references to Simon Bolívar and Che Guevara. He said his country needs to build a twenty-first-century socialism to overcome the poverty, inequality, and political instability that have plagued the Ecuadorian people. Both Chávez and Evo Morales were special guests at Correa's inauguration. With them at his side, Correa said, "Latin America isn't living an era of changes"; rather, "it's living a change of eras," and "the long night of neoliberalism is coming to an end" (Fertl 2007). Che would have been happy indeed to hear what Correa said afterward. He said, "A sovereign, dignified, just and socialist Latin America is beginning to rise." Exactly the kind of language Che used four decades ago.

Critical observers of Che's contemporary popularity in North America, Europe, and other regions outside Latin America are quick to point out that his iconic image has become a global brand, often devoid of any ideological or political significance when it is used to market certain products. They dismiss his continuing appeal to youth as merely a case of "adolescent revolutionary romanticism" and radical chic (O'Hagan 2004). However, while it is true that Che's image has become quite profitable and is used to market a wide variety of goods to young people in the United States and elsewhere, his image still has political significance. Consequently, his image was removed from a CD carrying case recently in the United States after it sparked considerable criticism in the media, in which Che was compared to Osama bin Laden and Adolf Hitler (Associated Press, December 22, 2006). Target Corporation, the large retail company responsible for distributing the product in question, felt compelled to withdraw the item and to issue a public apology for having sold it. This incident proves that Che's supposedly "apolitical" iconic image still has too much political significance for many shoppers in the global capitalist shopping mall.

Moreover, even in the United States, the center of global capitalism, Che still finds political admirers. When asked several years ago why his father is perceived as a "devil" by American corporations and believers in the free market, Che's son Camilo accurately pointed out that "he is a devil for the U.S. government and American multinationals" but that "many North-Americans admire and respect El Che" and that "they fight injustice in American society under his banner" (HUMO 1998). Thus, one sees Che Guevara images along the U.S.-Mexican border as manifestations of activism. Although Che Guevara was not Mexican, his image has been appropriated by activists in the Mexican community within the United States who seek more access to education and civil rights, and the use of his image can be seen as a critique of current U.S. immigration policy. Camilo also correctly noted that there are people in the United States who declare their solidarity with Cuba and seek to lift the U.S. economic blockade against his country.

Prominent public intellectuals such as Régis Debray in France, Jorge Castañeda in Mexico, Alvaro Vargas Llosa in Peru (son of the famous novelist Mario Vargas Llosa), Pacho O'Donnell in Argentina, and others have done their best to demystify and dismiss the significance of the enduring popularity of Che, particularly among young people. One of the most representative members of this group of critics is the British-born "liberal" savant Christopher Hitchens, who supported the Cuban revolution in the 1960s, but has since called himself a recovering Marxist. In a 1997 review article of Jon Lee Anderson's biography of Che and Che's posthumously published *Motorcycle Diaries*, Hitchens argued that Che's enduring popularity is a contemporary case of classic romantic idolatry. In what has become a familiar argument among intellectuals in the United States and Europe for dismissing Che's iconic popularity, Hitchens asserts that "Che's iconic status was assured because he failed. His story was one of defeat and isolation, and that's why it is so seductive. Had he lived, the myth of Che would have long since died" (Hitchens 1997).

Hitchens and other intellectuals who share his perspective thus claim that Che "belongs more to the romantic tradition than the revolutionary one," since "to endure as a romantic icon, one must not just die young, but die hopelessly," and, according to Hitchens, "Che fulfils both criteria." However, there is a fundamental factual inaccuracy and a false premise in this thesis. Che did not die young. Someone who dies at thirty-nine is hardly "young" (except to those who are over fifty). His death was untimely, to be sure, but he was not young when he died. Furthermore, Hitchens and the other intellectual demystifiers of Che's iconic "popularity" fail to comprehend the continuing political and ideological significance of his iconic legacy.

The waving banners, the graffiti on the walls, the posters, the T-shirts, the videos, the films, the books, the pamphlets, the photos, the songs, the tattoos, and the cries of "Che Vive!" on the lips of people around the world provide overwhelming evidence that Che Guevara represents a powerful symbol of one of the most outstanding examples in modern history of resistance to injustice, inequality, exploitation, and political domination. And this is true for people literally around the world. Che continues to be a "popular" hero for many people—of all ages—for the same reason that Evo Morales (who is in his late forties) says he admires Che: "I admire Che because he fought for equality, for justice," and "he did not just care for ordinary people; he made their struggle his own" (Rieff 2005).

As the art historian Trisha Ziff has astutely noted, "Che's iconic image mysteriously reappears whenever there's a conflict over injustice [and] there isn't anything else in history that serves in this way" (Lotz 2006). More than anything else, as Ziff acknowledges, Che is a symbol of opposition to imperialism and "in the end, you cannot take this meaning out of the image." Ziff is correct in asserting that the meaning of Che's image is that of the *"guerrillero heroico"*—the heroic guerrilla fighter against imperialism, and particularly U.S. imperialism.

But in contemporary Latin America, Che is more than a powerful symbol of resistance to U.S. imperialism; his values and many of his ideas continue to be extremely relevant to the current political reality and the shift to the left in Latin American politics. His views and revolutionary life are finding increasing resonance among the new political leaders, new political movements, and the rank-and-file political activists in the region. Che's vision of a socialist future and his ideas about how to get there appear directly relevant to their efforts to end the region's tragic pathology of distorted, neocolonial, and unequal development. His ideals and vision of a united, free, and socialist Latin America are a source of inspiration for their pursuit of emancipatory, equitable, and sustainable alternatives to the disempowering, inequitable, and unsustainable structures and values of twenty-first-century global capitalism. Che is much more than a popular symbol of uncompromising defiance to injustice and imperial domination; his revolutionary vision of the future and ideas about how to wage the struggle to get there are relevant to the contemporary efforts to bring about a revolutionary transformation of the basic economic, political, and social structures in Latin America and the Caribbean.

As a sign of how times have changes in the region, a little more than a month after Evo Morales paid a historic tribute to Che Guevara in La Higuera and Vallegrande, a similar unprecedented event took place in nearby Argentina. It will most likely become a legend of its own. Following an important meeting in Córdoba, Argentina, of the MERCOSUR (Southern Common Market) to which Cuba was invited and Venezuela was accepted as a new member, Hugo Chávez and Fidel Castro made a historic pilgrimage to Alta Gracia to tour Che's boyhood home.

Since 2001, the middle-class house, now called Villa Nydia, where Che lived as a boy has served as a local museum dedicated to his memory. On July 22, 2006, almost four decades after Che's death, two of the most important heads of state in Latin America paid a highly publicized visit to Che's boyhood home. When they arrived, the waiting crowd of several thousand people responded with a chorus of chants: Fidel, Fidel, Hugo, Hugo, and "Se siente, se siente, Guevara está presente"—"One feels it! One feels it! Guevara is present!" (Laprensagrafica.com July 22, 2006).

As they emerged from their vehicles, the two heads of state waved to the crowd and stopped at the entrance to the house in front of a bronze statue of Che made from a photograph taken when he was eight years old. They admired the statue and then went inside for an emotional encounter with the memorabilia of Che's boyhood and family life. Fidel was surprised to learn that Che's parents rented the house, and he asked how much rent they had paid. When the director of the museum said she really didn't know, Fidel jokingly reproached her for not knowing this important fact. At one point, Fidel broke down and cried in front of a large picture of Che's mother, Celia, with her young children around her, including Che. Then Fidel and Chávez met with some of Che's childhood friends who were waiting in the house, including Calica Ferrer, who made the 1953 trip with Che to Bolivia and Peru. Fidel and Chávez viewed Che's birth certificate, handwritten letters, and a motorbike like the one he rode across South America. Ariel Vidoza, a childhood friend of Che, answered Fidel's questions about Che's childhood. She said, "Ernesto didn't like the rich much. He preferred to play with us, the poor ones."

As they left the house, they posed for photographs with Che's boyhood friends in front of the statue of the young Ernesto. To the reporters waiting outside, Chávez said with a great deal of emotion in his voice: "I came to feed my soul. I am leaving with the batteries of my soul charged for 80 more years of revolutionary struggle and battles" (Venezolana de Televisión 2006). Fidel still had tears in his eyes, told the reporters and the crowd that he was sorry he and Chávez could not stay longer, and waved to the onlookers who were clapping and shouting Olé, Olé, Olé, Olé, Fidel, Fidel, Hugo, Hugo!

No one could possibly have imagined such an event forty years ago, even ten years ago. A historic scene: Che's comrade in arms, the famous twentieth-century revolutionary leader Fidel Castro (eighty years old at the time), and Hugo Chávez, one of the new revolutionary leaders of the twenty-first century, standing shoulder to shoulder at the threshold of the now immortal revolutionary Ernesto "Che" Guevara's boyhood home in Alta Gracia ("high grace"), Argentina. There they stood, surrounded by a cheering crowd of thousands. Unmistakable proof, to quote the Ecuadorian president Rafael Correa again, that "Latin America isn't living an era of changes; rather it's living a change of eras."

As the caravan of cars carrying Fidel Castro and Hugo Chávez left Alta Gracia for Córdoba, they passed a building in Che's boyhood hometown where someone had written on the wall in bold red letters, "Che Vive!"—"Che Lives!" It is quite possible they saw it as their cars speed by. Similar Che graffiti is on the walls of the laundry building in Vallegrande where Che's half nude body was displayed forty years ago (O'Hagan 2004). But on a wall of the public telephone building nearby is a new and even more powerful statement, one that brings us to the end of this story, but not the end of Che Guevara the heroic guerrilla. The graffiti on the wall in Vallegrande reads, "Che—alive as they never wanted you to be!"

REFERENCES

Anderson, Jon Lee. 1997. *Che Guevara: A Revolutionary Life*. New York: Grove Press.

Boff, Leonardo, and Clodovis Boff. 1988. *Cómo hacer teología de la liberación*. Madrid: Paulinas.

Castañeda, Jorge. 1997. *Compañero: The Life and Death of Che Guevara*. New York: Alfred A. Knopf.

Castro, Fidel. 2000. "A Necessary Introduction." In Ernesto Guevara, *Bolivian Diary*. London: Pimlico.

Chávez, Hugo, Aleida Guevara, David Deutschmann, and Javier Salado. 2004. *Chávez: Venezuela and the New Latin America*. Melbourne, Australia: Ocean Press.

Clarin.com. 2000. "Antonio Arguedas: Un destino latinoamericano." March 12, http://www.clarin.com/suplementos/zona/2000/03/12/i-00801e.htm.

Cooper, Marc. 2003. "Remembering Allende." *Nation*, September 29.

Debray, Régis. 1967. *Revolution in the Revolution?* New York: Grove Press.

———. 1975. *La guerrilla de Che*. Mexico City: Siglo XXI.

De Carlos, Carmen. 2006. "La historia oculta de las manos del Che." Posted April 16 at the Vulcanus Publications Internet website, http://www.vulcanusweb.de/dialogando/manos-del-Che.htm.

Delacour, Justin. 2006. "Bolivia's President Pays Homage to Che Guevara." *Latin America News Review*, June 14, http://lanr.blogspot .com/2006/06/bolivias-president-pays-homage-to-che.html.

Deutschmann, David, ed. 1994. *Che: A Memoir by Fidel Castro*. New York: Ocean Press.

———. ed. 1997. *Che Guevara Reader*. New York: Ocean Press.

Estellano, Washington. 2000. "Los archivos fatales de Antonio Arguedas." *Punto finâl*, March 24, http://www.puntofinal.cl/000324/ nactxt2.html.

Fertl, Duroyan. 2007. "Ecuador's Correa Calls for Socialist Latin America." *Green Left Weekly*, no. 695 (January 24), http://www.greenleft .org.au/2007/695/36103.

Gambini, Hugo. 1968. *El Che Guevara*. Buenos Aires: Paidos.

Gerassi, John, ed. 1968. *Venceremos: The Speeches and Writings of Ernesto Che Guevara*. New York: Simon and Schuster.

Goñi, Uki. 1995. "Las Manos del Che." December 1, http://www .geocities.com/CapitolHill/Lobby/4766/che16.html.

Guevara, Ernesto. 1961. *La guerra de guerrillas*. Havana: Talleres de INRA.

———. 1963. *Guevara, pasajes de la guerra revolucionaria*. Havana: Ediciones Unión.

———. 1968a. *Diario del Che en Bolivia*. Santiago: Punto Final.

———. 1968b. "Guerrilla Warfare: A Method." In John Gerassi, ed., *Venceremos: The Speeches and Writings of Ernesto Che Guevara*, ed. John Gerassi, 266–79. New York: Simon and Schuster.

———. 1968c. *Reminiscences of the Cuban Revolutionary War*. New York: Grove Press.

———. 1995. *The Motorcycle Diaries: A Journey around South America*. London: Verso.

———. 1996. *Episodes of the Revolutionary War*. New York: Pathfinder.

———. 2000. *Bolivian Diary*. London: Pimlico.

———. 2002. *Back on the Road: A Journey through Latin America*. New York: Grove Press.

Guevara, Ernesto, Aleida Guevara March, and Richard Gott. 2001. *The*

African Dream: The Diaries of the Revolutionary War in the Congo. New York: Grove Press.

Harris, Richard. 2000. "The Effects of Globalization and Neoliberalism on Latin America." *Journal of Developing Societies*, special issue (Spring): 1–28.

Harris, Richard, and Carlos Vilas, eds. 1995. *Nicaragua: Revolution under Siege.* London: Zed Press.

Hearman, Vanessa. 2003. "CUBA: Aleida Guevara—The Left Should Not Abandon Its Core Principles." *Green Left Weekly*, no. 546 (July 23), http://www.greenleft.org.au/2003/546/29908.

Hernández Navarro, Luis. 2006. "Caracas: Sexto foro social mundial." *International Relations Center Americas Program Report*, March 6, http://www.ircamericas.org/esp/3140.

Hitchens, Christopher. 1997. "Goodbye to All That." *New York Review of Books*, July 17.

HUMO (Belgian magazine). 1998. "An Interview with Camilo Guevara, Son of El Che, in Belgium," no. 43/3032 (October 16), English translation, http://www.thechestore.com/Che-Guevara-interview-Camilo.php.

Klein, Herbert. 1984. *Historia general de Bolivia.* La Paz: Juventud.

Kornbluh, Peter. 2007. "The Death of Che Guevara: Declassified." *National Security Archive Electronic Briefing Book*, no. 5, http://www.gwu.edu/~nsarchiv/NSAEBB/NSAEBB5/index.html (March 5).

Lotz, Corrina. 2007. "Che as Revolutionary and Icon." "A World to Win" online conference, http://www.aworldtowin.net/reviews/Che.html (accessed March 22).

Malloy, James. 1989. *Bolivia: La revolución inconclusa.* La Paz: Ceres.

Matthews, Herbert. 1961. *The Cuban Story.* New York: George Braziller.

Miami's Cuban Connection. 2006. "Che Guevara's Capturer Hugged Che before He Was Executed." Posted by ocorral@miamiherald.com on April 21, in Spy vs. Sly, http://blogs.herald.com/cuban_connection/spy_vs_sly/index.html.

Mirnoff, Nick. 2006. "How President Bush Has Unified Latin America." *San Francisco Chronicle*, March 26.

Munckton, Stuart. 2005. "Che Lives." *Green Left Weekly*, no. 616 (February 23), http://www.greenleft.org.au/2005/616/35329.

———. 2007. "Marxism and the Venezuelan Revolution." *Green Left Weekly*, no. 700 (February 28), http://www.greenleft.org.au/2007/700/36344.

O'Hagan, Sean. 2004. "Just a Pretty Face?" *Observer*, July 11, http://observer.guardian.co.uk/review/story/0,6903,1258340,00.html.

Prado, Gary. 1990. *The Defeat of Che Guevara: Military Response to Guerrilla Challenge in Bolivia*. New York: Praeger.

Rieff, David. 2005. "Che's Second Coming." *New York Times*, November 20, http://www.truthout.org/docs_2005/112005H.shtml.

Rodríguez, Félix (Félix Ramos). 1989. *Shadow Warrior*. New York: Simon and Schuster.

Rojo, Ricardo. 1968. *My Friend Che*. New York: Dial Press.

Rostow, Walter. 1967. "White House Memorandum to the President on Death of Che Guevara," October 11. In *National Security Archive Electronic Briefing Book*, no. 5, "The Death of Che Guevara: Declassified," by Peter Kornbluh, http://www.gwu.edu/~nsarchiv/NSAEBB/NSAEBB5/index.html.

Schlesinger, Stephen, and Stephen Kinzer. 1982. *Bitter Fruit: The Untold Story of the American Coup in Guatemala*. New York: Anchor/Doubleday.

Siles del Valle, Juan Ignacío. 1996. *La guerrilla del Che y la narrative boliviana*. La Paz: Plural Editores.

Smiley,Tavis. 2004. "Interview with Robert Redford," November 8, http://www.pbs.org/kcet/tavissmiley/archive/200411/20041108_redford.html.

Taibo, Paco Ignacío. 1996. *Ernesto Guevara: También conocido como EL CHE*. Mexico City: Editorial Joaquin Mortiz.

Tamayo, Juan. 1997. "The Man Who Buried Che." *Miami Herald*, September 19, http://www.fiu.edu/~fcf/cheremains111897.html.

Vilas, Carlos. 1996. "Fancy Footwork: Regis Debray on Che Guevara." *NACLA Report on the Americas* 30, no. 3 (November/December): 9–13.

INDEX